6.95

D1221453

DIAGNOSTIC TEACHING
OF READING

DIAGNOSTIC TEACHING OF READING

Ruth Strang

PROFESSOR OF EDUCATION
UNIVERSITY OF ARIZONA

McGRAW-HILL BOOK COMPANY

New York *San Francisco* *Toronto* *London*

DIAGNOSTIC TEACHING OF READING

II

PREFACE

In the discussion of reading problems, we often hear the words *identification, appraisal, diagnosis,* and *evaluation.*

Identification determines a student's reading status. It is a first step toward grouping pupils either within a class or in separate sections. Without identification of some kind, individualization of instruction is impossible. Many schools have not gone far beyond the process of identification.

An *appraisal* of a student's reading ability gives a more complete positive picture of his reading status and development. It emphasizes his potential in relation to his performance; it helps him to set attainable goals.

Diagnosis puts more emphasis on defining the nature of the individual's reading difficulties and the conditions causing them. However, diagnosis is also concerned with positive factors on which one may build. Even a tentative diagnosis gives the teacher a sense of direction and confidence in working with the individual. Without diagnosis, the teacher may miss important areas, may overemphasize others.

Evaluation stresses the desirability and worth of the reading instruction. It not only ascertains the progress that has been made toward specified objectives but also asks questions such as: "Are the changes that are being effected worthwhile?" "What values have they to the students and to society?" Evaluation looks beneath certain obvious or superficial results of reading instruction. For example, suppose a student brings his reading rate up to 400 words per minute. Looking at the student's improvement in rate, the teacher who evaluates this change may ask: "What purpose did the increase in speed of reading serve?" "At what cost has speed been gained?" "What has happened to the reader's habit of reflective thinking?" "How much strain or tension was involved?" "How much does such rapid reading contribute to his personal development?"

v

Appraisal, diagnosis, and evaluation have much in common. All involve (1) getting facts about the individual and his reading, (2) synthesizing and interpreting these facts, (3) arriving at hypotheses that are modified as new information is obtained, and (4) using the understanding gained to help students improve their reading.

Retardation in reading is another concept that needs clarification. When is a pupil retarded in reading? By one definition, a student who is two years or more below grade placement according to his scores on a standardized reading test is retarded in reading.

A second and more meaningful view of retardation is that it involves a discrepancy between intelligence and reading achievement—the student's reading is not in keeping with his mental potential. This ratio is difficult to determine because group tests of intelligence, and even the best individual intelligence tests, require verbal ability. The individual who is handicapped by reading difficulty may not be demonstrating his true mental ability. We shall see later in the book that tests of listening comprehension are useful in ascertaining an individual's reading potential.

A third kind of retardation is indicated by test results compared with day-by-day performance. Under test conditions and for a short period, the individual may score above average, but emotional conflicts, lack of purpose, visual discomfort, dull textbooks, and other factors may decrease his reading efficiency in everyday assignments.

A fourth kind of retardation occurs when the student's total reading score is satisfactory but his performance in some aspects of reading is very low. For example, he may be high in factual comprehension but deficient in making inferences and drawing conclusions.

Throughout the book, reference will be made to the concepts just defined. The focus, however, will be on a practical kind of diagnosis that contributes to the reading development of all the students.

Diagnosis is never an end in itself; it is only a means to more efficient learning. Gaining an understanding of the student's reading proficiency and difficulties takes time, but it also saves time. It saves time by enabling the teacher to focus his attention on the specific help the student needs, thus avoiding trial and error and unnecessary instruction and practice.

In this book diagnosis is viewed as an intrinsic part of teaching. Most of the information a teacher gains about a student's reading is not recorded; it is used immediately in helping the student to improve. The more familiar a teacher is with factors that may influence a student's reading development, the more alert he will be to note their presence as he works with individuals and with groups.

Another important emphasis is on student's self-appraisal. Diagnostic information is for the student as well as for the teacher or reading specialist. Increasing proficiency in self-appraisal is a major goal throughout school years.

The introduction gives a brief background of principles and points of view and an overview of diagnostic information, its sources, and synthesis.

Part 1 presents procedures such as observation, group tests, written reports, essays, and informal inventories that can be used with groups. These methods may also be used with individual cases. Other procedures, described in Part 2, must be administered individually.

This book should give the beginning teacher (1) a positive rather than a problem approach to the teaching of reading, (2) a feeling for the complexity of the process of learning to read, (3) a description of practical methods of appraisal leading to improvement in reading, and (4) an increased perception of children's struggles with reading difficulties. In the past, too many children have suffered from the "flaw focus" or faultfinding approach.

For the experienced teacher of reading we hope that the book will serve as a source of principles, diagnostic procedures, and materials essential in making decisions as to the improvements needed by a class or by individuals. As a reminder of a philosophy and psychology that sometimes becomes dim in the press of multiple duties, this book may also be useful.

The detailed descriptions of procedures and record forms suggested for teachers should be equally useful to the reading consultant or clinician. Unless the specialist's recommendations are practical enough to be carried out under classroom conditions, much of his diagnostic study is wasted.

In addition to its value to teachers and reading specialists, the book should also be helpful to principals, psychologists, and guidance workers.

The author owes much to a number of people: to the students whose lively participation in the author's course in Diagnosis of

Reading Difficulties at Teachers College, Columbia University and at the University of Arizona, over a period of six or seven years helped to identify and clarify important questions and problems; to Dr. Amelia Melnik who for several semesters as co-instructor has helped to develop the content of the course in Diagnosis of Reading Difficulties at the University of Arizona; to Debora Brink who read the manuscript as a whole; to Dr. Dorothy Withrow, Dr. Helen Carey, and Rosemary G. Wilson who have furnished information and record forms that they have developed in the reading program and clinic of the Philadelphia schools; to Erma Hotis for assistance with bibliographical work; and to Dr. Helen Robinson, Dr. George Spache, Dr. William Sheldon, Dr. Constance McCullough, Dr. Miles Tinker, and many others whose publications have contributed to the author's understanding of the role of diagnosis in the teaching of reading.

Ruth Strang

CONTENTS

PREFACE **V**

1. INTRODUCTION   3

PART 1. GROUP PROCEDURES

2. THE ROLE OF THE TEACHER IN DIAGNOSIS   27
3. OBSERVATION IN THE CLASSROOM   41
4. ORAL READING AS A DIAGNOSTIC TECHNIQUE   61
5. RETROSPECTIVE AND INTROSPECTIVE REPORTS   75
6. ASCERTAINING INTERESTS   97
7. CONTRIBUTION OF TESTS   117

PART 2. INDIVIDUAL METHODS

8. INTRODUCTION   153
9. PHYSICAL FACTORS IN READING DIAGNOSIS   163
10. READING TESTS ADMINISTERED INDIVIDUALLY   187
11. INDICATORS OF READING POTENTIAL   211
12. INTERVIEW TECHNIQUES   231
13. PROJECTIVE METHODS   253
14. INTERPRETATION AND SYNTHESIS OF INFORMATION   265

Appendix A.   Analysis of Several Widely Used Reading Tests   289
B.   Checklist of Instructional Needs   297

INDEX   303

GROUP PROCEDURES

INTRODUCTION

Inability to read is recognized as the most important single cause of school failure. It is also related to other problems, since children may respond to this handicap in devious ways. An undetermined number become emotionally disturbed, some become delinquent, others give up trying to do the impossible tasks assigned. Thus the teacher who maintains a sensitivity to the multiple causes of reading difficulty and implements his insights by providing appropriate instruction may contribute to many aspects of child development.

Appropriate instruction stems from accurate and pertinent diagnostic information in line with the broad view of the reading process. Pertinent information about the reader is of four kinds: (1) his reading ability; (2) factors in his reading achievement, such as learning capacity, linguistic ability, and listening comprehension; (3) personal characteristics, such as physical defects, emotional difficulties, interests, attitudes, and values; and (4) environmental factors, such as home and school conditions, influencing his achievement and causing reading difficulties.

GENERALLY ACCEPTED PRINCIPLES

The following fundamental principles underlying reading instruction cannot be too frequently stated:

1. Start where a child is, help him to progress as far and as fast as he is able so that he will eventually achieve his potential reading ability.

2. Success has a tonic effect; nothing succeeds like observed success. Too often the retarded reader has become convinced that he is dumb and cannot learn to read. Members of his family may have told him so. Teachers have become exasperated when he did not respond to their best efforts. He has demonstrated his inability to himself on material that was too difficult for him. His embarrassment and sense of failure are intensified when his classmates shout out the words he does not know and the teacher calls on another student who reads the passage fluently and knows exactly what it means. He needs the experience of success. In general, success is more stimulating than failure, reward than punishment, praise than blame.

3. Respect for the pupil increases his self-esteem. If the teacher listens intently to what the student is saying and shows that he understands how he is thinking and feeling, he thus conveys to the student his respect and genuine concern for him as a person. On the other hand, self-esteem is not usually achieved by superficial reassurance. The teacher does not say, for example, "Now don't worry about your reading. It doesn't matter so much." The student, if he is very much concerned about his reading, may

feel "The teacher doesn't understand. If she did, she would know that it *does* matter."

4. Learning takes place in a relationship. Rapport is a subtle thing. It has many ingredients. The teacher's confidence in his ability to help the student improve in reading inspires confidence in the student. One teacher, in his first interview with a nonreader, said positively, "I know I can teach you to read." And he did. Building rapport with an emotionally disturbed retarded reader is so delicate a process that no general rules can be laid down. The interviewer must feel his way; he often must listen with his "third ear."

Success with retarded readers depends largely on the ability of the teacher to establish a friendly, constructive relationship. In conveying a warm, friendly feeling the teacher's manner and actions are more important than his words. When the teacher's face lights up at the student's successful performance, when the teacher takes the trouble to find an interesting book or suitable exercises that will help the student improve, then the student knows that the teacher cares. If a student seems antagonistic or resistant, the teacher should not take this attitude personally; it may stem from previous coercion by parents and teachers and from many an unpleasant reading experience. When the teacher takes a relaxed attitude, the student has less need to resist; the teacher has become his ally rather than his enemy.

5. Success in working with seriously retarded readers also depends upon discovering what makes them tick. They seldom respond to the direct question, "What is your reading problem?" They want to forget it. They often are very ingenious in diverting attention from it. The teacher has to be alert to pick up the indirect and incidental clues that they let drop. If he can discover the conditions that are causing the student's difficulty, he can provide the special instruction and reading materials needed.

6. Fundamentally, success in teaching reading results from changing the dynamics of the situation. In the small reading group or individual conference the student is free from the classroom setting that he associates with failure, free from the teacher's disapproval and the ridicule of classmates.

7. Children react differently to what is apparently the same approach. One may love, while another hates, the same teacher. One may reject kindness as weakness, while another may respond

to it in an almost miraculous way. Criticism may motivate one student to do better, while it completely discourages another. There are even individual differences in students' responses to praise and recognition; it may embarrass some, motivate others. Consequently there is no substitute for the continuous effort to discern what the situation means to a particular individual.

DIAGNOSIS AND THE BROAD VIEW OF READING

Every promising path to improvement in reading demands an understanding of both the reading process and the reader. The broad view of reading includes an understanding of what constitutes effective reading, what contributes to effective reading, and what interferes with effective reading (Figurel, 1962).

Techniques of diagnosis vary with our theories of reading. If we think of reading as a visual task—seeing clearly the printed words—then we will focus on visual screening tests and eye examinations. These reveal some defects that prevent reading proficiency; other defects cause discomfort that decreases an individual's satisfaction with and enjoyment of reading.

If we think of reading primarily as word recognition, then our appraisal procedures will test auditory and visual discrimination, skill in using sound-symbol association to pronounce unfamiliar words, and facility in anticipating and checking their meaning by the context.

If, however, we think of reading as getting the meaning of the selection—and what could be more futile than merely pronouncing words without knowing what they mean—then we must ascertain the student's comprehension of what the author is trying to communicate. For this purpose we observe students as they read. We may also use many kinds of tests, both standardized and informal, some calling for free or composition-type, creative responses; some testing comprehension by means of objective exercises.

If we view reading as more than the literal comprehension of the author's thought, if we include the idea of reading between the lines and beyond the lines, then we must further expand the diagnostic procedure. We will find out whether the student can make inferences and generalizations based on the selection, draw conclusions, interpret literature, appreciate literary excellence, and sense the author's mood, intent, and purpose. It seems impossible to say where reading ends and thinking begins, impossible to separate the two processes.

Moreover, diagnosing difficulties in comprehension is much more complex than merely learning what the difficulties are. The reader's success in comprehending the meaning of a selection depends upon many factors: his visual efficiency and word recognition skills, his mental ability, his attitudes (including various emotional considerations), his background knowledge of the subject, and his familiarity with the structure of language. In diagnosing comprehension, we must regard the student as a person in relation to the material that he is asked to read. For example, a Puerto Rican pupil may not be able to comprehend *elevator* because he has never seen such a thing.

If our concept of reading embraces the reader's use of the material read, our diagnostic procedure becomes still more complicated. We are then concerned with how effectively the student uses ideas gained from reading in conversation, discussion, committee or individual reports, creative writing, drawing, and other modes of expression and communication. His purpose in reading largely determines his rate and method of reading.

If we go further and recognize that reading ought to change the individual's ideas, feelings, attitudes, and behavior, then we have set ourselves a truly difficult task. There are no standardized tests to measure these outcomes of reading. We must resort to informal methods which depend largely upon observation, interviews, and obtaining introspective reports from the students. Difficult as it is, however, this kind of diagnosis should be attempted, for one of the two main objectives of teaching reading is personal development through reading.

To present the broad view, diagnosis must be comprehensive. To be dynamic, it must yield understanding of the forces at work within the individual and the situation, forces that are attracting or repelling him. Such diagnosis recognizes the role played by the individual's previous experiences, his specific goals, preferably self-determined, and his progress toward these goals.

TWO APPROACHES TO DIAGNOSIS

There is some controversy about the proper approach to diagnosis. One school of thought advocates obtaining as much information as possible before beginning to work with the individual. Data are gathered from existing records; parents and students are interviewed; intelligence and achievement tests are administered, scored, and interpreted. This information is then reviewed and summarized before one attempts any remedial work. This approach is similar to the directive or counselor-centered approach in counseling. It is, of course, used when reading cases are referred to a clinic just for diagnosis.

In the other approach the teacher or clinician starts with the problem as the student presents it and begins immediately to help him solve it. As he observes and works with the student, he learns more about his manner of reading, the skills he has mastered, and those in which he is still deficient. If he feels the need for some special source of information, such as an intelligence test, a reading test, or a home visit, he secures it. Thus diagnosis is interwoven with instruction and practice in reading.

There are arguments for and against each of these approaches. Obtaining a fairly complete understanding of the individual before beginning to work with him has the advantage of permitting greater accuracy in selecting initial reading materials and procedures and of enabling the teacher to avoid doing or saying something that might be detrimental.

However, there are a number of possible disadvantages in prolonged preliminary diagnosis. An individual who is eager to improve his reading tends to become impatient if he must spend several hours without receiving any apparent help. At the end of every session, the student should feel that he has made some progress, that something has been accomplished.

Moreover, a person who is anxious about his reading and has feelings of inferiority about himself is likely to have these feelings intensified as he fails to answer the increasingly difficult questions on standardized tests. He may feel more strongly than ever that something must be very wrong with him. The skillful examiner, of course, can minimize these disadvantages, but he cannot eliminate them entirely.

Another objection to the routine preliminary diagnosis is that it may yield some information that is not relevant to the case and fail to turn up other information that is of special importance. There is also the possible danger of getting into deep water. The student may reveal psychological or medical problems about which the reading teacher would need expert assistance. It is one advantage of the second approach that, although the reading teacher is not a therapist, he may have a therapeutic effect on the individual as he works within the area of his own competence.

The disadvantage of the second approach, as we have already implied, is the danger of doing the wrong thing because of lack of knowledge. This problem is not likely to occur, however, if we follow the student's leads.

By combining diagnosis with instruction we give the student the satisfaction of accomplishing something in every period. The information obtained is immediately used. Most important, this approach gives definite responsibility for self-appraisal; it encourages the student to take the initiative in solving his own reading problems. Children and young people need to take more responsibility for their own development. They need to take an objective attitude toward their strengths and limitations. All in all, this approach of meeting the individual's needs as they are uncovered seems to be the more desirable.

RELATION OF DIAGNOSIS TO REMEDIATION

Diagnosis should lead directly to the improvement of reading through the reinforcement of the strengths and the remediation of the difficulties discovered. No gap should intervene between diagnosis and remediation. Some teachers and specialists seem to have little regard for the appropriateness of their remedial procedures to the diagnostic findings. One reading program uses games with all the students; another employs nothing but the kinesthetic approach; another finds in group therapy the cure-all of reading problems; still another gives all classes tachistoscopic training regardless of individual differences.

There are several reasons for this failure in following through. One is that the disproportionate amount of time spent on diagnosis and record keeping leaves little time for instruction. A second reason is that the processes are often carried on by different persons, neither of whom understands what the other is trying to do.

A third explanation is that some single cause of reading difficulty is overemphasized. As Spache (1955, pp. 18–26) so well pointed out, estimates differ widely as to the incidence of personality disturbances among retarded readers: 4 to 6 per cent in the St. Louis public school clinics and 39, 50, and 70 per cent in other clinics. Another clinic attributed 90 per cent of its cases of reading retardation to difficulties in the convergence-divergence ratio in vision. Some centers spend a disproportionate amount of time examining clients for organic defects, while others overemphasize the diagnosis of word analysis skills.

A fourth reason for the ineffectual use of diagnostic information is its inadequacy. Most quantitative data tell little about the child as a person, about the specific nature of his retardation, or about the dynamics of the difficulty. An astute teacher could obtain more immediately useful information of this kind simply by asking a child to read paragraphs of varying difficulty, to demonstrate his comprehension of them, and to try to explain both his successful and his unsuccessful responses (Dolch, 1951, pp. 124–125; Sheldon, 1958, pp. 545–546).

INFORMATION NEEDED

When a teacher is asked, "What do you know about Dick?" a ninth-grade student in his class, he is likely to say something like this: "Oh, Dick's an average boy. He causes no trouble," or "He's a disturbing element in the class. He's better in arithmetic than in reading." A more perceptive teacher may observe that, although Dick has a speech defect, he wants to talk and always has something to say. Another teacher, with a positive approach to children, may perceive primarily the things Dick does well and report that he is especially good in drawing and that she has used this ability to increase his self-esteem.

Dick's homeroom teacher has obtained facts about the boy's home background, attendance, school marks, test results, and educational plans from the cumulative records. By talking with one of his other teachers, she has learned that Dick was a poor reader, fidgeted a great deal, did not do his work, misspelled many words, wrote in a cramped hand, and was absent a great deal. He was given a buddy to help him, but this did not work out very well because the pair disturbed other children and Dick let his buddy do the work for him. It was significant that Dick was quite different on the playground; there he entered into the activities with enthusiasm.

In a half-hour interview alone with Dick after school, his reading teacher gained these additional tentative impressions and bits of information. Although he looked healthy, he had moved to this city because of a persistent cold. His mistakes on a vocabulary test, such as calling *hurt* for *hunt,* suggested the possibility of poor visual acuity. His poor memory and dull facial expression raised questions about his mental ability. He mentioned that his father was out of work; this and other incidental comments suggested possible anxiety or tension in his home. Here were a number of leads that a teacher might use in working with Dick.

In his daily observation and contacts with Dick, the teacher can obtain information of the following kinds:

How he approaches reading tasks

How well he reads at present

How he attacks unfamiliar and difficult words

How he feels about reading

How he responds to help

What his specific difficulties are

What enjoyment or satisfactions he gets from reading

What progress he is making

What he reads voluntarily

How much time he spends in reading

What his reading interests are

Why he reads

How far he can go in reading—what his reading potential is

How quickly he can learn

What home and school conditions are favorable to his reading development

What conditions seem to be causing his reading difficulty

Which of these conditions can be modified

Information of this kind can be grouped under four headings: reading status; reading potential; attitudes, interests, emotional difficulties, and values; and environmental conditions that may influence his reading.

Reading Status

In observing Dick's oral reading, the teacher would note his enunciation, his ability to recognize words in the basic sight vocabulary, his method of attack on unfamiliar words, his phrasing and attention to punctuation, his fluency, and his comprehension and interpretation of the selection read aloud.

When Dick reads silently, the teacher notes whether he can comprehend better than when he reads orally and why. Perhaps because of his speech defect or emotional difficulties, he becomes too embarrassed to concentrate on the meaning when he reads aloud.

His comprehension of the selection is shown by his ability to summarize or outline what the author said—to get the main ideas of a passage and the subordinate details, to distinguish essential details from those that are incidental or unimportant.

Comprehension also requires ability to see relationships such as comparisons, contrasts, and time sequences; to read between the lines and to sense the author's tone, mood, or intention in writing the material; and to evaluate—agree or disagree intelligently with the writer. Comprehension, as broadly defined, includes the ability to read beyond the lines, applying the author's ideas to one's present and future life and problems; to project oneself into the situations described and decide how one would have acted and why. Comprehension of descriptive passages in literature requires ability to imagine or picture what the printed word describes.

A thorough appraisal of Dick's reading status also includes information on his proficiency in the use of the dictionary, index, and other location of information skills. Can he locate sources of information in the library? After he has found a book or article on the topic, can he scan it to obtain the specific information he needs? After he has found the facts, can he analyze, synthesize, and communicate them? Does he know how to read graphs, maps, and tables?

Reading Potential

To gain understanding of Dick's reading potential, the teacher would need help from the psychologist or reading specialist. The three groups of abilities that Holmes (1961, pp. 111–122) found to have greatest weight in reading speed and power were (1) intelligence as measured by Thurstone's Primary Mental Abilities Test, (2) linguistic abilities, and (3) listening comprehension or auding.

Mental Ability as Learning Capacity. Other things being

equal, the less intelligent child will have the greater difficulty in reading. He is more likely to lack curiosity, which is basic to good reading. He lacks the reasoning ability to see essential relations in complex sentences. His lack of reading ability limits his acquisition of information, and this in turn makes it more difficult for him to put meaning into what he reads.

Learning capacity and learning rate are important aspects of intelligence that are often neglected in a diagnostic study. There are simple tests of learning capacity, such as that included in the Durrell-Sullivan Reading Capacity and Achievement Tests (1937–1945). However, more valuable evidence can be obtained by the clinician as he works with a case and by the classroom teacher as he observes students' responses to his instruction and keeps dated samples of their work.

Linguistic Abilities. Fluency and precision in speech, superior oral vocabulary and sentence patterns, "word sense," and familiarity with both colloquial and literary expressions are prognostic of success in reading. These abilities often are taken for granted. Children from homes where English is correctly spoken acquire correct language patterns naturally; children from foreign language backgrounds and illiterate homes require special linguistic instruction and/or much verbal association with English-speaking children.

Listening Comprehension. Ability to comprehend by listening, sometimes called *auding,* is one of the best single indications of potential reading ability. If an individual comprehends a passage read aloud much better than he comprehends a comparable passage that he reads silently, the prognosis for improvement in his reading is favorable. For prognostic purposes, tests of listening comprehension are being recommended in addition to individual intelligence tests (see Chapter 11).

Other Factors That Influence Reading Achievement

Dick, like most people, has unrealized reading ability. His potentialities exceed his achievement. Such discrepancy between capacity and performance may be due to his lack of interest, his attitudes toward himself and toward reading, inner conflicts, or other factors.

Interests. In addition to learning about Dick's favorite subjects, his general interests, and his reading interests, the teacher may obtain more objective information about his family's reading habits and the way Dick uses his leisure time. Does he have books available at home? Does he borrow books from the school and public libraries?

Attitudes. Even more important than this factual information are the student's attitudes and feelings about his reading. Does he see himself as a person who can read better? (Bianchi and Thompson, 1937.) Or has he become so discouraged that he thinks of himself as unable to learn to read? If Dick has a reading handicap, what need does it serve? What satisfaction does he get from being a retarded reader? Why does he hold on to his handicap? Why does he resist learning to read?

His method of coping with his reading difficulty often stems from his attitudes. Does he try to cover it up by aggressive or annoying behavior? Does he withdraw into a world of fantasy in which he is the best reader in the class? Does he withdraw from the whole situation by playing truant?

Emotional Difficulties. Various fears may lurk behind many plausible explanations of reading retardation. Is the student afraid of growing up, afraid to compete with more able readers, afraid of making mistakes? One psychoanalytical theory, not yet adequately substantiated, attributes reading retardation to fear of looking, avoidance of what might be a sexual object, or to hostility toward a parent, usually of the same sex (Walters et al., 1961, pp. 277–283). There are many emotional disturbances that may be involved in cases of serious retardation.

Values. The individual's value system underlies his attitude toward himself and his reading. What are his purposes in reading? Are they immediate—to win the approval of his parents, teachers, or classmates; to enjoy using his mind; to satisfy his curiosity; to learn how to make or do something? Does he also have long-term goals such as college entrance or vocational success?

Physical Factors. Of special importance in a child's early reading development are visual and auditory defects, lack of motor and eye-hand coordination, general immaturity, low energy level, endocrine disturbances, and malnutrition. Signs of these physical defects can be observed by the teacher. He may suspect visual and auditory difficulties if the child holds a book too near or too far from the eyes, if he pays no attention unless he is looking directly at the speaker, if he loses his place and skips lines in reading. Some of these visual factors are described in Chapter 9.

Home and School Conditions. These have a very important bearing on the pupil's reading development. In poor homes and homes where a foreign language is spoken, there is usually little opportunity for the child to develop a meaningful vocabulary or to master common English language patterns. Children who have learned to think verbally and express themselves fluently naturally have the advantage in learning to read. The parent-child and sibling relationships that prevail from infancy also exert a strong influence on the child's reading development.

Unfavorable school conditions and inferior instruction are responsible for considerable failure in reading. For some children, reading may have been introduced before they were physically, mentally, or socially ready to learn. The teacher's skill and the prevalent teacher-student relations may either facilitate or block a child's growth in reading.

Peer relations, especially during adolescence, play a prominent role in students' achievement. In many peer cultures (Coleman, 1962, pp. 4–7), popularity, athletics, and extraclass activities are more important to the students than scholarship. A significant negative relationship exists between peer prestige status and reading achievement status (Porterfield and Schlichting, 1961, pp. 291–297).

SOURCES OF INFORMATION

Information from many sources is obtainable about the individual's strengths and weaknesses in oral and silent reading; his capacity to learn; his attitudes, interests, and values. Conditions that interfere with his reading development may be observed. Insight of special significance may be obtained from the student's own appraisal and description of his reading progress and from his suggestions as to methods and materials that might help him to read better.

Some procedures can be used with an entire class; others must be administered individually. An overview of these procedures may be helpful at this point.

Group Procedures

These include the following:

1. Observation day by day, a basic technique by means of which one may gather much information about the student's manifest reading achievement, attitudes, and interests.

2. Interest inventories and questionnaires. The unstructured type of inquiry often yields more significant results than one that consists only of specific questions.

3. The reading autobiography gives clues as to the individual's reading development and the genesis of his difficulties, as well as revealing his present attitudes, interests, satisfactions, and dissatisfactions.

4. The daily schedule throws light on the student's interests and the pattern of his daily activities, including reading of different kinds.

5. The Dolch Basic Sight Word Test is useful to ascertain whether the student can recognize the most common words in one quick glance.

6. Informal reading tests should include at least two types of questions: those calling for a creative or free response, such as "What did the author say?" and short answer or objective questions on different aspects of reading. Informal tests can be used in a testing-teaching-self-appraisal procedure.

7. Standardized group intelligence and achievement tests give clues to the individual's level of ability and achievement in comparison with those of his peers. Subtest scores and analysis of the student's responses yield additional information.

8. Listening comprehension tests are useful in determining reading potential.

9. Classroom projective-type tests include incomplete sentences, incomplete stories, the draw-a-person technique, and free response to selected pictures. These techniques, used by a clinically trained person, yield clues as to feelings and relationships that may cause reading difficulties.

Individual Procedures

1. Visual screening tests.

2. Diagnostic reading tests: Durrell-Sullivan, Gray, Gates, McCullough, and others.

3. Individual intelligence tests.

4. Individual reading inventories.

5. Interviews with the student and with his parents. In interviews that encourage introspection, we may learn much about the individual's reading process and the intricate ways in which he arrives at the meaning of printed material.

6. Individually administered projective techniques presenting unstructured situations that evoke unique responses.

7. Case conferences on individual cases.

Combination of Procedures

The table on the following pages shows some sources of information and the kind of information that can be obtained from each.

SYNTHESIS AND INTERPRETATION OF INFORMATION

In analyzing and synthesizing the diagnostic information about a student, compare the different items to see which reinforce one another and which seem to contradict one another. Look for the genesis of the reading difficulty, try to see where it started and what conditions gave rise to it. Follow the individual's reading development through the years, and see how it influenced and was influenced by other aspects of his life such as character, personality, and success in school subjects.

Note also how the student's family and peers have reacted to his reading difficulty, how their attitude has affected him, and in what respects he is most handicapped by it. Try to ascertain his attitude toward reading at the present time, and summarize his reading strengths and weaknesses. Finally, form tentative hypotheses as to the causes of his reading difficulty with the intent to review and revise them as you gain new information and insight.

From the information collected about Dick, we learn that he is more than two years below his grade placement; yet he is intelligent enough to be a better reader. Until now he has been able to "get by" without much effort or concentration on reading. With appropriate instruction and with effort on his part, the prognosis for improvement is favorable.

Since school health examinations leave much to be desired, Dick should have his eyes tested by a competent ophthalmologist. A more systematic diagnosis of his perception and other word

Sources, methods, and instruments	Kinds of information obtained	What was learned about an individual student, Dick
1. School records	Scores on previous intelligence and achievement tests; school marks in all subjects; family size, economic and social background, language spoken, visual, auditory, and general health information; attendance; change of schools.	Dick is the oldest of seven children. His family is of low-middle socioeconomic status; white Irish and German extraction. Poor English, but no foreign language is spoken. Kuhlmann-Anderson IQ 110; no recorded health problems; good attendance at the same school. Dick has done consistently poor work through the first year of high school.
2. Classroom observation of students engaged in oral reading, in group discussion, and other classroom activities	Success in completing a given assignment; oral and silent reading performance; indications of attitudes toward reading, school, and himself; interests; relations with other students; speaking vocabulary and sentence structure; uses made of reading; changes in attitudes, points of view, and behavior.	Dick seems to make no real effort to learn new and difficult words. He glides over them and does not stop to analyze or remember them. Even after the teacher has pointed out obvious errors in spelling, Dick makes the same errors again. On the same page he will spell a word both correctly and incorrectly. Other pupils choose him in games. Woodworking is his favorite subject.
3. Interest inventories and questionnaires	Reading interests and other interests.	Dick's main interest is sports. He checked several reading interests but may just have thought this was the thing to do.
4. Reading autobiography and other introspective reports	Family reading habits, his own past and present reading interests, his analysis of his reading difficulties.	The family does little reading; Dick has read little in the past. At present he says he enjoys reading books on aviation.
5. Daily schedule	How he spends his time: in outdoor activities, TV, movies, chores, part-time work; alone, with friends, with	Most of Dick's free time was spent playing outdoors. After supper he usually watched TV. During the

Sources, methods, and instruments	Kinds of information obtained	What was learned about an individual student, Dick
	family; kinds and amount of reading.	days recorded he did no voluntary reading.
6. Dolch Basic Sight Word Test	Sight recognition of basic words, words that he needs to study.	Dick failed to recognize at sight about one-fourth of the Dolch basic vocabulary.
7. Informal tests and group reading inventory	The free or creative-type response yields information about the pupil's approach to reading and inferences as to how his mind works when he reads. The short-answer or multiple-choice questions give understanding of other aspects of comprehension.	Dick could not read independently books above sixth-grade level. He picked out a few scattered ideas but saw no relation or sequence among them. He was able to identify most of the main ideas and supporting details in the multiple-choice questions. He made no application of the ideas to his own life.
8. Standardized reading tests	Different tests yield different kinds of information: speed of reading easy material, speed-comprehension ratio, special vocabulary in each subject, sentence and paragraph comprehension, ability to use index and reference material.	On the subtests as reported on the Iowa Silent Reading Test, Dick's vocabulary, sentence meaning, and directed reading seem to be very poor. He used the index well but slowly, had surprisingly high ability to get the main idea of a paragraph. His total reading score was at the 33d percentile.
9. Listening comprehension tests	Relation between listening comprehension and silent reading comprehension on comparable material.	Dick comprehended much better when he listened than when he read.
10. Diagnostic spelling test	Grade level of spelling ability, kinds of errors made.	Dick's spelling is about sixth-grade level; he is not word-conscious.
11. Classroom projective techniques, e.g., incomplete sentences, pictures	Attitudes toward self, family, and clues as to emotional conflicts, worries, etc.	Dick gave repeated indications of fear of failure and dislike of school.

recognition skills (see Chapter 3) might reveal deficiencies in the basic learning-to-read sequence. By means of a test such as the McCullough Word Analysis Test (published by Ginn and Company), the teacher can put her finger on the deficiencies that are impeding the student's progress.

The following are some additional recommendations based on the initial tentative diagnosis and worked out jointly with Dick:

1. At home or in afternoon or evening study hall at school, encourage growth and expansion in his reading interests. Recommend and make available books, within his vocabulary and comprehension range, that will evoke other interests as well as cater to his present interests in reading about airplanes and aviation. By recording his reading on a form such as My Reading Design (Simpson, 1945), he would see his list of books grow and his interests become more varied.

2. To help Dick become more interested in words, teach him dictionary skills: how to use the pronunciation key and get some of the fascinating information that is found in dictionaries. Work with him on new words. Encourage him to keep a list of new words or a file of vocabulary word cards. He should get in the habit of jotting down new words that he meets in his reading, looking them up, figuring out how to pronounce them, and recording their meanings in his notebook or on cards.

3. Help him work out a schedule for studying his various subjects and, as time permits, give him help in reading the subjects in which he is deficient. Obviously he needs instruction and practice in the study-type of reading. The Survey Q3R (for a description, see Strang and others, 1951) formula would help him to organize, relate, and apply ideas gained from his reading.

These recommendations seem simple and obvious. On the other hand, there is danger of "overdiagnosing"—of reading into the information more than is warranted. There is danger of prematurely or erroneously labeling children as "remedial reading cases" and of confusing symptoms with causes. There is danger of focusing on faults to the exclusion of accomplishments.

USE OF INFORMATION

Procedures for working with pupils on their reading should stem from the understanding we have gained about them. Other-

wise there is no justification for spending time on diagnosis. Information such as that described in this chapter gives the teacher
or clinician clues to the individual pupil's reading development or
difficulty.

This information is often used in what has been called the
client-centered or student-centered approach to reading problems.
The teacher or clinician feels his way as he works with the individual. He offers the individual opportunities to explore the situation and present himself in his own way. The teacher notes and
responds to any expressions of interest and to other learning clues.
Activities in which the student takes initiative facilitate learning,
whereas required drill is likely to increase his resistance to authority or his sense of failure.

Descriptions of the treatment of several severely retarded
readers will illustrate this approach. Max liked to work with tools
as much as he disliked reading. The first thing he noticed when
he came into the room was a workbench on which were nails and
a hammer. After a little general conversation the teacher said,
"We need a bookcase. Could you make one for us? I'll help all I
can, but I'm not good at making things." They spent the first period making the bookcase. This accomplishment gave Max a
friendly feeling toward the room and the teacher and bolstered
his sense of worth. Such a fine new bookcase needed books in it.
To find appropriate books Max had to look over the pile that had
been donated by parents. He could read some words and, with
the help of the pictures, he selected those he thought his classmates would like to read. There were several books that interested
him particularly. During his reading period he asked for help in
learning to read them. Thus the reading instruction, stemming
from another interest, began.

David was extremely apathetic. He made no response to the
teacher's friendliness. He showed no interest in the picture books.
He did not accept the teacher's invitation to help her erase the
board. The first thing that aroused a flicker of interest was the
typewriter. "Would you like to write your name on it?" the teacher
asked. He chose a sheet of paper and typed his name, picking out
each letter carefully. This was the beginning of a book to which
he added stories each period that he came for special help. Typ-
ing was an opening wedge to teaching.

Charles was belligerent about reading. He would have none

of it. If the teacher continued the pressure that his parents and previous teachers had been putting on him, she would only intensify his resistance. She decided to play a waiting game and follow any leads he gave her. Seeing some paper and crayons, he began to draw. That was all he did for two periods. No words were introduced until he suggested that one picture ought to have a name. Then he printed the title he wanted to give it. This was the beginning of his picture dictionary. In this case it was fortunate that the teacher knew Charles had been nagged incessantly about his reading. Thus she avoided intensifying his rebellion. If he had been the sort of child who had been allowed to do as he pleased and had known no standards or firmness, the situation might have demanded quite a different approach; he may have needed to be made to do what he was capable of doing.

Stanley responded to vocabulary games. He showed much satisfaction in the growing pile of words that he could define and pronounce correctly and the increasing number of sentences he built. He was stimulated by objective evidence of progress.

These cases illustrate only a few of many possible approaches through interests, permissiveness, reasonable pressures, games, team learning, stories, practice exercises, and the like. A versatile approach that uses materials and methods in a flexible manner has been found to be most successful. The teacher uses information gathered about each student both prior to and during the teaching periods to maintain a continuous sensitivity to his needs and to his receptivity to learning.

CONCLUDING STATEMENT

Diagnosis is as complex as the reading process itself. The causes of reading difficulty are subtle and difficult to uncover. Often there is no clear line of demarcation between the causes and the effects of reading deficiency; it is sometimes hard to tell which is cause and which is effect.

On the basis of the information gained, the clinician makes inferences and formulates hypotheses leading to recommendations. The teacher goes through the same process in a less comprehensive, systematic way. Against his background of understanding of the student, the teacher often makes immediate use of the information he gains.

Without some diagnostic information, individualization of instruction is impossible. Diagnosis is a basic tool in providing for individual differences. Without such understanding, the teacher cannot help each pupil realize his potential reading ability.

Diagnosis should gear in with treatment. Finding out what is wrong should lead, as soon as possible, to doing something constructive about it.

Suggested Problems
Practice and Demonstration[1]

1. Have two students debate the pros and cons of the two approaches to diagnosis.

2. Give diagnostic information on a case and show how a teacher may use it in the classroom situation.

3. Dramatize an interview between a reading specialist and a teacher who has referred a reading problem to him. The reading specialist presents the results of his diagnostic study; teacher and reading specialist together plan a program of remedial work for the student.

4. Ask individual students to review research on the value of intelligence tests and listening comprehension tests in predicting reading achievement.

5. Summarize the diagnostic information in several case studies of reading difficulty and tell how it was obtained.

6. Obtain estimates from different sources of the percentage of reading cases in which there is emotional involvement; then discuss the possible reasons for such marked differences.

7. Make a chart showing common elements and differences in emphasis in the processes of identification, appraisal, diagnosis, and evaluation.

8. What is Conant's concept of retardation in reading? (See Conant, 1960, p. 21.) How does it compare with the other views presented in this chapter?

References

Bianchi, Martha Dickinson, and Alfred Leete Thompson (eds.): *The Poems of Emily Dickinson*, Little, Brown and Company, Boston, 1937, poem XCVII.

[1] In these sections, throughout the text, some of the suggestions are directed to college teachers of classes in reading methods; others are directed to the students taking such courses or to teachers studying the book independently.

Coleman, James: "Teen-agers and Their Crowd," *The PTA Magazine,* 56:4–7, March, 1962.

Conant, James Bryant: *Recommendations for Education in the Junior High School Years,* Educational Testing Service, Princeton, N.J., 1960.

Dolch, Edward W.: "Testing Reading with a Book," *Elementary English,* 28:124–125, March, 1951.

Durrell, Donald D., and Helen Blair Sullivan: *Durrell-Sullivan Reading Capacity and Achievement Tests,* two levels: grades 2.5–4.5, Primary; grades 3–7, Intermediate (Form A of Primary Test and Intermediate Reading Capacity Test, Forms A and B of Intermediate Achievement Test), Harcourt, Brace & World, Inc., New York, 1937–1945.

Figurel, J. Allen (ed.): *Challenge and Experiment in Reading,* International Reading Association Conference Proceedings, vol. 7, Scholastic Magazines, Inc., New York, 1962.

Holmes, Jack A.: "Personality Characteristics of the Disabled Reader," *Journal of Developmental Reading,* 4:111–122, Winter, 1961.

Porterfield, O. V., and H. F. Schlichting: "Peer Status and Reading Achievement," *Journal of Educational Research,* 54:291–297, April, 1961.

Sheldon, William D.: "Teacher Must Diagnose," *Education,* 78:545–546, May, 1958.

Simpson, Glenn O.: *Using My Reading Design,* Reading Circle, Inc., North Manchester, Ind., 1945.

Spache, George D.: "Integrating Diagnosis with Remediation in Reading," *The Elementary School Journal,* 56:18–26, September, 1955.

Strang, Ruth, and others: *Study Type of Reading Exercises, College Level,* Bureau of Publications, Teachers College, Columbia University, New York, 1951, pp. 8–14.

Walters, Richard H., and others: "A Study of Reading Disability," *Journal of Consulting Psychology,* 25:277–283, August, 1961.

Suggested Readings

Austin, Mary C., and others: *The Torch Lighters: Tomorrow's Teachers of Reading,* Graduate School of Education, Harvard University (distributed by Harvard University Press), Cambridge, Mass., 1961.

———— and others: *Reading Evaluation,* The Ronald Press Company, New York, 1961.

Betts, Emmett Albert: *Foundations of Reading Instruction,* American Book Company, New York, 1957.

Blair, Glenn M.: *Diagnostic and Remedial Teaching,* rev. ed., The Macmillan Company, New York, 1956.

Bond, Guy L., and Miles A. Tinker: *Reading Difficulties, Their Diagnosis and Correction,* Appleton-Century-Crofts, Inc., New York, 1957.

Brueckner, Leo J., and Guy L. Bond: *The Diagnosis and Treatment of Learning Difficulties,* Appleton-Century-Crofts, Inc., New York, 1955.

"Contributions to the Diagnosis and Remedial Treatment of Reading Difficulties; Symposium," *British Journal of Educational Psychology,* 30:146–179, June, 1960, and 31:79–105, February, 1961.

Diederich, Paul B.: "Design for a Comprehensive Evaluation Program," *School Review,* 58:225–232, April, 1950.

Gray, William S.: *The Appraisal of Current Practices in Reading,* Supplementary Educational Monographs, no. 61, The University of Chicago Press, Chicago, 1945.

Harris, Albert J.: "Diagnosis of Reading Disabilities," *Conference on Reading,* University of Pittsburgh, Pittsburgh, 1960, pp. 31–37.

———: *How to Increase Reading Ability,* 4th ed., David McKay Company, Inc., New York, 1961.

Hildreth, Gertrude: *Teaching Reading,* Holt, Rinehart and Winston, Inc., New York, 1958.

Josephine, Sister Mary: "Evaluation of Supervisory Programs in Reading," *Educational Administration and Supervision,* 40:434–437, November, 1954.

McCullough, Constance M.: "Changing Concepts of Reading Instruction," in *Changing Concepts of Reading Instruction,* International Reading Association Conference Proceedings, vol. 6, Scholastic Magazines, Inc., New York, 1961, pp. 13–22.

Meckel, Henry C.: "Evaluating Growth in Reading," *Reading in the High School and College,* National Society for the Study of Education, 1948, chap. 12, part 2.

Olson, Willard C.: "Reading as a Function of Total Growth of the Child," in *Reading and Pupil Development,* Supplementary Educational Monographs, no. 51, The University of Chicago Press, Chicago, 1940, pp. 233–237.

Robinson, Helen M.: *Why Pupils Fail in Reading,* The University of Chicago Press, Chicago, 1946.

Russell, David H.: "Evaluation of Pupil Growth in and through Reading," in *Reading in the Elementary School,* Forty-eighth Yearbook of the National Society for the Study of Education, The University of Chicago Press, Chicago, 1947, chap. 14, part 2.

Staiger, R.: "Organizing Corrective and Remedial Programs in Our Schools," *Conference on Reading,* University of Pittsburgh, Pittsburgh, 1960, pp. 135–142.

Strang, Ruth: "Evaluation of Development in and through Reading," in *Development in and through Reading,* Sixtieth Yearbook of the National Society for the Study of Education, The University of Chicago Press, Chicago, 1961, pp. 376–397.

————: "Controversial Programs and Procedures in Reading," *The School Review,* 69:413–428, Winter, 1961.

Vernon, M. D.: *Backwardness in Reading,* Cambridge University Press, New York, 1957.

Wrightstone, J. W.: *Appraisal of Growth in Reading,* Educational Research Bulletin 2, Board of Education, City of New York, 1941.

2

THE ROLE OF
THE TEACHER IN DIAGNOSIS

Any teacher can gain an understanding of his students that will help him to reinforce their desirable attitudes and competencies and to develop those which they lack. He need not wait for a specialist to give him diagnostic information; it is available to him in his daily work. According to Lytton (1961, pp. 79–94), teachers trained to detect individual differences have been as accurate in grouping retarded readers for remedial education as were group tests yielding IQs and AQs (accomplishment quotients). Through observation and interviews, teachers can be even more effective than tests in discovering the causes of their students' reading difficulties.

A skillful teacher continuously interweaves diagnosis and instruction. In every lesson he notes students' strengths and weaknesses in reading and tries to find causes of their lack of progress. By tabulating and summarizing the information about all the students, the teacher can gain understanding of the class as a whole.

The appraisal process pinpoints the student's present stage of development. Instruction starts from there and is guided by the teacher's knowledge of a psychological sequence of reading skills. (For a comprehensive chart of sequential development of reading see Strang and others, 1961, pp. 92–113.) If the student does not respond to group instruction, the teacher may use individual methods. As the teacher continues to work with the student on his reading improvement, he obtains additional information that suggests further methods and materials to be employed at each stage.

UNDERSTANDING GAINED DURING A READING LESSON

The teaching of any story or article offers opportunities for an informal kind of diagnosis. The following description of a typical reading lesson shows ways in which the teacher can learn about the background of experience that the student brings to his reading, his vocabulary knowledge, his reading habits, his comprehension of the selection, and his specific difficulties.

In orienting students to a selection, the teacher encourages them to talk about relevant experiences they have had. He notes background knowledge that they need to interpret the selection. He observes their ability to relate their previous experiences to the present reading situation. Their lack of understanding of certain words and concepts also becomes evident.

This preliminary discussion may indicate the need for instruction before beginning to read the selection. There may be a need to enrich the students' background of experience with pictures, explanations, or descriptions of the author and the setting. Usually the teacher helps them to set up a target—a purpose—

for reading the selection and makes sure that they understand the key words.

While the students are reading silently, the teacher can learn much about their reading habits. He will note that some seem to be reading rapidly with interest and attention. Others read slowly and show signs of difficulty—inattention, frowning, lip movements, finger pointing, and requests for help. Their questions indicate the particular difficulties they are having.

The group discussion that follows the silent reading will give additional information: How well have individual students accomplished their purposes for reading the selection? Which students were able to comprehend the selection accurately and easily? Which did not comprehend what the author said? Were there any that made creative comments and applications? Which profited by the instruction given? How did they answer the question, "How might you apply this story to your own lives or to the world today?"

To obtain more specific information about their vocabulary, word recognition, and comprehension skills, the teacher may ask individual students privately, while the others are still reading, to read a paragraph aloud, to state its main idea, to give the meanings of certain words in context, and to point out relationships or sequences.

If the teacher allows ample time for the reading of the selection, some students will finish before the time is up. How did they spend this free time? What initiative and self-direction do they show in finding something worthwhile to do? Some may begin reading another book; others may draw an illustration or write a poem or story suggested by the selection.

Reading experiences of this kind are a source of diagnostic information that the teacher may use immediately or later in planning individual and group instruction. He will vary individual assignments as to length and difficulty. To help each student progress at the rate and on the level appropriate for him, the teacher may use multilevel material such as The Science Research Associates Reading Laboratories (Science Research Associates, Chicago). To students who have similar difficulties, he will give instruction and practice individually or in small groups. To meet the needs of all students, he will draw on his reservoir of instructional procedures, materials, and ideas for creative activities. For the able learners, he will provide some challenging books in different fields, plays for dramatized reading, and opportunities to prepare and present special reports and programs.

For poor readers, the teacher will supply study guides, books, and other reading materials that are on their level. They need much easy supplementary reading to give practice in basic sight vocabulary and in the use of word recognition skills in context. Interesting books also serve as an incentive to acquire the reading skills that they need. To obtain additional practice, they may play vocabulary and word recognition games such as those published by The Garrard Press, Champaign, Illinois. Poor readers especially enjoy participating in choral reading and taking minor parts in the dramatized reading of plays. In interest groups, they can contribute to the study of special topics or problems by reading and reporting on a simple book, even a picture book. Motivated by a need to find out, a retarded reader sometimes makes sense out of material that the teacher thinks is too difficult for him. He uses clues the teacher may not recognize and puzzles out meanings in ways known only to himself.

The most seriously retarded readers cannot comprehend the texts provided for their grade. For these students the teacher may present orally the science and social studies content that is too difficult for them to read. He may make his presentation more vivid by the use of audio-visual aids. The students then dictate the main points, which the teacher will write on the board and have typed for them to read. If special reading classes are available, the teacher will refer these students for special instruction.

UNDERSTANDING GAINED THROUGH THE LANGUAGE EXPERIENCE APPROACH

In the language experience approach the student's account of his own experience or thoughts is used as reading material. From experience reading the teacher obtains several kinds of diagnostic information. In his story or poem the child may reveal his personal feelings and interests. For example, a first-grade child dictated to the teacher a little story that indirectly expressed her loneliness.

Another first-grade story suggests the frequent affinity of little boys for dogs: "When I was a little boy I had a dog. We do not have him now. While we were buying pizza, he ran away. His name was Winthrop."

As students try to read their experience stories, the teacher notes basic words that they do not recognize and any difficulties in recognizing in print words that are already in their speaking vocabulary.

UNDERSTANDING GAINED IN A SPECIAL READING CLASS

A period with a special reading class in a junior high school further illustrates how the teacher may gather information about individual students while teaching. According to group reading tests, the boys in this class were three or more years below their seventh-grade placement. Each boy was given a copy of the third-grade Reader's Digest Skill Builder to read. When they had finished the story, the teacher discussed it with them.

One boy, whom we shall call Bert, apparently had comprehended very little of it. Although he spoke well, he had little to communicate. When asked to read a few paragraphs aloud, he stopped at every word of more than three letters. When asked if he did much reading, he merely shrugged his shoulders. When sports were mentioned, he showed a little more interest. When asked if he liked animals, he became excited and took from his pocket two photographs of bears taken by his brother, who, he said, had a job feeding animals in the zoo. Although Bert was obviously enthusiastic about animals, he showed no interest in reading books or articles about them.

Near the end of the period Bert asked if they could do the *Reader's Digest* exercises next week. He told the others that he had got 100 per cent on the SRA Reading Laboratory's Power Builder Test. Actually, the teacher discovered, he had left the spaces blank and filled in the correct answers by consulting the scoring key; then he had proudly claimed to have scored 100 per cent.

He is very slow in all his reading and is extremely restless. He likes to distract others by his wisecracks and useless questions.

It became obvious in this single period that Bert could not comprehend second-grade material, that he needed to build up his basic sight vocabulary and acquire effective word recognition skills. He revealed his need to succeed in the group by making wild guesses and by copying the answers so he could boast about getting 100 per cent. His tension showed in restlessness and in his habit of playing with his fingers.

Using the understanding gained from this preliminary appraisal, the teacher planned to help Bert build a basic sight vocabulary and acquire word recognition skills so that he could achieve some real success. He could get this practice through a variety of games and activities that would also help to relieve his physical tension. The teacher planned to interest him in keeping a record of the words he learned so that he could see his progress. As he acquired sufficient reading ability, she would provide animal stories that he might enjoy if he could read them without frustration. Since recognition in the group was so important to him, the teacher planned to teach him the skills needed to participate successfully in some group activity, such as reading a few lines in a play.

In these small reading groups the teacher can also find out by which method a student learns best. Some students learn better by visual methods, others by auditory methods. Few students respond well to any method by which they have previously failed to learn.

A few retarded readers resist any direct instruction in reading. For example, a ninth grader who had been in remedial reading classes for four years was naturally resistant to further reading instruction. His teacher decided that she was not going to try to teach him reading. Instead, she spent most of the time allotted to him in talking about any subject that interested him. One day he showed an interest in skimming and they worked a little on that. Near the end of the term he told his teacher he had read his first book. To be sure it was required for a book report, but in the past he had always written his book reports from information elicited orally from other students. This time he had actually read the book himself. Since he is interested in art, the teacher is now looking for some books on art that he may be able to enjoy. In this case the best teaching seems to have been no teaching. The teacher tried successfully to convey to him the idea that no one can teach him to read if he does not want to learn. On the other hand, students who are eager to improve in reading may feel they are wasting time unless they can see that the instruction and practice in reading is really "getting them somewhere."

Some retarded readers respond neither to a direct attack on

the specific reading difficulties detected in the diagnosis nor to an indirect approach through games and other devices. They are often prevented by underlying emotional and social problems from learning the necessary skills or from mobilizing themselves to use their abilities.

UNDERSTANDING GAINED THROUGH INDIVIDUALIZING INSTRUCTION

While members of the class are reading independently suitable interesting books of their own choice, the teacher has time for individual conferences. In these conferences, he may ask the student to read a paragraph or two aloud. He first notes and approves something the student does well or better than before. Then he may give a little instruction and suggestions for practice in some skill in which the student needs to improve, such as phrasing—reading in thought units instead of word by word. With another student, the teacher may spend his ten-minute conference in finding out how well he has comprehended the selection and in showing him one or two ways of improving his comprehension. With a student who can read but does not, the teacher may spend his time introducing this reluctant reader to a book that he may be persuaded to read outside of class.

Sometimes the teacher may give a larger amount of time to an individual student whose lack of improvement is baffling. Group methods have not reached him. When there is no reading specialist or clinic to which to refer him, the teacher does all he can in the classroom setting.

Let us consider two individual cases. The first we shall call Alice, a sixteen-year-old girl. On the Wechsler Intelligence Scale for Children her verbal IQ was 72; her performance IQ, 79; and the full-scale IQ, 73. On the group Stanford Achievement Test her grade on paragraph meaning was 4.8; word meaning, 7.7; and average reading, 6.2. According to her test results, she was already reading beyond the fifth-grade level. Appraisal during class contacts with her indicated higher potential ability than was indicated by the individual intelligence test.

The teacher started with Alice's interest in a dog, Blackie, that she had lost four years ago. She still felt very sad about it. "Blackie was my best friend," she said. As she told about Blackie, the teacher wrote the story, typed it, and gave it to her to read.

Alice found little difficulty in reading her own language patterns and words whose meaning she already knew. This experience reading encouraged her to make a book about the care of dogs. She visited a friendly veterinarian who gave her some firsthand information. He also gave her some printed directions for selecting, feeding, and caring for dogs. She included this pamphlet in her book although it was above her tested reading level. As she read this pamphlet aloud, the teacher took the opportunity to observe:

Which words Alice knew at sight

How she attacked the pronunciation of unfamiliar words

Whether she understood the meaning of certain words and phrases: "substantiating your claims" she explained as "showing the reasons for your claims"; "grooming the dog," as "making the dog look nice"

How quickly she learned and how permanently she remembered the meaning of the new words she was being taught

Whether she could get the main idea of paragraphs

What her attitude was toward reading

How well she was able to express her feelings

Thus diagnosis and appraisal were byproducts of instruction. The advantage of this approach is that it gives clues that can be used immediately in the instruction of the pupil.

In the case of a thirteen-year-old boy with a reported Stanford-Binet IQ of 79, the teacher obtained the following diagnostic information just from hearing the boy read a story that interested him:

He read third-grade material haltingly and with difficulty.

He possessed very poor word recognition skills.

He failed to recognize some of the basic first-grade words.

He confused the name of the boat with the name of the place to which the invaders were going.

He could not make inferences or predictions about the story.

This boy might be expected to read fourth-grade material, yet his independent reading level was barely second grade. Observation of his reading indicated both strengths and weaknesses. The teacher helped him learn the words with which he initially had difficulty by giving him specific phonic instruction. For example, the teacher associated *fish* with words he already knew such as *dish* and *wish*. He used these words in humorous sentences, such as "He fished in a dish." He illustrated the word *trunk* with a sketch of an elephant's trunk and compared this with another meaning of the word: "He packed his trunk."

VALUES OF TEACHER DIAGNOSIS

Without these kinds of understanding, the teacher may either neglect practice and instruction on skills needed badly or give unnecessary instruction. He may also unwittingly reinforce an undesirable response as, for example, when he accepts and approves word calling or word-by-word reading or tells the student the meaning of a word he could have solved himself if he had used his newly acquired word recognition skills. There is a nice balance between "accentuating the positive" and insisting upon "errorless learning."

The reading program as a whole, as well as the progress of individual students, should also be evaluated. Is it balanced? Does it use the best features of various methods and materials as they are appropriate, e.g., drills from a phonic system if they are needed by some children and wide, challenging reading for the able learners? Are combined instruction and appraisal an essential part of the total reading program?

MORE TECHNICAL DIAGNOSIS

When severely retarded readers do not respond to classroom methods nor profit by individualized instruction within the class groups, the qualified teacher will try to make a more intensive study of their reading. In addition to making a more thorough analysis of their reading difficulties, he will be alert to personality and cultural factors which are often the key to serious reading problems. To get concerted action on the case, the teacher may share with parents, counselors, and other teachers his awareness of the student's needs. Through the proper channels he will also seek whatever expert assistance in the technical aspects of diagnosis that is available from psychologists, psychiatrists, reading and mental health clinics, and social agencies.

CONCLUSIONS AND CAUTIONS

To help the teacher make effective use of all sources of assistance, we offer the following suggestions and cautions, each of which will be developed in more detail in subsequent chapters.

The intelligence test that is used to appraise the student's reading potential should involve little or no reading.

A listening comprehension test may give a better estimate of reading capacity than the intelligence test. A discrepancy between listening comprehension and reading comprehension would indicate that lack of reading comprehension may be due to inadequate basic reading skills.

Teacher-made tests have several advantages over standardized tests: (1) they measure or describe reading ability over a wider range of content and skills; (2) they can be used flexibly to obtain diagnostic information; and (3) because they are similar to the student's daily reading tasks, they impress him as being more useful than the majority of standardized reading tests.

The visual screening tests given by the school nurse or family physician have often been inadequate for reading diagnosis because the nurse and physician generally used the old Snellen Chart, which tests distant vision rather than vision at reading distance. There are more adequate screening instruments now on the market that can be operated by reading teachers and nurses carefully trained in their use (see Chapter 9).

Observation, the reading autobiography, and the interview, used by perceptive persons, yield more understanding of students' needs, interests, and attitudes toward themselves and toward reading than do group personality inventories.

Facts about the student's family background, the community attitude toward education and reading, and the school atmosphere often help to explain reading problems. Knowing deficiencies in the student's background, the teacher is in a better position to supply experiences that appeal to his interests, satisfy his needs, and help him to progress toward the goals he has set for himself. These factors often play a vital role in successful instruction. Gains made by retarded readers are often traceable to the change from a classroom in which they have experienced nothing but failure to a small group in which they experience success.

The evaluation pattern should be suitable to each situation. It is better to select a few reliable instruments that the teacher can interpret and apply than to use many instruments whose results are poorly interpreted and used. Many teachers underestimate the value of their day-by-day contacts with students.

The teacher's concept of himself as a person and his skill as a teacher are the central factors in the total situation. Techniques are tools, always used by a person.

Fortunately, the teacher does not bear the entire burden of helping a student improve his reading. Administrators, counselors, librarians, and other staff members each make some contribution to the diagnosis and remediation of reading difficulties and to the appraisal of students' progress in reading (Early, 1962, pp. 1–6).

Suggested Problems
Practice and Demonstration

1. Use the method of having pairs of students interview each other and report to the group what they have learned about the other's interests, background, need for the reading course, etc. Then summarize the kinds of understanding of individual students that a teacher may gain in one period from this procedure: their use of language, organization of ideas, social sensitivity, poise, feelings of inferiority, interests, hobbies, purpose, personal relations, and other items.

2. Describe different classroom situations and point out the kind of information about pupils that may be obtained in each.

3. Demonstrate the teaching of a directed reading lesson to a class. Then summarize the kind of information that may be obtained during this process.

4. Present a detailed report of work with an individual case and discuss the way in which understanding of the individual grew as treatment proceeded.

5. Dramatize the procedure of referring a child with a baffling reading problem for special services.

6. What channels of referral should be used in a school?

7. What is the responsibility of the specialist for reporting back on the case to the teacher?

References

Early, Margaret J.: *Providing Leadership for Secondary Reading Programs,* Council for Administrative Leadership, Albany, N.Y., June, 1962.

Lytton, H.: "An Experiment in Selection for Remedial Education," *British Journal of Educational Psychology,* 31:79–94, February, 1961.

Strang, Ruth, and others: *The Improvement of Reading,* 3d ed., McGraw-Hill Book Company, Inc., New York, 1961.

Suggested Readings

Anderson, Irving, and Walter Dearborn: *The Psychology of Teaching Reading,* The Ronald Press Company, New York, 1952.

Artley, A. Sterl: "Classroom Help for Children with Beginning Reading Problems," *The Reading Teacher,* 15:439–442, May, 1962.

Barbe, Walter B.: *Educator's Guide to Personalized Reading Instruction,* Prentice-Hall, Inc., Englewood Cliffs, N.J., 1960.

Bloomer, R. H.: "Effects of a College Reading Program on a Random Sample of Education Freshman," *Journal of Developmental Reading,* 5:110–118, Winter, 1962.

Burton, William H.: *Reading in Child Development,* The Bobbs-Merrill Company, Inc., Indianapolis, 1956.

Carter, Homer, and Dorothy McGuinnes: *Teaching Individuals to Read,* D. C. Heath and Company, Boston, 1962.

DeBoer, John J., and Martha Dallman: *The Teaching of Reading,* Holt, Rinehart and Winston, Inc., New York, 1960.

Deighton, Lee C.: *Vocabulary Development in the Classroom,* Bureau of Publications, Teachers College, Columbia University, New York, 1959.

Gray, William S.: *Improving Reading in All Curriculum Areas,* Proceedings of the Annual Conference on Reading, The University of Chicago Press, Chicago, 1952.

———— and Bernice Rogers: *Maturity in Reading,* The University of Chicago Press, Chicago, 1956.

Kottmeyer, William: *Teacher's Guide for Remedial Reading,* Webster Publishing Company, St. Louis, Mo., 1959.

McKim, Margaret G.: *Guiding Growth in Reading in Modern Elementary Schools,* The Macmillan Company, New York, 1955.

Mearns, Hugh: *Creative Power,* Dover Publications, Inc., New York, 1958.

Newton, John R.: *Reading in Your School,* McGraw-Hill Book Company, Inc., New York, 1960.

Robinson, Helen M.: *Corrective Reading in Classroom and Clinic,* Proceedings of the Annual Conference on Reading, no. 79, The University of Chicago Press, Chicago, 1953.

Russell, David: *Children Learn to Read,* Ginn and Company, Boston, 1961.

———— and others: *Reading Aids through the Grades,* Bureau of Publications, Teachers College, Columbia University, New York, 1956.

Spache, G. D.: "Diagnosis of Reading Problems in the Classroom," *Education Digest,* 26:47–49, November, 1960.

Strang, Ruth, and Dorothy Bracken: *Making Better Readers*, D. C. Heath and Company, Boston, 1957.

Strang, Ruth, and Donald Lindquist: *The Administrator and the Improvement of Reading*, Appleton-Century-Crofts, Inc., New York, 1960.

Tinker, Miles A., and Constance M. McCullough: *Teaching Elementary Reading*, Appleton-Century-Crofts, Inc., New York, 1962.

Tyler, Fred (ed.): *Individualizing Instruction*, Sixty-first Yearbook of the National Society for the Study of Education, The University of Chicago Press, Chicago, 1962.

Weiss, Jerry M.: *An English Teacher's Reader, Grades 7–12*, The Odyssey Press, Inc., New York, 1962.

Witty, Paul (ed.): *Development in and through Reading*, Sixtieth Yearbook of the National Society for the Study of Education, The University of Chicago Press, Chicago, 1961.

Wolfe, Don M.: *Language Arts and Life Patterns, Grades 2–8*, The Odyssey Press, Inc., New York, 1962.

3

OBSERVATION
IN THE CLASSROOM

An elementary school teacher who stays with his class four hours a day for over 150 days has a total of about six hundred hours of possible time for observation. If he has fifty pupils in his class (which heaven forbid!), theoretically he would have twelve hours to devote to each pupil. Of course he must spend some of his time in giving instruction to the class as a whole. But even

41

then, he may be noticing how the class and certain individuals in it are responding to the instruction. It seems possible that most teachers can develop greater skill in understanding their pupils through observation, either specific and objective or more subjective and impressionistic.

A teacher readily identifies a student who cannot read: He often looks away from his book; he tries to avoid reading. He gets better marks in subjects that do not require reading. Sometimes he comprehends what he hears better than what he reads. As the teacher observes more closely, he discovers specific difficulties in vocabulary, word recognition, and comprehension. From further observation in the classroom and from interviews he may infer that certain emotional difficulties are interfering with the student's achievement in reading.

Observation is a basic technique. It is employed every day by every teacher. It does not require extra time or materials. Day by day the teacher observes pupils in his classes as they engage in learning all the language arts. Most of his observations are never recorded; they are used immediately or at the first opportunity to help the student. For example, a child hesitates over the initial sound of an unfamiliar word. The teacher says, "What other words do you know that begin with the same letters?" Thus the child identifies the initial sound of the word. This clue may enable him to pronounce the word. As a check on the correctness of his pronunciation, the teacher asks, "Does the word you pronounced make sense in the sentence?"

LIMITATIONS OF OBSERVATION

Although observation is excellent for gaining understanding of the way a student reads, it does not directly tell us why he reads this way. From our observation we can only make inferences about the causes of the student's reading failures or successes. To guide the student in improving his reading, we need inferences or hypotheses based on a number of observations plus all the other relevant information that is available.

As safeguards against misinterpreting recorded observations, four principles should be kept in mind:

1. Since the student is always changing and growing, an ob-

servation that was made last year may not describe his present reading performance.

2. A teacher can observe only a small part of a student's total behavior. On the basis of such limited information, the teacher can make only tentative generalizations about the student's reading.

3. Observations made by a teacher may tell more about the teacher than about the student. His first impression of the student, his philosophy of education, and many other factors may color what he sees.

4. Ideally, observations should be interpreted in conjunction with interview, test, and other data. However, observations often are the only data that are available at the moment, and sometimes action should not be deferred.

DETAILED ANALYSIS OF CLASSROOM SITUATIONS

Teachers are daily confronted with many common classroom situations in which they may gain much understanding of their students' reading. A detailed analysis of these situations serves as a guide to observation; it alerts the teacher to significant reactions which she might not otherwise notice. We may either start with the situation and describe the kind of understanding we can obtain from it or start with the kind of understanding we need and indicate the situations in which such understanding can be obtained.

The analyses on the following pages show kinds of information about students' reading that may be obtained in different classroom situations. To save space we have run the items on the same line; however, it would be easier for the teacher to set each one up on a separate line, e.g.:

Language abilities:

Vocabulary
    Meager _____
    Rich   _____
    Accurate _____
    Incorrect _____

Sentence structure
    Incomplete sentences _____
    Simple sentences   _____
    Complex sentences   _____

Oral Report Periods

In kindergarten and the lower grades and in oral English periods in the upper grades, students are offered many opportunities to tell their experiences. As the teacher listens, he learns about their vocabulary and language patterns, their interests and personality traits. Glimpses of home conditions also are frequently revealed.
Specific observations:

Language abilities: vocabulary: meager ____, rich ____, accurate ____, incorrect ____

Sentence structure: incomplete sentences ____, simple sentences ____, complex sentences ____

Imagination: creative ____, bizarre ____

Organization: recounted events in proper sequence ____, well organized ____, disjointed ____

Sense of humor: enjoyment of humor ____, makes others laugh ____

Intelligence: is alert mentally ____, sees relations ____, solves problems ____, learns slowly ____

Interest: wholehearted ____, indifferent ____, apathetic ____

Personality: self-confident ____, shy ____, socially poised ____

Family relations and background: affectionate home relations ____, unhappy home ____

Peer relations: well liked by classmates ____, ignored by classmates ____, rejected ____

Appearance: habitually happy ____, sad ____; well dressed and well groomed ____, poorly dressed ____, inappropriately dressed ____, disheveled ____

While Listening to the Teacher Read a Story

Note parts of story that evoke keenest interest: keenly interested ____, eager to talk about it ____

Comprehension: accurate ____, detailed ____, inadequate ____

When Students Read Aloud

This situation gives the teacher opportunity to observe each student's word recognition skills, pronunciation, phrasing, and expression. One can quickly detect "word callers" by asking several searching questions on the selection they have read. The student may also reveal his attitude toward reading and toward himself as a reader. It will be evident whether he approaches reading with enjoyment, indifference, dislike, anxiety, resistance, or hostility.

Dramatized reading of a story or play shows still more clearly the student's ability to read aloud with expression, to bring out appropriate feeling and meaning, to interpret clues of character, and to evoke the interest of the audience.

Specific observations:

Method of word attack: sounds out words ____, tries to analyze structure ____, uses context clues ____

Word recognition problems: skips words ____, reverses letters, words, phrases ____, substitutes words ____, guesses wildly ____

Substitutions yield valuable clues. If the student substitutes a word that makes sense in the sentence, we may infer that he is reading for meaning. If, however, the word he substitutes makes no sense, we may infer that he is merely pronouncing words with little concern for the meaning of what he reads. The teacher should also note what kinds of words cause the student difficulty. Are they little common words such as those in the Dolch basic vocabulary or longer words; words within his experience or words foreign to him? It is also important to observe how he goes about getting the meaning of unfamiliar words.

Phrasing: reads word by word ____, reads in phrases or other thought units ____, loses place easily ____, reads clearly and with expression ____

Comprehension: recognizes basic vocabulary at sight ____, shows an understanding of material read ____, sees relationships and sequences of ideas ____, can discuss what he has read ____, shows originality in interpretation ____

Attitudes: volunteers to read orally ____, reads only when called upon ____, appears to enjoy reading orally in different situations ____, reads aloud to others in free time ____

Reaction of classmates to student's oral reading: eager to have him read ____, show interest ____, attention wanders ____, restless ____, disinterested ____, rudely interrupt ____

Silent Reading in Library, Free Reading, and Study Periods

The student's choice of books in a free reading or library period may show his reading interests and level. His behavior during the period indicates his silent reading habits and power of concentration. In addition to the specific observation, teacher or student may make an attention-distraction chart. Such a chart may make the students more aware of the time they are wasting. Of course, it would be necessary for the students to have a chance to discuss what goes into their attention-distraction charts. Were they just idly daydreaming, or were they staring into space while pondering thoughts evoked by their reading? If they were distracted, what caused it? Was the book too hard? Were they thinking about tonight's party?

Specific observations:

Attitude toward silent reading: _____

Approach to books: leafs through many books _____, chooses quickly _____; looks first at chapter titles and/or table of contents _____, pictures _____, printed pages _____; tends to choose small books _____, large books _____, one kind of book _____, a particular author or series _____; is rather uniform in choices _____, chooses a variety of books _____; chooses books at his own age level of interest _____, below _____, above _____; takes books home often _____, seldom _____, never _____; reads them through _____; can discuss what he has read _____; returns books on time _____, undamaged _____; asks for books he does not find on shelves _____

Uses library just to look at magazines _____; reads little of newspapers except the sports page and "funnies" _____; always carries a big stack of books home _____; asks for permission to take a new book home over the weekend _____

Can locate sources of information _____, finds suitable material _____, makes notes on relevant material _____

When a new book is distributed receives it enthusiastically _____, groans and shows other signs of rejection _____, turns pages aimlessly _____, systematically examines book _____, asks questions about book _____

Voluntary reading: reads more than required _____, includes a variety of material _____, comments on reading are clear, original, thoughtful _____, shows depth of appreciation beyond his grade level _____

Visual habits and posture: frowns _____, blinks often _____, squints _____, rubs or wipes eyes _____, other _____; holds book at average distance _____, too close _____, too far _____; good general posture _____

Uses reference tools such as glossary and dictionary: freely _____, seldom _____, never _____, effectively _____, as an excuse for leaving seat (as evidenced by attitude, approach, results) _____; independently _____ or with assistance _____

Reads by himself _____, talks to others _____; if the latter, in cooperative study _____ or as a disturbance _____

Amount of work completed: about same as classmates _____, noticeably more _____, noticeably less _____; if assignment is completed early, goes on to more of the same _____, stops and is idle _____, does something else _____, related (such as drawing pictures to illustrate the story) _____ or unrelated to classwork, disturbs others _____

Asks for teacher's help: _____

Group Instruction and Discussion

The teacher will observe that some students "catch on" quickly while others need to have an explanation repeated several times. The student who learns quickly should not have to mark time while the slow learners gain sufficient comprehension to go on. Sometimes, in a question or comment, a quiet student will reveal undetected ability. In response to a picture or incomplete story, a student may show exceptional originality.

Interaction in the group also may be observed. A great deal of learning takes place as a result of group interaction. Students may stimulate and encourage one another to read better; they may share their most effective reading methods, recommend stories they have liked, and otherwise facilitate each other's learning. On the other hand, interaction in some groups may be detrimental to growth in reading. Many retarded readers have told of being embarrassed when classmates shouted out the words they did not know, laughed at their mistakes, or made fun of the easy books they were reading. The bright child who enjoys reading may suffer in equal measure from an anti-intellectual spirit.

Specific observations:

Attitudes: eager to participate _____, interested _____, indifferent _____, withdrawn _____

Work habits: works well alone _____, with others _____

Thought habits: follows sequence of story or discussion _____, organizes thought well _____, recognizes cause and effect relations _____, summarizes well _____

Learning capacity: quick to catch on _____, needs to have directions or questions repeated _____, asks searching questions _____, relates ideas _____

Oral expression: expresses thought clearly in well-constructed sentences _____, uses words accurately _____, has good enunciation _____, uses a wide range of oral vocabulary _____

Discussion techniques: contributes relevant facts _____, analyzes the situation _____, shows breadth of information _____, listens to others and builds on what they have said _____

Creativity: inventive _____, shows imagination _____, is intellectually curious _____, shows maturity of interests _____

Personal involvement: tense _____, noncommittal _____, nervous and ill at ease _____, enjoys discussion _____, listens well but contributes little _____, applies vicarious experience to himself _____

Making and Giving Oral Reports

Individually or in a small group the students may show their interest in certain topics, their acquaintance with sources of information, their ability to evaluate and compare sources and to extract relevant information from them, organize it, and report it effectively. Observation of the audience gives indication of their ability to listen and evaluate tactfully the reports given.

Individual Contacts at Recess and Other Times

Positive attitudes: toward school ____, toward reading ____, toward self ____, toward parents ____

Negative attitudes: toward school ____, toward reading ____, toward self ____, toward parents ____

Favorite school subjects: _____

Subjects disliked: _____

Best friends: younger ____, older ____, brighter ____, duller ____

Significant events in the student's past: _____

Observation of Interaction between Student and Teacher

Since the influence of teacher behavior on children's spontaneous, cooperative, and self-initiated behavior and on their learning and achievement has been demonstrated by a number of research studies (see Anderson, 1939; Withall, 1960; Flanders, 1960; Moustakas and others, 1956), we should not only observe the individual student or teacher, but also the interaction between them and between students. In this way we can gain an understanding of the effect of teacher behavior and methods and of peer relations and values on individual students' attitudes and reading skills. In addition to our records of students' proficiency in reading, we would then learn more about what the teacher does that gets certain results.

Some teachers may think that this detailed analysis of observation in classroom situations is bewilderingly complex. Others may think it is "much ado about nothing." Obviously, a teacher cannot observe all the items about every student. But if he is familiar with kinds of understanding of students' reading that a teacher may gain during the school day, he becomes more alert to certain significant responses that individual students may make.

During a Silent Reading Period

Sixth-grade boys were reading books of their own choice during an individualized reading period.

Bruce, a large boy who was repeating the grade, laughed out loud as he was reading *Rufus M.* by Eleanor Estes. Most of the other students paid no attention to him; a few of his immediate classmates looked up, some annoyed, some amused. Occasionally he smiled to himself. It was almost four minutes before he turned the page. His lips were moving as if he were pronouncing each word to himself. In the second period he was still struggling through his book; he had completed two-thirds of it, still reading in the same slow way.

This observation raises questions about the meaning of Bruce's behavior: Did he really appreciate the humor of the book or was his loud laughter an attention-getting device? Do his classmates ignore or reject him? What are the causes of his slow reading—lack of a basic sight vocabulary? Inability to apply the word recognition skills he has been taught? Poor reasoning ability? Failure to use his knowledge of sentence structure to get meaning? Overemphasis on phonics that has led to persistence of the habit of sounding out every word? Further observation and conversation with Bruce is necessary to answer these questions.

Mack, the slowest student in the group, sat with the open book he had chosen—*Kidnapped*—looking into space. He did not get beyond page 9. He had previously read and enjoyed a simplified version of *Treasure Island* and wanted to read another book by the same author. But this time he had got hold of the original edition and could not understand it. Once in a while he roused himself and tried hard to read it but made little progress. He was glad when the period ended. Next time he chose an easy new illustrated book and enjoyed looking at the pictures. This observation made the teacher realize the importance of helping Mack choose a book that he could read independently without frustration. A too difficult book might destroy his recently acquired interest in reading and his effort to improve.

John had selected *Robinson Crusoe*. He squinted and grimaced as he read. He told the teacher he had a headache. He said he often got a headache when he read in school. Although he said he had been to an eye doctor who told his mother there was nothing wrong with his eyes, in view of these signs of visual discomfort the teacher decided to ask the school nurse to make a follow-up of his eye examination. The teacher also recognized that John's inability to read the books that his friends were reading might account for symptoms he had observed.

These examples illustrate a few kinds of understanding that a teacher may gain from observation. They also show the limitations of observation alone; one needs additional information to interpret most observations.

In Daily Talk Contacts with Students

Students' casual comments often clarify objective observation of their behavior and give clues to home conditions, parent-child relationships, and attitudes toward reading; for example, "At home there's no good place to read. . . . There's always something going on," and "Mother helps me get the problem started; she reads the problem to me to make sure I know what to do."

Some comments indicate the nature of the student's interest in a book: "This book is just right for me. I'm writing a paper on New York state highways. But it would also be interesting to the fruit growers and dairy farmers around here because it shows on charts how many apples and dairy products are shipped over our highways."

Other comments may explain fluctuations in the student's performance, as in the case of a girl who says that she wants to continue in school but that her mother wants her to leave and go to work.

RECORDING OF TEACHER OBSERVATIONS

Although most observations are not recorded, some systematic recording of the most significant behavior is useful to the teacher, the student, the parent, and the student's next teacher.

The recording may take either of two forms: (1) dated observations of individual students or anecdotal records that are recorded and then may be collected in each child's cumulative record folder and summarized periodically or (2) a checklist. The checklist may be used for a single pupil or as a record for the entire class. A checklist may contain some blank spaces for recording additional observations or explaining items checked.

A Checklist Record Form

An example of the checklist type of guide to observation in the classroom is given on the following pages. We may judge such a guide by these criteria:

1. It is organized around classroom situations with which the teacher is confronted.

2. Its items refer to specific behavior that can be observed rather than to generalizations or inferences about behavior.

3. It provides space to add further observations and impressions.

4. It is selective; i.e., it does not contain so many items as to make it unwieldy.

The following directions for using this form of record are suggested:

1. The teacher will have one of these checklist forms for each student, arranged alphabetically. He will also have in mind the kinds of observations that may be made in different classroom situations.

2. In each of the situations described, the teacher will note the most significant features in each student's performance. For example, it is Mary Jones's turn to tell about her weekend. The teacher takes Mary's checklist from the pile, listens and observes as Mary gives her report. He makes these comments on it: "Mary spoke very clearly and distinctly. I liked the way she told about each event in her weekend in just the order in which it happened— what happened first, next, and last. You were all interested in her story, weren't you? There was one new word she used that we can all learn to pronounce correctly. . . ." As the teacher summarizes the good points and the criticisms, he makes a tally on Mary's record as follows:

Speech	Language patterns	Reaction of peers
1 Distinct, clear	1 Good organization	1 Interested

Under *insights,* the teacher may write the word mispronounced and his impression of any progress she has made. By putting the first tally to the extreme left and the tallies for each subsequent

CHECKLIST RECORD OF CLASSROOM OBSERVATIONS ON PUPIL'S READING

Name _____ Grade _____ Teacher _____ Pupil _____

Directions: Tally significant observations day by day. Space at bottom of each situation can be used for noting specific errors, interpretation, general impression, evidence of progress, and recommendations.

I. When Giving Oral Reports

Vocabulary	Speech	Language patterns	Interests	Reactions of peers	Emotional factors
___ Rich	___ Distinct, clear enunciation	___ Complete sentences	___ Reads at home	___ Interested	___ Poised
___ Words mispronounced	___ Inaudible	___ Simple sentences	___ Uses library	___ Uninterested	___ Relaxed and happy
___ Meager	___ Stuttering	___ Complex sentences	___ Has own library	___ Sympathetic	___ Tense and anxious
___ Meaningful	___ Incorrect sounds	___ Good organization	___ Special collections	___ Friendly	___ Self-confident
	___ Monotonous	___ Repetition of ideas	___ Sports	___ Critical	___ Shy and embarrassed
	___ Expressive	___ Interpretation of ideas	___ Trips with family	___ Hostile	___ Antagonistic
		___ Imaginative	___ Science		___ Unhappy
			___ Art		
			___ Music		
			___ Shop		

Insights

_____   _____   _____   _____

52

II. Oral Reading and Group Instruction Periods

Word recognition skills

___ Basic sight vocabulary
___ Tries to sound words
___ Tries to pronounce by syllables
___ Tries to analyze structure
___ Substitutes another word
___ Makes wild guess
___ Reverses letters
___ Reverses words
___ Reverses phrases
___ Uses context clues

Comprehension

___ Answers factual questions correctly
___ Gives main ideas
___ Tells whole story accurately
___ Draws conclusions
___ Makes generalizations
___ Follows directions
___ Gives sensible reasons on thought questions
___ Gives fantastic, irrelevant reasons on thought questions
___ Relates reading to experiences
___ Unable to relate reading and experiences
___ Expression in reading

Insights

Peer relationships

___ Gets along well with girls
___ Gets along well with boys
___ Respects others
___ Disturbs others
___ Works alone only
___ Works well with one other child

Location of information

___ Uses index
___ Uses table of contents
___ Uses dictionary
___ Uses maps
___ Uses diagrams
___ Uses encyclopedia

53

CHECKLIST RECORD OF CLASSROOM OBSERVATIONS ON PUPIL'S READING (Continued)

III. Dramatization of Stories

Reading skills

____ Reads with expression
____ Interprets behavior of character accurately
____ Shows little understanding of character
____ Interprets sequence accurately
____ Reads too slowly
____ Reads too rapidly

Personal development

____ Poised
____ Relates characters and story to own experience
____ Interest evident
____ No interest
____ Shy, ill at ease

Insights

IV. Silent Reading Situation (Free-choice Reading or Library Time)

Attitude toward reading

____ Engrossed in book
____ Enjoyment evident
____ Independent
____ Dependent upon others
____ Uninterested, resists or avoids reading

Reading level

____ Primer
____ First
____ Second
____ Third
____ Fourth
____ Fifth
____ Sixth

Physical factors

____ Holds book up
____ Holds book close to face
____ Lip movements
____ Squints
____ Blinks eyes
____ Eyes red or watery

Interests

____ Animals
____ People
____ Science
____ History
____ Adventure
____ Fairy tales
____ Sports

Location of material

____ Finds suitable book quickly
____ Follows suggestions of other children
____ Has teacher help
____ Uses library classification
____ Uses table of contents

____Takes useful notes
____Selects too advanced books
____Unable to find any book of interest to him

____Easily distracted
____Other

____Seventh
____Other

____Complains of headaches
____Complains of dizziness
____Bends over book
____Fatigue posture

____Art
____Music
____Cars, planes, trucks, boats
____Rockets
____Armed services

Insights

_____
_____
_____

V. Listening to Story Read Aloud

Interest

____Listens attentively
____Listens part of time
____Easily distracted
____Restless and preoccupied

_____
_____
_____

Comprehension

____Evident appreciation of story—talks about it
____Asks related questions
____Responds to humor and excitement
____Answers factual questions
____Tells main ideas
____Tells whole story accurately
____Relates ideas to own experiences

55

observation a little further to the right, the teacher can get some indication of the student's progress.

In each period, the teacher will not attempt to record his observations of all the students. Instead he will focus his attention on a few students and record his observations on their records. Thus, in time the teacher may systematically accumulate observations of behavior significant for reading improvement. In some instances it may be easier for the teacher to jot down his observations on a scratch pad and tally them later on the checklist.

If, as suggested, the teacher calls attention to, or asks the students to point out, the individual's strengths, he will reinforce the good reading habits of the other students. If he gives instruction in an error noted, as when the teacher taught the pronunciation of a new word, the entire class profits by the analysis of one student's performance.

In addition to this immediate use, the checklist serves as a periodic appraisal of a student's progress. The teacher may go over the record with the student, who thus becomes more aware of his reading goals, the progress he is making toward them, and the practice he needs to correct certain faults or deficiencies. Such a record, passed on to the next teacher, supplies a wealth of initial understanding of the students in the new class.

A Global Approach

What might be called a "global approach" is another possible way of recording observations plus interpretation, plus recommendations. It describes the most significant aspects rather than checking separate items.

This method is effective only when used by an experienced person, a person who has gone through the process of specific analysis many times and is thoroughly familiar with the detailed guide to observation and skillful in seeing relationships and drawing inferences from the observed behavior. Such a person can sense the central factor and the related factors that are affecting the student's responses.

For example, the teacher might write about Mary Jones's oral report: "Mary speaks clearly and distinctly. This ability and her sense of sequence in reporting her stories help her to hold the attention of the class. She likes to use new words but does not always pronounce them correctly. We shall encourage her to listen carefully to new words and to be precise in her pronunciation of them."

INTERPRETATION OF OBSERVATIONS

The most difficult part of the technique of observation is interpreting what one sees. For example, it is easy to observe that a poor reader wants to read aloud at every opportunity and attempts to answer questions that are too difficult for him, but what is the motive underlying this observed behavior? Is it family pressure to be an outstanding student? Desire for attention? An inaccurate self-appraisal? Or is there some other explanation?

Manifestations of inattention may indicate language difficulty, visual or auditory defects, resistance to authority, inner conflicts, lack of immediate as well as long-term goals, or failure to recognize one's need for the knowledge and skills that are being taught —to mention only some of the many possible interpretations.

Ideally, interpretation should be attempted only after a number of observations have been made, and then it should be supplemented by interviews and other sources of information. Actually, however, an experienced teacher, against the background of his accumulated impressions, often may use a single observation as the basis for giving immediate help to a student.

CONCLUDING STATEMENT

There is no substitute for skill in observation. The understanding of students' reading development and difficulties that can be obtained by this technique is pertinent, specific, and often immediately applicable to the instruction being given.

However, the limitations of observation should be recognized. Other sources of information are needed to interpret the facts and to answer questions raised by observation of the students' behavior. What appears to be the same behavior may have different meaning to different students.

Although the teacher uses most of his daily observations immediately in instruction or merely adds them to his general impression of his students, there are some items significant enough for him to record. The checklist form of record serves both as a useful guide to classroom observation and as a summary of information he has gained from day to day. The global or descriptive account may be more useful after he has become very familiar with the kinds of details that may be most significant. Then he may prefer to write a brief description of the highlights of his observation and interpretation. Both types of records are of value only insofar as they are used in helping students to improve their reading.

Suggested Problems
Practice and Demonstration

1. Observe children in any common classroom situation and record significant facts about individual children's reading.

2. Experiment with different methods of recording your observations, e.g., using a checklist for each pupil or jotting down notes which you summarize later.

3. In what situations can you as a teacher record observations of individual children's reading most easily? In what situations can you gain the best impression of the reading ability of the class?

4. How can you use a checklist as a guide to observation?

5. Give examples of the immediate use of observations made by the teacher.

6. Suggest possible interpretations of a number of observations of students' reading. Dramatize interviews in which you obtain indications of the meaning of the observed behavior to the individual.

7. Simulate classroom reading situations in which the members of the diagnostic class can practice recording their observations of individual students either on a checklist form or in a descriptive summary.

Suggested Readings

Anderson, Harold H.: "The Measurement of Domination and Socially Integrative Behavior in Teachers' Contacts with Children," *Child Development,* 10:73–89, June, 1939.
————: "A Study of Certain Criteria of Teaching Effectiveness," *Journal of Experimental Education,* 23:41–71, September, 1954.
Crombach, Lee: *Essentials of Psychological Testing,* 2d ed., Harper & Row, Publishers, Incorporated, New York, 1960, pp. 506–538.
Driscoll, Gertrude P.: *How to Study the Behavior of Children,* Bureau of Publications, Teachers College, Columbia University, New York, 1956.
Durkin, Dolores: *Phonics and the Teaching of Reading,* Bureau of

Publications, Teachers College, Columbia University, New York, 1962.

Flanders, Ned A., and Sulo Havumaki: "The Effect of Teacher-Pupil Contacts Involving Praise on Sociometric Choices of Students," *Journal of Educational Psychology,* 51:65–68, April, 1960.

Hinds, L. R.: "Better Reading: Spur to Effective Teaching," *Arizona Teacher,* 50:16–19, January, 1962.

Moustakas, Clark E., and others: "An Objective Method for the Measurement and Analysis of Child-Adult Interaction," *Child Development,* 27:109–134, June, 1956.

Strang, Ruth: *The Role of the Teacher in Personnel Work,* 4th ed., Bureau of Publications, Teachers College, Columbia University, New York, 1953, chap. 8.

Thorndike, Robert, and Elizabeth Hagen: *Measurement and Evaluation in Psychology and Education,* 2d ed., John Wiley & Sons, Inc., New York, 1961, pp. 399–421.

Withall, John: "Research Tools: Observing and Recording Behavior," *Review of Educational Research,* 30:496–512, December, 1960.

Wright, E. Muriel J.: "Development of an Instrument for Studying Verbal Behaviors in a Secondary School Mathematics Classroom," *Journal of Experimental Education,* 28:103–121, December, 1959.

4

ORAL READING AS
A DIAGNOSTIC TECHNIQUE

The modern use of oral reading differs in several ways from the oral reading of a century ago. It is not used nearly so exclusively, even in the primary grades. It is used only occasionally in the upper elementary grades and then mostly in audience situations. In the first grades the main purpose of oral reading is to give the teacher opportunity to study the child's reading. The second purpose is to encourage well-phrased, expressive reading. The third purpose is to share one's enjoyment with others.

In the primary grades, where the basic sight vocabulary and word recognition skills are acquired, oral reading is essential as a basis for diagnosis. As the child reads aloud, the teacher notices proficiency and progress as well as difficulties and errors. The latter might go uncorrected in an individualized silent reading program.

DIAGNOSIS THROUGH ORAL READING IN THE ELEMENTARY GRADES

To obtain a quick general idea of the oral reading ability of a new class, the teacher is justified in asking each child in turn to read a paragraph aloud. In this way he will quickly spot those who read fluently on the grade level, those who have to puzzle out even the basic sight vocabulary, those who have no ready word recognition skills, and those who feel embarrassment and frustration in the reading situation. To avoid causing embarrassment on the part of sensitive students, the teacher will make some encouraging remark and will plan to make a more thorough analysis of their reading in private.

If the teacher has a double-spaced typed copy of the paragraphs to be read, he can quickly mark the errors for each student according to the following code (see also Gray, 1963):

1. Encircle all *omissions* (whole words, syllables, letter sounds, endings, etc.).

2. Insert with a caret ($\wedge$) all *insertions*.

3. Underline and write in all *mispronunciations* (writing in the mispronunciations indicates whether the child uses initial-sound clues, shape-of-word clues, or no perceptible clues at all).

4. Draw a line *through* words for which substitutions were made; write in the *substitution*. (Note whether it makes sense, indicating that the child is reading for meaning, or whether it is irrelevant to the context.)

5. Use dotted or wavy line to indicate *repetitions*.

Illustration

Spot was a good dog. He never ran after the boys and girls or automobiles. But Woof was a naughty dog. He ran after dogs and girls horses and automobiles, and he barked at all of them.

The teacher may add a comprehension check after each paragraph, for example:

1. What is the story about?
2. What kind of dog was Spot?
3. How was Woof different from Spot?
4. Why was Woof a bad dog?

It is best to write each student's answers to the questions because the quality of these answers may vary widely within the limits of correctness. In a period of this kind, the teacher is very active— quite different from the teacher who lazily listens as the children stumble through their basic reader.

If the teacher can provide books for independent reading or other worthwhile work for the class as a whole, he can ask the students individually to read aloud to him. This method is obviously superior to having the students take turns reading aloud before the class. The student profits not only from gaining insight into his oral reading skills, but also from the morale-building effect of having an adult's exclusive attention.

Incidentally, the individual conference has been found to be an effective way of working with discipline problems. The teacher may expect the seriously retarded reader to display considerable frustration in a reading period (Natchez, 1961, pp. 308–311). As in other frustrating situations, he may react by becoming dependent, aggressive, or withdrawn.

Instruction may follow diagnosis immediately. If a student is weak in word recognition skills, the teacher shows him how to use several methods of word attack—if one does not solve the word, the good reader tries another method until he experiences success in analyzing the word in context. If this instruction is given in the class as a whole, or better, in small "seminar" groups of students having the same difficulties, the other students can listen (Russell, 1959) and learn. Everyone in the group should give as close attention to the instruction being given to an individual reader as though it were being given to him personally.

TESTS OF BASIC SIGHT VOCABULARY AND PSYCHOLINGUISTIC ABILITIES

To supplement the information obtained from the student's oral reading, the Dolch Basic Sight Word Test (1942) may easily be given to any class or subgroup within a class that seems to lack the ability to recognize common words quickly at sight. The test presents 220 words "which make up 70 per cent of first readers and 65 per cent of second and third readers" (Dolch, 1942). The children circle the one word on each line that is read by the teacher. It is desirable to know how many of these essential sight words the children can recognize immediately and which words they need to study and practice further. The Dolch and other vocabulary games (Russell and Karp, 1956; *Good Ways to Strengthen Reading Skills,* 1956; Spache, 1955) are useful for children who need practice on this basic vocabulary in order to become more rapid, effective readers.

To find out more about the factors that are causing poor oral reading, it is necessary to study the student's specific word attack skills. The teacher pronounces each test word—*build, danger, tumble,* etc.—distinctly and asks the students to write the letters representing the single and double initial sound consonants and the final sound of each word. The student's knowledge of endings —*s, d, ed, ing;* the possessive form—*'s;* compound words; prefixes, suffixes; contractions; and syllabication may be tested by asking him to separate the root from the endings or from the prefixes and suffixes and to write the two words that make up a compound word.

A more thorough appraisal is possible with the McCullough Word Analysis Test (1962), which combines phonics with structural analysis. This test also measures the student's understanding of seven rules of syllabication, of prefixes and suffixes, and of how consonant blends and vowel sounds are combined to make a word. Since the test is based on words familiar to fourth graders, it can be used in the fourth grade and above. The teacher gives one part of the test a day. Their errors call children's attention to the aspects of instruction that each particularly needs.

A more elaborate, unified schema for studying the psycholinguistic or reading development of children has been described by Samuel A. Kirk and James J. McCarthy in an article entitled "The Illinois Test of Psycholinguistic Abilities: An Approach to Differential Diagnosis" in the *American Journal of Mental Deficiency,* 56: 399–412, November, 1961. This test consists of five dimensions: (1) auditory and visual stimuli, (2) reception of meaningful visual and auditory stimuli, (3) association of these stimuli with past learning, (4) motor or vocal expression of the ideas, and (5) abilities that help to integrate the other learnings. For application of this procedure to slow learners, see Samuel Kirk, "Reading Problems of Slow Learners" in *The Underachiever in Reading,* pp. 62–69, compiled and edited by H. Alan Robinson, Supplementary Educational Monographs, no. 92, The University of Chicago Press, Chicago, 1962.

DIAGNOSIS THROUGH ORAL READING IN HIGH SCHOOL AND COLLEGE

High school and college students' difficulties in basic vocabulary, word recognition skills, phrasing, and expression have important diagnostic value. Lack of a basic sight vocabulary and efficient word recognition skills are often an explanation of slow reading. Poor phrasing may reveal ignorance of language patterns. Research has shown that errors in pronunciation may be related to errors in comprehension. Auditory defects may be associated with poor reading, especially in children who have been taught by the phonetic method.

To gain some understanding of these problems on the high school and college level, the four oral reading paragraphs in the Reading Diagnostic Record for High School and College Students (Strang and others, 1952) may be used. Paragraphs A and B are at about fifth- or sixth-grade level of difficulty. Paragraph C is about college freshman level. Paragraph D is from Dewey's *Human Nature and Conduct* and will be comprehended only by the more mature readers. The four paragraphs are as follows:

READING PASSAGE A. Fear, like anger, stops the flow of the digestive juices. In India a test was once used to tell whether or not a prisoner was guilty of a crime. The man was given a handful of dry rice to put in his mouth. He was told to keep the rice in his mouth a few minutes. If the prisoner had committed a crime and was very much frightened, his saliva would stop flowing and the rice would remain dry. If he was not guilty and had no fear of being punished, his saliva would flow as usual and the rice would be wet.

READING PASSAGE B. The earth has written its own story. Like all the books in the world, it cannot tell everything. Like all very old books, this book of the earth has missing pages. In places the words are dim or in a language men have not yet learned to understand. But the book is there—a thrilling story of strange and mysterious things, of living creatures so small they have to be imagined, and of monsters the like of which we shall never see alive. The pages of the book are the layers of rock that lie one on top of another.

READING PASSAGE C. The widespread realization of the importance of "the human factor" is a striking feature of present-day civilization. More and more attention is being paid to psychological characteristics of human beings. In industry we attempt to discover the main temperamental qualities and abilities that influence an individual's adjustment to his job, and we explore the attitudes of employees to working conditions or to their employers. In education we try to guide parents and teachers as to the best means of dealing with children at home and at school, and treat the maladjusted and the delinquent at Psychological and Guidance Clinics.

READING PASSAGE D. Actual social change is never so great as apparent change. Ways of belief, of expectation, of judgment, and attendant emotional dispositions of like and dislike are not easily modified after they have once taken shape. Political and legal institutions may be altered, even abolished; but the bulk of popular thought which has been shaped to their pattern persists. This is why glowing predictions of the immediate coming of a social millennium terminate so uniformly in disappointment, which gives point to the standing suspicion of the cynical conservative about radical changes. Habits of thought outlive modifications in habits of overt action.

The directions to students are simple: "Read the following paragraph aloud as you usually read orally." While the student reads, the examiner records errors by the method already described. He also observes phrasing, intonation, stress, and pauses that indicate the student's understanding of the language structure of the selection. It is easy to detect word-by-word reading, mechanical division of sentences into parts of phrases and clauses and other evidences of failure to read in thought units. More subtle aspects of expression also should be noted. Performance may cover a range from colorless monotone to the richness of feeling and significance that a great actor gives to every line.

The student's comprehension is first tested by an unstructured, creative-response question, such as "What did the author say?" This free-response question is followed by specific comprehension questions to test the ability to get the main ideas and important details, to interpret, to draw inferences and conclusions, and to explain key words and phrases.

To obtain additional understanding of the relation between the student's oral and silent reading comprehension, the examiner may ask him to read the same paragraph silently. This procedure may indicate whether the student comprehends the paragraph better on rereading it—whether a second reading gives him greater mastery of the printed words.

Attitudes are revealed by the student's remarks and expressive movements. The poor reader frequently shows embarrassment at being asked to read orally. He is apologetic and insecure. Occasionally a student seems to exercise no critical judgment; he seems content with an exceedingly poor performance. A few students take an objective attitude toward their reading and express interest in the diagnostic procedure.

The student's ability to express in his own words what he has just read orally gives still more information about the way his mind works while reading and communicating what he has read. The wide range of responses to the question "What did the author say?" may be rated from 0 to 5 on a scale such as the following:

Rating	Response
0	No response
	Inability to understand the paragraph: "I never know what I read aloud." "I can't explain."
	Inability to remember what one has read: "I don't remember."
1	Totally inadequate—gives no idea of the content of the paragraph. Examples:
	Passage A: "It was an interesting story."
	Passage B: "You get knowledge from books."
	Passage C: "Everybody is doing something for human beings."
	Passage D: "Things change."
2	Very inadequate—very brief, fragmentary, general, or partly inaccurate. Examples:
	Passage A: "India has a test of guilt."
	Passage B: "The rocks are pages of a book."
	Passage C: "That the psychological factor of people is studied."
	Passage D: "Opinions of people do not change."
3	Inadequate—accurate but too brief. Examples:
	Passage A: "Fear stops the flow of saliva."
	Passage B: "The earth has written its own story."
	Passage C: "The human factor is important."
	Passage D: "Habits of thought are hard to change."

Rating	Response

4   Adequate—accurate summary of the passage. Examples:

Passage A: "Fear stops the flow of saliva. This fact was used in India to tell whether a person was guilty or not."

Passage B: "The author has compared the earth to a book. What is found in the layers of rock is compared to the writing in a book. He feels we can read the history of the world from rock formations."

Passage C: "There is at present an emphasis being placed on understanding the individual by employers, parents and teachers. Maladjusted individuals are being studied in clinical situations."

Passage D: "Attitudes remain and are harder to change than the more outward aspects of culture."

5   Superior—main points and details summarized somewhat creatively. Examples:

Passage A: "Anger and fear stop the digestive juices. A recognition of this fact caused the rice test to be used in India as a test of guilt. A man suspected of a crime was given a mouthful of rice. If the rice became just moist it showed lack of fear and he was judged guiltless."

Passage B: "The author compared the geology of the earth (its rock formations) to the pages in a very old book— some of them missing, and others not entirely clear."

Passage C: "We are becoming increasingly interested in the individuality of people. In industry attempts are being made to understand the factors of the adjustment of the individual to his job. In education we cooperate with parents in the study of children through psychological and guidance clinics."

Passage D: "Ways of belief and judgment are not easily modified after they have taken shape. There is always a lag between social change and popular thought—that is, institutions change but people's attitudes change more slowly."

The student's attempts to summarize these paragraphs give insight into his ability to comprehend and communicate what he has read. Some students who are able to identify statements as false or true and to answer multiple-choice questions correctly cannot coherently express an author's thought in their own words. Other students who make no errors in pronunciation and read fluently reveal, when checked for comprehension, that their reading has been little more than word calling and that they have not learned to read with the intent to understand, remember, and communicate.

Individuality in the approach to reading is also indicated by the free response. The rating of 3 may be obtained by a student who habitually makes a terse, precise summary. Such a response is often appropriate, and the student should be commended for this ability. At the same time, it should be pointed out that ratings of 4 and 5 are given for more complete and creative summaries.

This type of free or creative response, unlike the questions in the usual standardized test, is purposely unstructured so as to reveal more about the student's habitual approach to reading. Does he pick out a few scattered details or the main ideas? Does he try to condense the author's thought into a short, succinct statement? Does he comprehend the author's whole pattern of thought? Does he enhance the author's thought by reflection and reference to his own experience? Information of this kind could also be obtained by having the group read the paragraphs silently.

To obtain more comprehensive diagnostic information, a wider variety of paragraphs should be used. These would include poetry, other types of literature, and selections from each of the content fields.

Oral reading paragraphs, of course, do not yield a complete appraisal, but they do occupy an important place in the total diagnostic procedure.

If time permits, the teacher may give instruction after the student has read and responded to the paragraphs. In the first paragraph the structure is clear-cut: the topic sentence, followed by a block of illustration:

Fear and anger stop digestion.
A test of guilt in India illustrates this generalization.

In the second paragraph, the main idea is again found in the first sentence. The topic sentence is followed by statements of limitation. In the last sentence the main idea is reinforced:

The earth is like a book.

> It has these limitations:
>> It cannot tell everything.
>> It has missing pages.
>> It is dim in places.

But | It has these strong points:
>> It is a thrilling story.
>> It is a story about mysterious things and strange creatures.

Its pages are layers of rocks.

In the third paragraph, the first two sentences express the main idea. The remaining two sentences give illustrations of it:

The "human factor" is increasingly important.

> In industry
> In education

The fourth paragraph requires detailed analysis of each sentence. The first sentence is the topic sentence. The next two explain the two main concepts contrasted in the first sentence. The next sentences support the main idea, and the last sentence repeats the main idea in different words.

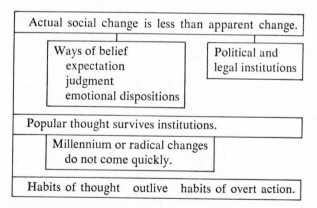

Actual social change is less than apparent change.

Ways of belief expectation judgment emotional dispositions	Political and legal institutions

Popular thought survives institutions.

> Millennium or radical changes do not come quickly.

Habits of thought outlive habits of overt action.

Instruction in sentence and paragraph structure is basic. In simply written paragraphs of a traditional pattern, the main idea can be quickly recognized. In paragraphs such as D above, packed with ideas, one must analyze the contributions made by each sentence to the structure of the thought.

CONCLUDING STATEMENT

In the primary grades children get the meaning of printed words when they pronounce words whose meaning is already familiar to them. For this reason any opportunity for children to read aloud enables the teacher to appraise their comprehension of the sentences as well as their word recognition skills. Observing children read aloud may also give clues to word calling, to fluency as compared with word-by-word reading, and to interest and attitude toward reading. In an audience situation, proficiency in skills of interpretation is indicated by the reaction of the audience to the child's reading as well as by direct observation of the reader. In the primary grades, oral reading is an important diagnostic procedure; the teacher is far from being a passive listener when the child reads aloud.

In the upper grades the teacher's observation of the student in situations in which he needs to read aloud yields important understanding of his phrasing and interpretation of the passage, his attitude toward reading and toward himself, and the audience's response to his reading. To test his comprehension of factual material, he should be asked both an unstructured and a specific, searching question concerned with vocabulary, sentence and paragraph structure, and higher levels of interpretation and critical reading.

Standardized oral reading tests, which are described in Chapter 10, aid the teacher in appraising an individual's oral reading more precisely and with reference to the performance of others of his age and grade.

Suggested Problems
Practice and Demonstration

1. In what ways may a teacher quickly obtain information about the oral reading of each new student without causing embarrassment to the poor reader?

2. Demonstrate the procedure of having a pupil read a paragraph orally while each member of the teacher-education class marks the

errors he makes, as suggested in the first section of this chapter. Do this several times until the class has gained proficiency in the techniques. Also ask them to make an interpretation of the pupil's oral reading and recommendations for helping him to improve.

3. Ask each member of the teacher-education class to make an analysis of his own reading, using The Reading Diagnostic Record for High School and College Students referred to in this chapter. In class, let each member read the four paragraphs silently, respond to the question, "What did the author say?" and rate his answers on the five-point scale suggested.

4. Using these paragraphs, demonstrate instruction in paragraph structure following the reading and rating procedures.

References

Dolch, E. W.: *The Basic Sight Word Test,* The Garrard Press, Champaign, Ill., 1942.

Good Ways to Strengthen Reading Skills, Scott, Foresman and Company, Chicago, 1956.

Gray, William S.: *Gray Oral Reading Test,* The Bobbs-Merrill Company, Inc., Indianapolis, Indiana, 1963.

McCullough, Constance M.: *McCullough Word Analysis Test,* Ginn and Company, Boston, 1962.

Natchez, Gladys: "Oral Reading Used as an Indicator of Reactions to Frustration," *Journal of Educational Research,* 54:308–311, April, 1961.

Russell, David: *Listening Aids through the Grades: One Hundred Ninety Listening Activities,* Bureau of Publications, Teachers College, Columbia University, New York, 1959.

———— and Etta E. Karp: *Reading Aids through the Grades: Three Hundred Developmental Reading Activities,* Bureau of Publications, Teachers College, Columbia University, New York, 1956.

Spache, George D.: *Resources in Teaching Reading,* Reading Laboratory, University of Florida, Gainesville, 1955.

Strang, Ruth, and others: *Reading Diagnostic Record for High School and College Students,* Bureau of Publications, Teachers College, Columbia University, New York, 1952.

Suggested Readings

Brooks, Nelson H.: *Language and Language Learning,* Harcourt, Brace & World, Inc., New York, 1960.

Dawson, Mildred A., and Marion Zollinger: *Guiding Language Learning,* Harcourt, Brace & World, Inc., New York, 1957.

Della-Piana, Gabriel: "Analysis of Oral Reading Errors: Standardization, Norms, and Validity," *The Reading Teacher,* 15:254–257, January, 1962.

Gray, William S.: *On Their Own in Reading,* 2d ed., Scott, Foresman and Company, Chicago, 1960.

Herrick, Virgil, and Leland Jacobs: *Children and the Language Arts,* Prentice-Hall, Inc., Englewood Cliffs, N.J., 1955.

Hill, E.: "Diagnosis and Correction of Oral Reading Skills," in *Conference on Reading,* The University of Pittsburgh Press, Pittsburgh, 1960, pp. 151–154.

Illinois Test of Psycholinguistic Abilities, Box 2141, Madison, Wisconsin.

Pronovost, Wilbert L.: *The Teaching of Speaking and Listening in the Elementary School,* Longmans, Green & Co., Inc., New York, 1959.

Roberts, Paul: *English Sentences,* Harcourt, Brace & World, Inc., New York, 1962.

Robinson, Helen: *Oral Aspects of Reading,* Proceedings of the Annual Conference on Reading, The University of Chicago Press, Chicago, 1955.

Ruesch, Jurgen: *Therapeutic Communication,* W. W. Norton & Company, Inc., New York, 1961.

5

RETROSPECTIVE AND INTROSPECTIVE REPORTS

Teachers and students are partners in the diagnostic process. Asking students to appraise their own reading shows the teacher's faith in the resources within each individual. Nobody knows better than the reader himself how he feels about reading and what makes reading easy or difficult for him. To be sure, some students may be reluctant to express themselves freely. Some may distort their true feelings. Some may lack the ability to analyze their reading problem. On the other hand, most students, when encouraged to write their educational autobiographies, subjective essays, or other kinds of self-evaluation, seldom fail to show considerable insight. Most of the techniques described in this chapter are appropriate for students above elementary school level.

THE READING AUTOBIOGRAPHY

The most common kind of retrospective-introspective report is the reading autobiography. What is a reading autobiography? What kinds of information can be obtained from it? How can it be used?

A reading autobiography is an oral or written developmental history of a student's reading experiences. Students with limited writing ability prefer the oral autobiography. Some of the most seriously retarded readers will welcome the opportunity to express their resentments, discouragements, and embarrassment about their poor reading. The personal attention of an adult who listens with interest and accepts what they say often stimulates them to try to find out what is wrong with their reading and how they can improve.

The kind of information that is obtained from the reading autobiography will depend upon the directions that are given. These may take the form of a series of specific questions such as the following:[1]

	Yes	No	
1.	__	__	Do you remember the name of the first book you ever read?
2.	__	__	As a child, did you prefer books that were illustrated?
3.	__	__	Do you like to have the radio or record player on while you read?
4.	__	__	Did you learn to read before you came to school?
5.	__	__	Did any members of your family try to teach you to read?
6.	__	__	Do you always have something other than school work that you are currently reading?
7.	__	__	Do you have a public library card?
8.	__	__	Do you read in bed?
9.	__	__	Do you reread a book you particularly enjoyed?

[1] Questionnaire developed by Mr. Paul Eagan and his tenth-grade class at Tucson (Arizona) High School.

Yes No

10. __ __ When you are reading a book in which you are particularly interested, do you often neglect your duties to read it?

11. __ __ Do you ever read to younger children?

12. __ __ Do you often find you have been reading without comprehending the meaning?

13. __ __ Does your mother or father ever read aloud to the family?

14. __ __ Does your family have group discussions of current events?

15. __ __ Is more than one language spoken in your home?

16. __ __ Do you read for pleasure during vacation times?

17. __ __ Do you dislike English classes?

18. __ __ Do you have a personal library of your own?

19. __ __ Does your family subscribe to book clubs?

20. __ __ Do you prefer reading the "digest" form of a novel in preference to the unabridged version?

21. __ __ Do you read at the breakfast table?

22. __ __ Do you find yourself reading the advertising on food packages at meal times?

23. __ __ Do you agree with the girl who said, "Although I am in many clubs and engage in other activities, reading a good book is 'my first choice' "?

24. __ __ When confined to bed with minor illnesses do you look forward to reading?

25. __ __ Do you have a car available for your use?

26. __ __ Do you ever read while riding in cars or buses?

27. __ __ Do you read books or stories aloud with a friend?

28. How would you classify yourself as to reading speed: (Average reading speed for high school texts is around 250 wpm.) __ Average reader __ Slow reader __ Fast reader?

29. Does reading make you sleepy? __ Yes __ No __ Sometimes

30. Do the members of your family recommend reading material for each other? __ Yes __ No __ Sometimes

31. I go out approximately _____ evenings a week.

32. I spend _____ hours per week on extracurricular activities (clubs, sports, publications, etc.).

33. We have _____ television sets in our home.
                (number of)

34. I (do) (do not) watch television more than I read for pleasure.

35. Original composition (has) (has not) helped my interest in reading.

36. I have usually obtained (better) (worse) grades in English than in mathematics.

37. Circle the parts of the newspaper that you usually read.

A. Comics   C. Sports   E. Society
B. News items   D. Editorials

38. In your spare time which of the following do you do most? (Number 1 to 4 in order of frequency.)

    Watch television   Visit with friends

    Read   Other

39. Circle the types of books read aloud in your home.

    A. Juvenile literature   D. Current events

    B. Novels   E. None

    C. Short stories   F. Other (tell what kind)

40. In our home there are the following types of reading material:

    A. Hard-back books consisting of

        1. Approximately ＿＿＿ novels (number of)

        2. Approximately ＿＿＿ scientific

        3. Approximately ＿＿＿ research

        4. Approximately ＿＿＿ other

    B. Paperback books ＿＿＿

    C. Magazines as follows (list the names)

        ＿＿＿＿

        ＿＿＿＿

        ＿＿＿＿

41. I make use of our

    A. Public library ＿＿＿ times a month.

    B. School library ＿＿＿ times a week.

42. When I read for my own pleasure I choose mostly (check):

    A. Novels   D. Science fiction

    B. Short stories   E. Essays

    C. Comic books   F. Other (name them)

43. Does the fact that you are expected to make a report on a book: ＿ detract from your enjoyment of it, ＿ deepen your understanding and enjoyment of it, ＿ neither answer applies in all instances.

44. As far as your reading speed is concerned, do you: ＿ read everything at about the same speed, ＿ frequently "scan" certain types of reading material, or ＿ change your speed with the kind of material and your purpose?

45. Do you prefer: ＿ to read aloud, ＿ to be read to, ＿ to read to yourself?

46. When a "pleasure" book fails to interest you after twenty-five pages or so, do you: ＿ go ahead and finish it anyway, ＿ stop reading it, ＿ decide to read it at a later date?

47. Our family participated in reading aloud in the following ways:

    A. My ＿ mother ＿ father read to us at preschool age.

    B. My ＿ mother ＿ father have always read to us.

    C. My ＿ mother ＿ father never read to us.

48. How many schools have you attended since the first grade?

49. When I come across a word I don't know: I ＿ look it up in the dictionary, ＿ try to guess at its meaning from the context, ＿ try to pronounce it by

dividing it into syllables, ___ try to pronounce it by sounding it out, ___ skip over it. (Check more than one if they apply.)

50. Circle the following practices you follow when reading school work:
    A. Summarize material after you read it
    B. Raise questions before or when reading and then read to find the answers
    C. Underline key statements in your text during study
    D. Take notes for future reference: after reading a section ___, while reading ___

If these questions have called to your mind any comments you would like to make, please use the remaining space to do so. Any additions to this reading survey that you may be able to suggest would be greatly appreciated.

Although the checklist form of autobiography is easy to write and can be quickly tabulated, it does not give unique, personal insights or show relationships between separate items or indicate their relative importance. Unstructured questions that invite spontaneous creative response usually give more significant information.

To obtain a sequential and circumstantial written account of a student's reading development, one may ask questions that suggest the desired content, as in the following form:

Name_____Age_____Grade_____Date_____

MY READING AUTOBIOGRAPHY

Here is a chance to write the history of your reading. Begin with the very first reading you did. How did you learn to read? Tell about your reading in school and out of school in the first grade, second grade, and so on through each year of elementary school. Tell about your reading right up to today. What do you read? What do you like to read? Is reading hard or easy for you? Do you find reading in the junior high school harder than reading in the elementary school? Why?

Another approach is to give pupils a few questions to guide them in writing a free autobiography, such as:

Early experiences:
    When did you start to read?
    What did you read? (titles)
    Did you enjoy reading?
    What have been your reading interests through the years?

Present experiences:

What kind of reading do you enjoy now—books, magazines, newspapers, short stories, poetry?

What do other members of your family like to read?

What kind of reading do you dislike?

When and where do you do most of your reading?

What kind of reading material do you have in your home?

When do you use the library?

How do you read—fast or slow, eagerly or reluctantly, etc.?

Future experience:

Are you dissatisfied with any of your reading habits, such as speed, or with your ability to understand and remember what you have read?

If you have any trouble with reading, what kind of trouble is it, and what do you think can be done about it?

The students do not answer these questions specifically; they read them beforehand to get an idea of what should be included in a developmental history of their reading experiences and then write freely.

In a heterogeneous class, the teacher will obtain autobiographies that cover a wide range of content and writing ability. The following are samples of the reading autobiographies of students, ranging from slow learners to gifted students. The spelling and wording are unchanged.

A. In find my tow in read wend I was in the three grade and I didt know how to read wrold.

in school my mand traper is in English therr we have to read alouter. An I dont like to stande up to read at any time.

The only book I read is a motorcycle and a car book. I get the book one every month. And my tray to read much better because wend I get old eneft I wind like to become of StateTooper. And in that you have to have a high school deplomur. Our get in the motor cycle part of the army.

I sterp to have read troullz wend I was 13 year old and sent thin I have tropz.

B. When I was in the 1th and 2th grade I was all right but when they skip me to the 3th grade I fell back and failed.

One book I like was *Builders of the old world* It was very good it tell how the people of the old world live.

C. The first time I can recall my reading anything was the book I was given in grade school. The book was of a boy and his horse. The every day life of the two were told. My reading was poor ever since I can remember. All through grade school I was given a book which was a half-term lower than the grade in which I was. My marks were not of the highest when I finished grade school.

High school was not to grate a change for me because I was use to being with older people than myself. I had a deftinit gold when I entered high school which was to go thru high school with the highest makes I could get. I which to go to college and the only way that would be possible would be to get a scholarship for my gymnistics. If I did get the schollarship I would have to go to gym workout, therefor I would have to be able to do my classrork much faster than the other students.

D. Reading most people think your suppose to know or any way by the time you get out of grade school. As far back as I remember I have always had trouble reading but just realized it recently. This happened because I was never tested for it. I always had books around the house which I would start and put down. I would say it is boring, uninteresting or some excuse. My mother always would say "pick up a book." I would for five minutes and put it down again. My parents both read a great deal.

E. I am a first year student in high school. I feel that to be a good student I need a great deal of help in English. It is difficult to spell some werds, to pronounce them, and to use werds properly.

I feel that English would help me lot with my Latin and Science.

F. I shall try to give you a brief outline of my reading ability. As I told you yesterday I do very little reading. In the past few years my reading matter included magazines, comic books and newspapers. In the newspaper, I used to read the front page and the sport section. Since we have television in our house, I rely mostly on that to give me the world affairs of today. When there is an article about sports I like to read it especially if it is about baseball.

I am not too interested in doing any reading for school. Most of the time I leave my required reading for the last minute.

When I start to read I find that I am reading words and not getting the gist of the particular passage. The aid I am seeking is to help me to read with more understanding and care.

I expect to go to college and I understand that reading is very important there, if I expect to do college work.

G. I guess I started to read some time during the 1st grade but before that both of my parents had read a great deal to me. I can remember having *To Think That It Happened On Mulberry Street* read to me and later reading other books by Dr. Seuse and so by the time I began to be taught to read in school the stories about "Jack & Jane" were more than a little dull.

My father continued to read to both my brother and I untill I was about 12 and even now occasionally will read us a passage of a good book.

My reading interests from the time I was eight to about eleven consisted primarily of glancing through *Popular Mechanics, Popular Science,* and various flying magazines. At this time my interests turned towards science fiction & adventure. I think I went through all the Steven W. Meder & Howard Pease books in the Branch Library in my neighborhood & also several books by Robert Heihline. My reading became more narrow in the period between 12 & 14 and confined itself almost exclusively to science fiction. I read from cover to cover almost every issue of *Galaxy* & *Astounding Science Fiction* & many novels & short stories in that vein.

My interest recently have been mostly of a more classical nature because, for the first time, I am looking about my own house for reading material. For the purpose of giving you an idea of the nature of my most recent reading I'll list a few:

Stendhal by Matthew Josephson
Martin Eden by Jack London
Cross & the Arrow by Albert Maltz
Spoon River Anthology by Edger Lee Masters
Inside Africa by John Gunther
Insolent Chariots by John Keats

I hadn't until recently used the Library to any extent but I was driven to it by the research necessary on my term theme & I find it not at all unpleasant. Since then I have spent a great deal of time studying & reading at the library because it is directly across the street from the high school.

I don't think there is any kind of reading that I dislike unless it is written in an elementary or overly technical fashion but I do tend to stay away from those subject which are unfamiliar to me.

During the school year my reading is done mostly just before I go to sleep or just after I wake but during the summer I just sit myself down with a book & read cover to cover unless it is of a technical nature and then it becomes to much to read in one sitting.

It seems to me that my reading is slow & it takes me forever & a day to get through only a few pages & when it comes to assigned reading, book reports, & the like it requires enormous amounts of my time although I enjoy most of what I read. This seems to be where my trouble lies I understand & enjoy most of what I read but I read far to slowly.

I don't know exactly what corrective measures I will undergo here but if they can speed up my reading without an appreciable drop in comprehension I would be more than satisfied.

What a vast difference in reading ability and in general maturity is represented in this small sampling of autobiographies! And what a wealth of diagnostic information they give about spelling and handwriting, vocabulary, organization of ideas, sentence structure, and overall richness of expression and depth of thought! Some accounts give admirable detail concerning the subject's early reading experiences, when and how he was taught, the range and variety of his reading, his home background, and his use of available resources. Other autobiographies reveal the writer's attitude, his special reading interests, and his difficulties. Sometimes they include his ideas about ways to overcome the difficulties that he has recognized.

Autobiography C, for example, was written by a seventeen-year-old boy whose Stanford-Binet IQ was 112 and whose scores on the survey test of the Diagnostic Reading Tests (Committee on Diagnostic Reading Tests, 1947–1958) were at the 2nd percentile in rate and at the 18th percentile on total reading. On the Nelson-Denny Reading Test (1929–1960), his paragraph comprehension was at the 20th percentile and his vocabulary at the 40th percentile. He called his autobiography "The Story of My Reading"; it showed a long history of reading difficulty, recognized by the boy himself. His marks in elementary school reflected his reading inability and possibly other conditions that were affecting his achievement in other school work. His expressed desire to succeed in high school and to go to college helped the reading teacher to understand this boy's motivation and to take steps to help him realize his potentialities and achieve his goals.

In a number of autobiographies a typical developmental picture emerges: a keen interest in reading in the first grades, which was lost for several years and then regained in the teens when the practical importance of reading became more evident.

Some students make steady progress toward increasingly mature reading. Such progress was described by a gifted tenth-grade girl:

When I first started to read I read very widely. I was kind of a bookworm in my younger days, and I accepted what I read completely as fact. But once I started to go into a subject—the life of Queen Elizabeth I, for instance—I read many books about her. After I had read five or six, I began to run up against contradictions. Then I began to think for myself a little more, and I think that is what makes a mature reader.

The reading autobiography often calls the teacher's attention to learning clues that should be followed up in an interview or in class instruction. It may suggest instruction that is needed in specific reading skills, either by individuals or by groups. Writing an educational autobiography may help the individual to get perspective on his reading, set goals for himself, and round out and fill in gaps in his reading development.

INTROSPECTIVE STUDY OF THE READING PROCESS

In Connection with the Reading Autobiography

The reading autobiography sometimes enables the teacher to understand a student's difficulties in learning. In the following autobiography, a sixteen-year-old girl tried to explain why she had difficulty in reading history:

To begin with, I don't like to read to myself. Probably because I'm not a good reader. It takes me quite a while to read and know what I just read. I am an especially poor reader if the subject doesn't interest me.

Last year I didn't do well in World History because I found it very boring. It was very foolish of me to have decided from the beginning of the year that I couldn't do it. I think if I had tried harder I could have absorbed some lessons at least. The teacher I had talked away over my head. I didn't retain a thing he said because I couldn't understand his method of teaching.

This year I think I am going to do much better. I am very interested in American History. Because I like the subject I can get interested in the reading assignments. If I really put my mind to a chapter I can learn it. The only thing wrong is that I read so slowly. If I want to learn what is in that chapter I have to read it carefully. Then after I've been reading for a while I get tired and start thinking of the other homework I've got or the dirty dishes that have to be washed. Then I get disgusted and start skiming through the chapter trying to find the answers to the questions.

To sum it all up, I love American History and the way that you teach it but if I can't give my undivided attention on the assignment I'm sunk.

Other able learners try to describe and analyze their reading processes, as in the following quotation:

When I am up against some text material or something else that is concentrated and difficult to get immediately, I sometimes will go on reading without really coordinating my mind with the task; I will keep on reading the words without thinking about them at all. When I have come to the end of a page, I wouldn't be able to say what was on it. I have read it but it seems as though my eyes were working separately from my brain.

By Means of Retrospective Questions
Following a Reading Exercise

Immediately after reading a selection and answering the comprehension questions on it, the teacher may ask students certain questions about their reading process:

What did you do to get the main ideas?

What did you do to get the details?

What did you do when you met a word you did not know?

These and other questions have elicited responses such as the following from junior and senior high school students:

If the selection is familiar to me and simple to understand, I read through it fast or skim over it.

When I read a paragraph, I try to pick out the main points and establish them in my mind; after that I look for and try to remember important dates and details.

When reading a news story, I read all details, for a headline just tells what happened; it doesn't give the details or tell why.

When I do not know a word, I go back over the paragraph and try to find its meaning.

I read carefully and slowly and try to remember the main points from each part.

I read very fast, even a history book. I get quite a good deal out of it, even at a fast rate. I do not go over my reading. Sometimes, however, I go through the pages I have read and look at the headings, recall as much as I can about each heading.

If there is a complicated section that I don't understand, I read it over until I get it.

If the lesson is a hard one, I reread it, very quickly to see if I've got everything out of it.

I read more slowly than most people, but very seldom do I read the book over again, unless it is history or geography. Then I only read it again if I have forgotten important facts and statistics.

Comments like these, made after the students have corrected their own answers to the comprehension questions, evoke a lively and profitable discussion of reading methods that do or do not achieve the best results.

By Means of Introspective Study While Reading

The most difficult type of introspective study is made while reading a given selection. There is always the danger here that simultaneous introspection may interfere with the student's normal reading process, thus creating an artificial, distorted picture. However, some students have made enlightening responses to the invitation to introspect while reading; at least their analyses suggest hypotheses to be tested further.

Following are the directions for introspective study given to mature high school and college students:

Name_____Teacher_____Date_____

HOW I READ!

Should you like to discover how you actually read, watch yourself as you read. It may not be easy at first, but you will soon find it interesting and helpful. After you have made some discoveries about your reading process, you may wish to share them with the rest of the class and discuss ways to improve.

Directions: Select a story, article, or section at least three pages long from a school book. As you read your selection, try to observe what you do as you read. For example, do your eyes move backward over the line of print? If so, why? Do they ever miss a line? Do you look at every single word? Do your eyes move faster than your mind? Do your thoughts wander? Where do they wander? Do you think of the meaning of each word or group words in phrases and thoughts?

When you have finished your reading, write down immediately everything you noticed about your reading. You may be surprised at what you discover about your own reading.

Name of selection_____No. of pages_____

Type of selection_____Source_____

How I Read This Selection

Responses to This Exercise on How I Read: The selection was four pages on reptiles taken from the students' ninth-grade science textbook.

A superior reader wrote: "When I read, my eyes follow the lines and sometimes go a few lines ahead of what I am reading. I don't look back. I don't get help on words. I don't read every word but I don't skip any lines. I read all the way through the article without stopping."

A very poor reader made this analysis: "Sometimes I miss a line. I look at almost every word. My eyes move faster than my mind can read. Sometimes my thoughts wander. Sometimes I think about what I read. I usually read too fast. I don't often think about the ideas in the lesson I am reading. I don't concentrate on my reading."

Such responses serve as content for class discussion. The students who read most quickly and well can give the others, in words that they can readily understand, suggestions about their most practical reading methods.

OTHER FORMS FOR SELF-EVALUATION

A set of questions to guide students in their self-appraisal of study skills has been found to differentiate between college students of diverse proficiency. Successful readers responded affirmatively to the following items more often than did retarded readers:

1. Do you skim material before reading it in detail?
2. Do you summarize material after you read it?
3. Do you raise questions when reading and then read to find the answer?
4. Do you underline key statements in your text during study?
5. Do you review the previous assignment before proceeding to read the current one?
6. Do you make an effort to read as rapidly and as carefully as you can when you study?
7. Do you plan a study schedule in advance and adhere to it?

8. Do you immediately reread sections of your assignment which are not clear?

9. Are you careful not to skip graphs, tables, and charts when you read your assignment?

10. Do you take notes or underline key statements in your text during the study?

For slow-learning students, self-evaluation questions should be exceedingly simple, clearly stated, and very few in number. For example:

1. Why do you want to read better?
2. What advantage would it be for you to be a better reader?

Eleven boys aged nine to eleven, with an IQ range of 80 to 95, were asked the above questions. Their ability to communicate was extremely limited; their retardation in reading and writing was extraordinary. They particularly disliked direct questions. Every one of these boys was withdrawn and uncommunicative.

The teacher asked the question in a casual way during a reading session. He would say, for example, "That was a fine job, Roy. You really have come quite a way in reading. Do you feel there is an advantage for you in becoming a better reader?" In some cases he added, "Why do you want to be a better reader?"

Three of the boys did not know the meaning of the word *advantage* until it was explained. Without exception, all the boys spontaneously and, as a matter of fact, quite truthfully replied, "I don't know." However meager this reply, they revealed some information by variations in their tone of voice. Some seemed to feel great discomfort and anxiety; some answered with a "don't-bother-me and leave-me-alone" tone; a few with an open, frank tone; one with a mocking undertone. Three boys were more explicit. In answer to the question, one said, "Not to be stupid"; two said, "To get better jobs," and one of these added this significant statement, "So nobody can cheat me."

Meager as these answers were, they revealed three dominant motivations for reading, as these severely retarded readers perceived them: to maintain self-esteem, to be successful in a vocation, and not to be defenseless in a predatory society.

Another approach to slow-learning students which, incidentally, is also useful in building their language patterns, is to ask a few simple questions about their reading environment, such as the following:

Question	One pupil's response
What I read	Funnybook
When I read	I dot know when
Where I read	Home
What books are in my house	All kinds off book
My mother reads	My mother reads the newspaper
My father reads	(Student wrote "all kinds" then crossed it out and wrote "My father reads the Bible.")
My brothers read	My brother reads the funnybooks
My sisters read	My sisters read storey book

This simple exercise gives a glimpse of the student's reading interests and the reading background of his home. It also shows up difficulties in sentence structure and grammar.

SUBJECTIVE ESSAYS

A wider variety of information may be gained from subjective compositions. The following are topics that have elicited fascinating details about students' reading:

What Makes a Book Easy or Difficult to Read?

How Does Interest Affect My Reading?

How an Uninteresting Book Captured My Interest

How My Parents Helped or Hindered My Reading Development

How Books Have Influenced My Point of View, Attitudes, or Habits

How I Feel When I Read Aloud in Class

Children's perceptions largely determine their behavior. They are usually motivated by the acceptance and approval of the important persons in their lives—adults and peers. Their behavior is influenced by their perception of themselves and their perception of the way other people feel toward them. Davidson and Lang (1960, pp. 107–118) reported a positive correlation for fourth-, fifth-, and sixth-grade pupils between the children's perception of their teacher's feelings toward them and the children's perception of themselves. "The children who had a more favorable or more adequate self-concept, that is, those who achieved a higher self-perception score also perceived their teacher's feelings toward them more favorably" (p. 109). There was also a positive relation between children's favorable perception of the teacher's feelings toward them and their academic achievement and classroom behavior. Introspective reports are a direct means of gaining understanding of perceptions that may be the key to serious reading problems.

By means of autobiographies, questions about the reading process, and essays about his reading attitudes and habits, the student may become more aware not only of reading methods but also of conditions that are favorable or detrimental to reading improvement. For example, in their essays on the manner in which early childhood experiences affected their reading, high school students often attributed their interest in reading to listening to children's classics and other books read aloud to them during the preschool years. One wrote: "Among other things, I remember most the times I would sit by my mother as she read Bible stories and other books such as *Heidi* to me."

Another high school student described his early experience in more detail:

If I had to pick one person who influenced my reading most . . . I would pick my grandmother. She is the one who really started me reading. She used to sit and read to me by the hour when I was little. Now that I can read by myself, she just makes sure I have enough to read. She gives me about four or five books a year for my birthday or Christmas or some other occasion.

I am quite an avid reader now and I think she is largely responsible for it (Strang and Eagan, 1961, p. 10).

Another boy gave this warning:

In creating an interest in reading, I think it is important for adults to stay in the background. If they constantly badger the child by saying, "Why don't you read a book," they will build up an opposition to reading. On the other hand, they should set a goal for the child to strive toward (p. 11).

Other essays give insight into the role of the teacher in reading improvement:

Because my teacher thought I was particularly good in reading I took a greater liking to it.

The first person who stands out in my memories [as contributing to his reading development] would be my third grade teacher. . . . At this time I was having a little trouble pronouncing words. As I remember, she was the first teacher who was interested enough to stop and spend time on me. She explained how to pronounce words by syllables first and then put the syllables together (p. 11).

These few quotations give only a glimpse of the kinds of understanding that both teachers and students may gain from subjective essays.

STUDENTS' EVALUATION OF READING INSTRUCTION

Students can participate in improving reading instruction. No one should have a better basis for appraising a reading course than the students who have just taken it. Like the autobiography, evaluation forms may call for a wide range of responses—all the way from writing a completely unstructured appraisal to filling out a checklist.

One method of evaluation is to present the students with a list of the experiences they have had in the course and ask them to rate each according to its value in improving their reading. They should also tell why or in what way they think the experience was or was not helpful.

Each question on the following rating sheet calls for a statement of the reason for the particular answer:

Name_____Section_____Date_____

READING CLASS RATING SHEET

To each pupil: Please answer the following questions as completely and honestly as you can. By telling your teacher what you really think of this reading course, you will be helping him to improve the course for other boys and girls. Your answers will in no way influence your grade for the course; you need not even sign your name if you do not wish to. Thank you very much for your help and cooperation.

1. This course has helped me (underline one):
   (a) a great deal, (b) much, (c) some, (d) little, (e) not at all.

2. Please give your reasons for answering the first question the way you did. (You may use the other side of this sheet if necessary.)
3. Which activities helped you most? Explain.
4. Which activities helped you least? Explain.
5. I usually found the classes to be (underline one):
   (a) very interesting, (b) interesting, (c) of some interest, (d) of little interest, (e) of no interest. *Please tell why.*
6. Did this class in any way change your attitude toward reading? Please explain.
7. I am glad I took this course (check one): Yes ___, No ___. Why?
8. I believe a reading course next year for eighth-grade pupils would be helpful (check one): Yes ___, No ___. Why?
9. If an advanced course of this type were offered as an eighth-grade elective subject next year, I (would, might, wouldn't) elect to take it. (*Underline one word in parentheses.*)
10. Please write any other reactions to the course that you wish to add.

Obviously, the results of any subjective appraisal are valid only if the teacher obtains the interest and cooperation of the students.

DAILY SCHEDULE OR DIARY RECORD

The student may also contribute to the understanding of his reading by keeping a record of his daily activities for a week. For accuracy's sake he is asked to make entries all during the day, not to try to remember at the end of the day just what happened in the morning. If he is asked to include details about *what* he reads as well as *when* he reads, much may be learned about his reading habits and interests.

"Time is of the essence." It is our most common and valuable commodity. How do we spend it? "I'd like to read more, but I don't have the time." This is the excuse most frequently given by students who do little or no voluntary reading.

How can students become more aware of the way they use time? How can teachers gain information as to how much and what kind of reading their students are doing outside of school and what other activities are competing for their time?

The quickest and easiest way to obtain such information is to interest the class in keeping a record of their daily activities for a school day and for a weekend. In presenting this idea, the teacher may use various appeals to ensure accuracy:

Keeping this diary record is a way of helping you to save time for things you want to do.

Other students have said, "It's fun to see how you spend your time, but it's sort of a nuisance to have to carry the record around with you all day."

If you want to be scientific, you must be accurate in recording exactly what you do during the day.

As with all other kinds of personal documents, the daily schedule is worthless if the students are not interested and cooperative. No student should be forced to write a subjective-type record or composition if he objects to doing so. He can be given another kind of assignment.

The form for recording one's daily activities is simple. Plain lined paper may be used. The following directions and headings have been used successfully:

DAILY SCHEDULE

Directions: It is sort of fun to see how you spend your day. This is the way to keep a day's record or diary: Begin at 6:00 in the morning. Your first activity in the middle column will probably be "sleeping." When you get up, put the time on the second line under 6 A.M., and write in the middle column "got up, washed, and dressed." Then add the next thing you do and so on through the day until you go to bed at night. Carry this sheet around with you and write your activities as you engage in them during the day. Do not wait until the end of the day. Tell in detail what you do. For example, do not write just "read," but tell what you read. Do not say just "played," but tell what you played and with whom.

Time	What I Did in Detail	No. of Minutes in Each Activity

Is this the way you usually spend a school day and a weekend? ____
If not, how is it different? _____

If the teacher wants to help students individually with their use of time, he asks them to sign their names on their schedules. If he wants to get an overview of the daily activities of his class or to use the records for research purposes, he may ask the students not to sign their names and thus avoid the inaccuracy that results from people's unconscious tendency to want to make a good impression.

It is amazing how much a teacher can learn about a class by spending an hour or two reading their daily schedules (Strang, 1953, pp. 336–357). He can learn how much or how little time students spend in reading, what they read, when they read, where they read, and what other activities are competing with their reading.

Some students include no reading at all. In other cases voluntary reading time is usurped by long assignments given by teachers who require a disproportionate amount of homework. Some students' days are overscheduled; they take private lessons in dancing, music, or French and attend numerous social activities. With others, part-time employment occupies what might be leisure time. A few seem to be reading excessively to the exclusion of outdoor activity and social experiences.

A class period may be profitably spent in discussing some of the students' schedules in a kind of "daily schedule clinic." The teacher reads a schedule aloud, anonymously, of course, and the class members point out its good features, propose ways in which the individual might save time, and suggest the best times to fit in some voluntary reading. Such a discussion helps the student to make desirable and reasonable modifications of his original schedule. In individual conferences, the student may delve more deeply into the reasons why he is wasting time and reconsider his values and philosophy of life in relation to his use of time.

CONCLUDING STATEMENT

Each of these self-evaluation reports has possible therapeutic value for the person who writes it. The autobiography invites the writer to take an objective view of himself; it gives both student and teacher perspective on his reading development. Compositions on various personal subjects give the individual a chance to express thoughts that may have been awaiting expression for a long time. The daily schedule shows the person how he is spending—or wasting—his time. These ways of self-appraisal may be used, as appropriate, throughout the high school and college years.

Suggested Problems
Practice and Demonstration

1. Write your own reading autobiography as a part of the study of your reading. What insights did you gain from it?

2. If you are teaching at present, obtain reading autobiographies from students in your class who are interested in writing or dictating them. As you read them, underline especially significant statements and file them in each student's cumulative record folder.

3. In the teacher-education class, present several autobiographies or essays obtained from students of different reading abilities, together with other available data about each student. Discuss the significant information in each and note details in the introspective reports that were not found in other sources.

4. Ask each member of the class to try to obtain one set of essays on any topic, such as those suggested in the section on Subjective Essays. Analyze and categorize these essays and summarize for the class the students' ideas on each of the topics.

5. Obtain the interest and cooperation of a group of students in keeping a daily schedule for one school day and one weekend. Categorize the various activities and calculate the number of minutes spent in each activity. Have students make bar graphs showing the average number of minutes spent per week in study; voluntary reading; looking at television; informal social activities with friends; conversation with members of family; listening to the radio; playing out of doors; part-time work or chores; group activities such as clubs, parties, trips, and excursions; sleep; and daily routines such as eating, washing, dressing. From these quantitative summaries draw conclusions as to which activities are encroaching upon students' voluntary reading time. Make recommendations for a better-balanced schedule.

6. At one time in the history of psychology, extensive use was made of introspection in research; later this method was somewhat discredited, but recently it has been used more extensively. Summarize the advantages and disadvantages of introspective and retrospective reports.

7. Work out at the beginning of your course, and later apply, a form for evaluating the instruction you give. Decide on the behavioral objectives and work out methods of obtaining evidence of whether these objectives have been attained.

References

Committee on Diagnostic Reading Tests (Frances Oralind Triggs, chairman): *Diagnostic Reading Tests,* Committee on Diagnostic Reading Tests, Inc., Mountain Home, N.C., 1947–1958.

Davidson, Helen H., and Gerhard Lang: "Children's Perceptions of Their Teacher's Feelings toward Them Related to Self-perception, School Achievement, and Behavior," *Journal of Experimental Education,* 24:107–118, December, 1960.

Nelson, M. J., and E. C. Denny: *Nelson-Denny Reading Test* (rev. by James I. Brown), for Grades 9–12, College, and Adults, Forms A and B; measures vocabulary, comprehension, and reading rate, Houghton Mifflin Company, Boston, 1929–1960.

Strang, Ruth: *The Role of the Teacher in Personnel Work,* Bureau of Publications, Teachers College, Columbia University, New York, 1953, pp. 336–357.

———— and Paul J. Eagan: "Teen-age Readers," *The PTA Magazine,* 55:10–12, June, 1961.

Suggested Readings

Bonsall, Marcella R.: "Introspections of Gifted Children," *California Journal of Educational Research,* 11:159–166, September, 1960.

Bullock, Harrison: *Helping the Non-reading Pupil in Secondary School,* Bureau of Publications, Teachers College, Columbia University, New York, 1956.

Inhelder, Barbel, and Jean Piaget: *The Growth of Logical Thinking from Childhood to Adolescence,* Basic Books, Inc., Publishers, New York, 1958.

Letton, Mildred Celia: "Individual Differences in Interpretive Responses in Reading Poetry at the Ninth Grade Level," unpublished doctoral dissertation, Department of Education, University of Chicago, Chicago, June, 1958.

Ogden, Charles Kay, and I. A. Richards: *The Meaning of Meaning,* Harcourt, Brace & World, Inc., New York, 1949.

Piekarz, Josephine A.: "Individual Differences in Interpretive Responses in Reading," unpublished doctoral dissertation, Department of Education, University of Chicago, Chicago, June, 1954.

Richards, I. A.: *How to Read a Page,* Beacon Press, Boston, 1958.

Russell, David H.: "Contributions of Reading to Personal Development," *Teachers College Record,* 61:435–441, May, 1960.

Strang, Ruth: "Reactions to Research on Reading," *The Educational Forum,* 26:187–192, January, 1962.

6

ASCERTAINING INTERESTS

Interest is often the key that unlocks effort; it has a dynamic effect on the way students read. Consequently, a study of students' reading and other interests is an important part of any diagnostic procedure. Many methods of studying children's interests have been used, and many reports of the reading interests of children of different ages have been published.

97

INTEREST AS A DYNAMIC FORCE [1]

We have all observed the dynamic effect of interest on children's reading. A first-grade class's interest in a little white kitten who strayed into their classroom helped them to quickly recognize the words in the story about it that they dictated to the teacher. A class of mentally retarded children, who generally had a defeatist attitude toward reading, made progress in reading simplified versions of newspaper stories and articles which they themselves had selected as especially interesting. A group of older boys who had left school without learning to read went to work in earnest after they became aware of the importance of reading in getting and holding a job. They made remarks such as the following:

> I'm in a rut in my job because of my poor reading. There's no future in it and I'm afraid to take a good job that requires reading. I don't want to be a day laborer all my life. I'm twenty years old and if I don't learn to read now, I never will. It's now or never for me. I wouldn't dare to get married because I'd never feel secure in my job.

Another said:

> My boss wanted me to take a job in the office, but I knew I'd have to read letters and bills so I told him I was more valuable to him in the shipping room. He kept asking me and I kept stalling for about nine months; then he hired someone else.

An emotionally disturbed boy, who at first unconsciously was resisting all attempts to teach him to read, read with keen enjoyment a story the teacher had written especially for him. The story was written in his own idiom and expressed his feelings of hostility and anxiety. Because the boy had previously refused even to open a book, the teacher ingeniously wrote the story on cards, a sentence or two on each card.

Students' View

Young people agree with psychologists on the efficacy of interest in learning. Direct quotations from the students support psychological theories of the dynamic effect of interest. In twelve

---

[1] Much of this section is quoted with permission from an article previously written by the author (Strang, 1957).

different schools and communities, 250 youngsters from the sixth through the twelfth grades, with IQs of 82 to 150, were asked, "How does your interest in a book or assignment affect what you read, the way you read, and what you learn?" With very few exceptions they confirmed our impression of the dynamic force of interest. When asked, "What makes a book easy to read?" a large proportion of them said, "If it's interesting."

They described a pattern or sequence: If the book is interesting, they read it eagerly and with enjoyment. Their interest enlists their attention and impels them to read fast but effectively. Because they are concentrating harder than usual, they comprehend what they read. They learn and remember what they have read. The whole process is satisfying. This satisfying experience may lead them to read other books by the same author, look up more information on the same topic, and otherwise widen their interests. As one bright twelve-year-old boy said, "My interest in books and reading them broadens my knowledge of many things and increases my vocabulary. And the more interest, the more reading; the more reading, the more knowledge."

Students confronted with dull, drab, uninteresting reading material show the opposite pattern. They read reluctantly, their minds wander, they skip and skim so that they can "get it over with" more quickly. Consequently, they do not comprehend, learn, or remember much of what they read. Since this experience is so lacking in satisfaction, it does not lead to further reading or related worthwhile activities.

Interest and Effort

Interest evokes effort. More than half a century ago, John Dewey clarified the concept of interest and effort. His view that interest and effort go hand in hand has been reinforced. If a book or article has meaning, use, and purpose for the individual, he will put forth effort to read it. The country boy who was considered a "remedial reading problem" in school puzzled out the meaning of a difficult agricultural bulletin because he wanted to learn how to raise a prize pig. However, interest cannot completely compensate for lack of reading skills. The person whose reading ability falls below a certain critical point cannot get the meaning of a passage no matter how much interest he may have in the content.

Students express in various ways their ideas of the relation of interest to effort: "If you're not interested, you don't care whether you succeed or fail," and "If the assignment doesn't interest me, it may take me an hour when it would only take me twenty minutes if I were interested."

A thirteen-year-old girl in the ninth grade made this more comprehensive comment: "The assignment affects what I read in this way: If it's on something that I'm interested in, I'm likely to read everything I can find on the subject. If I'm not interested, I'll read just as much as I have to. Also, if I'm interested in it, I'll concentrate so deeply that it would take an atom bomb to divert my attention."

Interest creates readiness, which is the precursor of effort. A seventh-grade boy expressed it in this quaint way: "If I am interested in a subject I am much more susceptible to knowledge. I will read much better and easier. On the other hand, if I am not interested and the subject is boring, I may have some sort of a mental block. This is very foolish and I am trying to correct it. We sometimes have to work on things we don't like."

Interest is selective. It chooses one of the many things that lie within our field of perception at a given moment and directs our attention to it. Interest also intensifies the degree and lengthens the span of our attention.

Interest and Personality Development

Interest may be related to personal development in several ways. The student's basic interest in self-improvement may be reflected in his reading. His drive toward self-realization may be reinforced by biography and autobiography, by authentic historical novels, and by true-to-life accounts of people's strivings and frustrations, thoughts and actions in the modern world. He will tend to identify himself with characters who are vigorous, courageous, sincere, kind, helpful, successful. A dominant interest helps him to organize his experiences. A wholehearted interest in a book has an integrating effect on his personality. It is good for a young person to become absorbed for a time in something bigger than himself and beyond himself, to identify himself with an admirable character, to feel with another person, whether real or fictional.

Interest and Wide Reading

Interest in one book may also lead to further reading. A student selects a book because of some initial interest: A friend recommended it; he heard friends talking about the characters; the teacher read an excerpt that caught his interest; the title was appealing. A satisfying experience with this book may form the nucleus of a reading pattern; the student may go on to other books on the same topic, books with a similar appeal, or books by the same author.

Interest, Comprehension, and Memory

Interest aids comprehension and memory. Some psychological experiments have demonstrated that interesting content is comprehended and retained better than uninteresting content. Bernstein (1953) selected two stories which she made equivalent in readability as measured by the Flesch, Lorge, and Dale-Chall formulas. One story was full of action and suspense; it portrayed teen-age characters in situations of interest to teen-agers. The other selection, from a famous novel, was a long, wordy description of adult characters. The ninth-grade students who read both stories comprehended the first more quickly and more accurately. As would be expected, they rated it as more interesting than the other selection.

In another research, Wharton (1957) replaced the vague, general expressions in a college history text with more precise, picture-forming words; this, too, had a favorable effect on comprehension. Similarly, improvements in the organization and interest of a high school history text clearly facilitated comprehension (Peterson, 1954).

Many students firmly believe that interest underlies learning and remembering. When new material is related to the individual's past experience and to his expectations for the future, it is firmly anchored in his memory.

"If you are interest in sometink," wrote a seventh-grade youngster with an IQ of 72, "you will learn, but if you are not interest in what you reading you will not learn." An able learner in the tenth grade said, "If I'm really interested in a subject and am eager to learn it, I find myself learning as fast as I can read the knowledge off the page." A ninth-grade boy described his reaction to uninteresting books more concretely: "When I read a book that isn't interesting, I become very bored and start daydreaming or even sleeping. I begin to twiddle around with other things because I am not interested in what I'm reading. I learn very little unless the book is interesting and informative."

Students link enjoyment with efficient reading. A fourteen-year-old girl with an IQ of 126 emphasized her inability to remember books that she does not enjoy: "If I know I must read a particular book, I read it whether I enjoy it or not; although to tell you the truth, if I don't enjoy it, it goes in one ear and out the other . . . although I've read every word."

Certainly the dynamic force of interest should be more fully used, both in the development of reading ability and in personal development through reading.

CULTIVATION OF INTEREST

Few students seem to recognize the hard fact that one must sometimes read books one does not like. Most youngsters spoke with an air of finality about the importance of interest. Very few assumed any responsibility for building interest in an initially uninteresting subject. However, one put it this way: "Books or assignments are interesting only if you make them so."

When specifically asked, "How can you get interested in something you were not interested in at first?" a class of eighth-grade students offered many sound suggestions, such as the following:

First of all, you have to go at it with the attitude that it can be interesting. If you start out thinking it won't be interesting or fun, the chances are slight that you will end up liking it.

Second, you have to remember that a book may sound as if it wasn't going to be interesting but the more you find out about it, the more you will realize that it is really interesting. Before you say that it isn't interesting, you must know about it.

Third, try to find out the things about a subject that are interesting and concentrate mostly on these (Strang, 1962, p. 85).

INTEREST AND READING ABILITY

Few students mention reading inability as a cause of lack of interest; practically none see a relation between interest and general mental ability. The following quotations express a few of their ideas about these relationships:

A retarded reader said: "If you're used to books with little words and you're assigned a book that you can't make head or tail of, well, that affects your interest."

The hostility toward reading expressed by an eleventh-grade boy, who was reading at third-grade level, crowded out any consideration of interest: "The subject that I read makes no difference to me. Because I think reading is strictly for the birds. I hate anything to do with reading, such as books, teachers that make me read, etc."

Another poor reader pointed out that "If I read a book I must have a great interest in it because I don't like to read." The lower the reading ability, the higher must be the interest in the book. This statement highlights the need to provide highly interesting material for retarded readers.

Another explanation for lack of interest in a book or assignment mentioned by a fifteen-year-old girl in the tenth grade was distracting thoughts: "Sometimes I have things on my mind and that interferes a lot in my reading. If there is some way to get all that's in your mind out I know it would be a big help. But is there a way?"

Boredom is often a cause of lack of interest among gifted youngsters. One teen-age boy expressed their common feeling about repetitious material: "Doing too much of a certain thing, whether you liked it or not at first, will become tiring and boring."

WAYS OF ASCERTAINING READING INTERESTS

Observation

Of the many ways of studying students' reading interests, observation offers the alert teacher many opportunities in the course of his daily class contacts. The teacher notes which books a child chooses, the degree of concentration and enjoyment with which he reads them, his eagerness to talk about them, his desire to read more books of a like nature or books by the same author. When the teacher is reading a story aloud, he can easily sense the students' interest or lack of it by the quality of their attention, the degree of their eagerness to talk about it, and the insistence with which they ask for more.

Reviews Written by Students

More detailed information about reading interests may be gained from the reviews written by older students. If the reviews have the social purpose of acquainting others with interesting books, they are likely to be written carefully and thoughtfully.

Records of students' reading may take different forms, from a simple listing of books read to a comprehensive review such as one finds in newspapers and magazines. The type of review varies with the kind of book and the purpose for which it is read. The following is one of many forms that have been used in schools:

READING PROGRAM BOOK INFORMATION

Pupil_____Age_____Grade_____

Name of book_____

Author_____

Publisher_____ ___ ___ _____

No. of pages_____ Year of publication_____

Pictures_____(none, few, many)

Other books I have read on the same subject or by the same author_____

_____

_____

Description of the most important character_____

_____

_____

One incident that occurred in this book (try to pick an interesting one.) _____

_____

_____

Five new words I learned in this book _____, _____, _____, _____,

_____

Interest rating I would give this book on a five-point scale—reason for the rating_____

_____

_____

An illustration I would like to draw for this book (optional)

In many schools students have become quite resistant to the formal book report. The practice of copying other students' reports or published reviews of the book seems to be quite prevalent. Students greatly prefer discussions to written reviews of books. They are often stimulated by the comments of their peers to read more widely.

Charts of Reading Progress

For a graphic method of showing the scope of a student's interest, one may use a published leaflet called My Reading Design. This record form has a page on which the student lists and numbers in order the books he has read. In the appropriate space on a pie graph, each segment of which represents a type of book, such as biography, art and music, science, horses, fairy tales, etc., the student writes the number of each book.

Choice of Favorite Stories

Students' actual choice of books is usually evidence of their reading interests. One eighth-grade teacher asked each student in a class of able learners, who had access to many magazines in their homes, to bring in one story or article that interested him very much and would interest his classmates. These youngsters brought in more nonfiction than fiction. Their selections represented a wide range of mature interests, including politics, science, music, and psychology.

As an alternative, students may be asked to summarize in their own words their favorite story, mention certain highlight features of it, and tell how they happened to read it. Using this technique, Gaier and Collier (1960, pp. 431–451) found that girls and boys aged nine or ten particularly liked stories about travel, tales of exciting, dangerous pursuit and escape, and stories about "social situations involving subterfuge and surprise, or humor and comical enjoyment." Their interest was heightened by memorable characters, illustrations, or style. Next to fiction, girls preferred fairy tales; boys preferred factual material. Girls preferred leading characters of their own age or only slightly older; boys preferred characters older than themselves. The favorite themes of girls were mystery, pleasant social relationships, and "small helpless children or animals who triumphed over stronger, older, usually male characters." Boys, on the other hand, chose stories whose characters showed remarkable physical or mental adequacy and settings remote in place and time. Animal stories were still favorites. These results are similar to those obtained in other studies of children's interests (Witty, 1961).

Although much information may be obtained by this technique, the results probably depend to some extent upon what books are available. For example, the interest in informative books might have been higher for both girls and boys if they had had access to some of the attractive new factual material.

Rating Titles or Selections

Instead of asking the student about his favorite stories, one may offer him his choice of actual or fictitious annotated titles. An ingenious and unique study of reading interests was made by Thorndike and Henry (1940, pp. 751–763). In order to present each child with a uniform situation, uninfluenced by his previous experiences with books, the investigators prepared a large number of fictitious titles and annotations. For example:

| Yes | No | ? | *Lonesome Laddy Finds a Friend.* How a stray dog found a new master and showed his true love. |
| Yes | No | ? | *Pilot Peters on Patrol.* The adventures of an airplane scout. What was the mystery plane that roared by in the dawn? |

The child was asked to mark the titles which he would *really like to read.* Some children, particularly susceptible to social pressure, might feel they ought to mark *Famous Sermons by Famous Preachers, History of the Lutheran Church,* or *Brush Your Teeth,* even though they would never read such books. Slow-learning children, who are generally more susceptible to suggestion, chose more titles of this kind than did the fast-learning children. On this type of questionnaire, sex differences were much greater than differences in intelligence. There were "few individual titles that showed reliable differences between the bright and the dull children" (Thorndike and Henry, 1940, p. 762). However, comparison with the actual reading done by the same pupils showed marked differences between the slow and the fast groups in the number and quality of books read. The fast-learning group read twice as many books, covered a wider range of titles, and read books of better quality than the slow-learning children. Of the 282 items rated by the slow group, 100 were comics, whereas comics made up only 23 of the 560 items rated by the fast learners.

Instead of offering the student fictitious titles and annotations, one may ask him to rate actual selections. This technique was used effectively by Coleman and Jungblut (1961, pp. 221–228) in a study of the reading preferences of 750 children in grades 4 to 6. The students read and rated 81 selections, 225 to 400 words in length, on the following scale:

Could you read the selection? Yes ___ No ___
If you could read it, please put a cross (X) in the circle which tells best how you feel about this selection.

O   Like very, very much
O   Like quite a lot
O   Like a little
O   Dislike a little
O   Dislike quite a lot
O   Dislike very, very much

Each selection was also rated by adults for its appeal to children of a given age and its value with reference to educational goals. The investigators also appraised the difficulty of each selection by means of the Lorge Readability Index. The children's interest-aversion ratings provided an important supplement to the readability index and the judgments of experienced adult educators.

Interest Inventories

There are also numerous interest inventories of the checklist type. These may list reading habits, types of books, characteristics of books, or actual titles to be checked, usually under the headings of Like, Dislike, or Indifference.

One of the earliest and most comprehensive of the interest inventories was developed by Witty and Kopel (see Witty, 1949, pp. 302–305). It included many items on interests and activities other than reading; it also elicited background information and called for short answers to specific questions.

An example of the short-answer type of questionnaire that covers several areas of reading interest is given on page 108.

Creative-type Questionnaire and Essay

A unique form of questionnaire elicited some fascinating specific information about reading interests: the preferred type of book, its appeal, and style of writing (Strang, 1946, pp. 477–482). An example of this form, as filled out by a girl in the eighth grade, is reproduced on page 109; it will give an idea of the kind of insights that may be gained from this technique.

From this type of questionnaire and from essays written on specific topics, one finds many common and many unique expres-

MY READING INTERESTS

1. Name_____Age_____Grade_____
2. Check the library or libraries below that you can use. Double check those you do use.
   Community library ____   School library   ____
   Church library   ____   Any other library ____
3. How many books have you borrowed from friends during the last month? ____

   Give titles of some _____
   _____
   _____

4. How many books have you loaned to friends during the last month? ____
   Give titles of some_____
   _____
   _____

5. Give the titles of some of the books in your home. _____
   _____

6. From what sources, other than libraries mentioned above, friends included above, and your home, do you obtain books? Check below:
   1. Buy them ____   3. Rent them ____
   2. Gifts   ____   4. Exchanges ____
7. What are your hobbies and collections? _____
   _____

8. What do you intend to be? _____
   Are you going to college? ____ Where? _____
9. Name the five magazines you like best. _____
   _____

10. Name the three movies you last saw. _____
    _____

11. Name the three radio or TV programs you like best. _____
    _____

12. Name the state or country farthest away that you have visited. _____
    _____

13. What sections of the newspaper do you like best? Check below.
    1. Sports ____   4. News   ____
    2. Funnies ____   5. Editorials ____
    3. Stories ____   6. Other   ____
14. Which of the following have encouraged you to read? Check below.
    1. Parents   ____   6. Pals   ____
    2. Teacher   ____   7. Club leader ____
    3. Librarian ____   8. Relatives   ____
    4. Hobby   ____   9. Club work   ____
    5. Friends   ____   10. Other   ____

TO THE STUDENTS

Year in school_____eighth_____Boy_____Girl____x____
Name (you need not sign your unless you want to.) ___C.S.K.___

You have, right now, the best possible information about what high school students like to read. Will you share it with us by answering as thoughtfully and fully as possible the following questions:

1. What do young persons like you most want to read about? Adventure and mystery

2. What kind of a book or article would you choose to read above all others? Books about teen-age romances, etc.

3. Suppose you were going to write a book or article that persons of your age would all want to read, what would be its title? The Typical Teen-ager

4. Write a paragraph or two showing how you think this book should be written to appeal most to the boys and girls in your class.
    The book should be written in such a fashion that it would be both humorous and adventurous; appealing and interesting.
    Life of a teen-ager, not babyish stories, story of romance, adventure, mystery and pleasure.

5. Think of the books or articles you have read this year that you just could not stand. What was it in them that made you dislike them so much?
    In some books they skip from one subject to another. In mysteries they sometimes don't have any endings. Books that are mushy and foolish are also very unpopular. Stories that abuse animals I don't like.

6. Think of the books or articles you have liked most this year. What was it in them that made you like them so much?
    First of all they had a plot which made them interesting. I like dog stories, adventure, mystery, and almost anything in modern life that is written in typical teen-age level.

7. Which book or article that you have read during the last year interested you most keenly? Give the author, Margaret Vail, title Yours Is the Earth, magazine or publisher _____, and date _____ (if you remember it). Then write as much as you can about the book or article and why you liked it so much. (Use other side of page.)
    The book is an autobiography of part of her life in France.
    Margaret Vail married a French soldier. She was in Paris when her daughter was born. Then the war broke out.
    It is the thrilling tale of how she escaped France and got into Spain, climbing the mountains with her daughter, then four years old.
    The book had a plot. It was interesting and every page held me in suspense till the end. It was a war story, but not a gory, bloody tale.

sions of dislike for certain kinds of books and styles of writing:

"Hate anything like Dickens"
"Too much beating around the bush"
"Stories not true to life"
"Sob stories about teen-agers"
"Too much talk—just a bunch of people yakking"

Lack of action and suspense is frequently mentioned. Equally interesting are the reasons students express for liking a book:

"Grown-up but with words you can understand"
"Gives the feeling that you are there"

To Sign or Not to Sign

The question of whether or not students should sign their names to these questionnaires often arises. The more personal the data, the more sensitive the individual is to the impression he is making. However, there is not the same problem with reading interest as with personality inventories. Usually students will answer questions about their reading interests thoughtfully and frankly, whether they do or do not sign their names. If the information is to be used for individual guidance in reading, obviously it is necessary that the blanks be signed.

USING INFORMATION ABOUT INTERESTS

Information about students' interests may be used by teachers, librarians, and parents in guiding the reading of individuals, in introducing books, and in capitalizing on some common interest of a group. Observation of students' interests may be used immediately in guiding their choice of books. A third-grade child chooses a book from the class library to read in his free time. If the book is one that he can read independently, the teacher approves his choice. If it is too difficult for him, the teacher may say, "That's a good book to read later, Jimmy. Here's another book about cowboys you'd like to read right now." If a student is enthusiastic about a book he has just read, the teacher may suggest another book that treats a similar topic, has the same appeal, or is by the same author.

If a student shows no interest in reading any book, the

teacher may try to uncover some other interest or activity to which reading might contribute. For example, a boy in a social studies class (Shepherd, 1961, pp. 140–142) did not choose any of the supplementary books on the early explorers which the teacher had brought into the classroom. Most of the other students, having made their choices, had started reading. The teacher asked John about his outside interests. When the teacher learned that John was absorbed in building a boat with his father, he said, "There's a book here I'm sure you would like. It's about the adventures of an early explorer who went around the Cape of Good Hope in a small boat." John took the book and later made an enthusiastic report on it to the class. By tying reading in with students' outside activities, the teacher utilizes the impetus of their interests.

In addition to daily observation, interest inventories filled out by all the members of a class guide the teacher in ordering new books or in getting books for the class from the library or bookmobile. Without this information the teacher might not be aware, for example, that his young adolescent boys are most interested in certain features of war, sports, and science and in stories about real people and that the girls are interested in mysteries and stories about teen-agers like themselves. If several students mention special interests such as medicine or current problems, the teacher may make available books that contribute to these interests.

Reports of reading interests such as the one reproduced in this chapter may give clues to personality patterns and sources of emotional tension. For example, an adolescent may reveal his attitude toward life, his preoccupations and anxieties, or the quality of his human relationships by such comments as the following:

I especially like stories of people who find out what their career is going to be. Stories of people such as Florence Nightingale and *The Life and Thought of Albert Schweitzer* get you to thinking and wondering about jobs in the field of medicine. Characters who work hard and show a great deal of courage make you want to be more like them. Some books make you want to work harder and do a better job at what you're doing. . . . Books that make you happy and make you laugh are very good to read when you feel downcast or afraid. These books can cheer you up and lift your spirits and make you less afraid (Strang, 1961, p. 391).

After reading a set of these papers, the teacher becomes more aware than ever of the unique personality of each member of his class.

Questionnaires, reviews, and compositions such as have been described in this chapter, when read anonymously to a class, serve as a basis for discussion. By hearing about one student's enjoyment of certain books, others may be stimulated to broaden their reading interests. Class discussion of what makes a book interesting and worthwhile may help students to build criteria for book selection.

Last but not least is the value of a study of their reading interests to the students themselves. It encourages them to appraise their choices of reading materials and to challenge the assumptions that underlie their interests or lack of interests.

CONCLUDING STATEMENT

In general, junior and senior high school students feel strongly about the importance of having interesting reading material and interesting assignments. If the material is uninteresting, they will skim over it quickly, not caring what it says nor whether they finish reading it, getting little or nothing out of it, not noticing the important points, not remembering it, and consequently getting low marks in the subject. If they are interested they will enjoy reading, read carefully and eagerly, comprehend with less effort, note the important facts, get more out of their reading, remember it, search for more material on the same topic, and desire to learn more about related matters.

Being able to recommend the right book for the right child at the psychological moment is basic to success in teaching reading. The child's first experiences with books influence his attitude toward reading. The books recommended to an adolescent determine whether he views reading as "strictly for the birds" or as "one of life's inexhaustible pleasures."

Suggested Problems
Practice and Demonstration

1. Tell or read a story to a group of children and note the points at which they laugh, lose interest, become restless, want to ask ques-

tions, show keen interest. From a number of records of this kind summarize the style of writing, kind of story or article, difficulty, content, and other characteristics of stories that are most and least interesting for a certain age and grade group.

2. Give an interest questionnaire such as the creative-type questionnaire described in this chapter to an intermediate or secondary school class and summarize the understanding of students' interests gained from their responses.

3. In individual cases recommend books you think would be especially interesting and valuable for improvement in reading or for personal development.

4. Study students' comprehension of two passages differing in their interest appeal but otherwise comparable.

5. Read Dewey's *Interest and Effort* to obtain his main line of thought on this subject.

6. Give the same interest blank to two comparable classes. Ask students in one class to sign their names; tell students in the other not to sign their names. Are there any marked differences in the kind of responses that might be due to the factor of signing their names?

7. Have students in the teacher-education class fill out a form such as "My Reading Interests" in this chapter about their own reading interests.

References

Bernstein, Margery R.: "Relationship between Interest and Reading Comprehension," unpublished doctoral project, Teachers College, Columbia University, New York, 1953.

Coleman, J. H., and Ann Jungblut: "Children's Likes and Dislikes about What They Read," *Journal of Educational Research,* 44:221–228, February, 1961.

Gaier, Eugene L., and Mary Jeffrey Collier: "The Latency-stage Story Preferences of American and Finnish Children," *Child Development,* 31:431–451, September, 1960.

"My Reading Design," *The News-Journal,* North Manchester, Ind. Forms A, B, C, and D for primary, intermediate, junior high, and high school, respectively.

Peterson, Eleanor M.: *Aspects of Readability in the Social Studies,* Bureau of Publications, Teachers College, Columbia University, New York, 1954.

Shepherd, David L.: *Effective Reading in the Social Studies,* Harper & Row, Publishers, Incorporated, New York, 1961.

Strang, Ruth: "Reading Interests, 1946," *English Journal,* 25:477–482, November, 1946.

————: "Interest as a Dynamic Force in the Improvement of Reading," *Elementary English,* 34:170–176, March, 1957. Used with the permission of the National Council of Teachers of English.

————: "Evaluation of Development in and through Reading," in *Development in and through Reading,* Sixtieth Yearbook of the National Society for the Study of Education, The University of Chicago Press, Chicago, 1961, pp. 376–397.

————: "Prevention and Correction of Underachievement," in H. Alan Robinson (ed.), *The Underachiever in Reading,* Report of the Twenty-fifth Annual Conference on Reading, The University of Chicago Press, Chicago, 1962, pp. 79–86.

Thorndike, Robert L., and Florence Henry: "Differences in Reading Interests Related to Differences in Sex and Intelligence Level," *The Elementary School Journal,* 40:751–763, June, 1940.

Wharton, William P.: "Picture-forming Words and Readability of College History Texts," unpublished doctoral dissertation, Teachers College, Columbia University, New York, 1952.

Witty, Paul: *Reading in Modern Education,* Ginn and Company, Boston, 1949.

———— (chairman): *Development in and through Reading,* Sixtieth Yearbook of the National Society for the Study of Education, The University of Chicago Press, Chicago, 1961, chap. 8.

Suggested Readings

Figurel, J. Allen (ed.): *Reading for Effective Living,* International Reading Association Conference Proceedings, vol. 3, Scholastic Magazines, Inc., New York, 1958.

Larrick, Nancy: *A Parent's Guide to Children's Reading,* Doubleday and Company, Inc., New York, 1958. Also, Pocket Books, Inc., New York, 1958.

————: *A Teacher's Guide to Children's Books,* Charles E. Merrill Books, Inc., Columbus, Ohio, 1960.

Mackintosh, Helen K.: "Children's Interests in Literature and the Reading Program," *The Reading Teacher,* 10:138–145, 1957.

Norvell, George W.: *What Boys and Girls Like to Read,* Silver Burdett Company, Morristown, N.J., 1958.

Robinson, Helen M.: *Developing Permanent Interest in Reading,* Proceedings of the Annual Conference on Reading, The University of Chicago Press, Chicago, 1956.

Strang, Ruth: *Helping Your Child Improve His Reading,* E. P. Dutton & Co., Inc., New York, 1962.

———— and others: *Gateways to Readable Books,* The H. W. Wilson Company, New York, 1958.

Wollner, Mary Hayden Bowen: *Children's Voluntary Reading as an Expression of Individuality,* Bureau of Publications, Teachers College, Columbia University, New York, 1949.

7

CONTRIBUTION OF TESTS

Tests add precision and completeness to the teacher's classroom observations. When the teacher uses tests, he controls the stimuli to which the students respond. Since a test presumably presents a common stimulus to all students, comparisons of their differing responses are possible.

APPRAISAL BY TEACHER-MADE TESTS

The most informal way to screen a class for speed and comprehension is to ask the students to read silently a selection of four or five pages in their textbook. As each one finishes, he looks up and closes the book. This identifies the fast and the slow readers. When all have finished, the teacher asks questions based on the selection; the students write their answers. This test of their comprehension shows how well students can understand and remember the selection that they have just read. Some students will find it easy; others, too difficult.

More definitely designed are the paragraphs such as those described in Chapter 4. These may be multigraphed and given to an entire class. They then serve as an informal silent reading test of ability to recognize paragraph structure and use it as an aid to efficient reading.

Tests of Reading for Different Purposes

Many kinds of informal tests may be used for different purposes. To call attention to the importance of recognizing the author's intent, mood, and purpose, the teacher may use several short selections or even advertisements of such a nature that the reader who does not sense the writer's purpose will seriously misinterpret them. For example, he may take seriously a poem or short essay written with a humorous intent. Or he may accept at face value easily detected misstatements of a writer whose aim is to persuade the reader to buy certain products. With selections of this kind the reader should ask three questions:

What does this paragraph say?

What attitudes is the author trying to induce in the reader?

How does he use words to serve his purpose?

To test ability to skim quickly for a certain bit of information, the teacher may use news stories or other short articles in which the reader is asked to find a single fact, such as the score of the football game or who won the race on a certain date. All the students begin reading when the signal is given and look up as soon as they have found the answer. Those who have succeeded most quickly then describe their methods to the others.

To test ability to select the main idea or ideas in a selection, the teacher should first use well-constructed, well-organized articles. The test exercise may call for answers to multiple-choice questions or for a list of the main ideas: (1) _____, (2) _____, (3) _____.

To test for thoroughness of understanding of a factual article or an assignment in history or other subject, the teacher may ask for a summary or outline. This exercise would include the relationship between the main ideas and their supporting details.

Tests of ability to make deeper interpretations of different kinds of material would be based on selections from literature or from other content fields that require interpretation of character and critical thinking.

Informal Tests in Each Subject

Every subject teacher needs to find out how well the students in a new class can read the books he expects them to read. He wants to know: What is their purpose or purposes in reading a given selection? What is being communicated to them—what have they learned and remembered from reading this section of the text or reference book? How well can they communicate orally or in writing the ideas gained? An informal "teaching test" in each subject will answer these questions.

These teaching tests have several advantages: They are closely geared to instruction, whereas a formal diagnosis is too often divorced from instruction. The test results are easy for the teacher to apply in his daily instruction. The free or unstructured response shows how students approach a reading assignment, what they remember from reading it, and how well they communicate the ideas in it. These tests also promote student self-appraisal. By encouraging the student to take the initiative in analyzing his own reading process, they motivate learning. A series of similar tests followed by a discussion of progress made enables the student to assess his ability to profit from instruction.

Informal tests are fairly easy to construct and administer. The teacher selects a section of about a thousand words from a text which the students have not read. The student reads the selection and computes his speed. He may time himself or the teacher may write the time on the board in ten-second or larger intervals, erasing each number as the next comes up. As soon as the student finishes reading, he looks up and writes the number that he sees. This figure is his reading time in seconds.

He then answers the questions without referring to the selection. Thus retention as well as comprehension is tested. This is a student's most natural response after reading an assignment.

The first question calls for a free or creative response. It may ask simply for information: What did the author say? Or it may ask for information plus opinion: What did the author say? What did the author mean by this? Or it may combine information, opinion, and consideration of the author's motive: What did the author say? What did he mean by this? Why did he say it? After obtaining answers to the first question only, the teacher will be amazed at the wide range of responses in a single class.

The free response may be supplemented by short-answer or objective questions. Some of these test the reader's ability to recognize the main ideas and supporting details; others, his ability to draw inferences and conclusions, to define key words, and to appreciate humor, character portrayal, or other qualities of literary style. The test exercises can be varied to serve different purposes, such as to see how well students can answer questions they have formulated before beginning to read, or how effectively they can extract ideas relevant to a particular topic.

Some students in a heterogeneous class will do very poorly on this kind of informal test. The text for the grade is obviously too difficult for them. But they can learn to get some ideas from it, and they usually want to have the same book as their classmates.

As students participate in the class discussion of one another's answers to the questions, they see more clearly why their free response rated only 1 or 2, whereas others deserved ratings of 9 or 10. They become aware of the reasons why some definitions of words are more precise and clear than others. They learn how to get the main idea more quickly by analyzing the ways in which paragraphs are built.

The informal reading test may be expanded into an informal group reading inventory and into a comprehensive, integrated, diagnostic self-appraisal teaching procedure.

Group Reading Inventory

The group reading inventory is used to determine the reading proficiency of every student in a given subject class. The most important part of the inventory is the informal test already described. To this are added questions on study skills, location-of-information skills, and other skills needed in reading the particular subject. Ability to apply the ideas gained from the passage to current events or to personal problems may also be appraised in this informal group inventory.

Students mark their own papers to see for themselves their strengths and their difficulties in reading. Junior high school students are especially interested in themselves as persons and like to know about their reading efficiency. When the student has corrected his inventory, he tabulates the results on the front page, for example:

Parts of book
Speed of reading
Vocabulary meaning
Contextual meaning, and so on

A check may indicate either skills in which the student needs instruction and practice or, if preferred, the skills he has mastered.

The grade level at which the student is able to read is not so important as the analysis of his reading skills. If, however, a student scores 65 per cent below the grade level, he should be given an individual reading inventory.

Detailed directions for making group reading inventories for English, social studies, and science classes were worked out for teachers by Dr. David Shepherd when he was serving as reading consultant at the Norwalk (Connecticut) High School. They are reproduced here with his permission. Permission for reprinting parts of the social studies and science inventories was also obtained from Harper & Row (Shepherd, 1960).

ENGLISH: Group Reading Inventory

Directions for making and administering a diagnostic survey test of reading skills using an English literature textbook:

1. Use between 35–40 questions.
2. Use questions designed to measure the following reading skills in the proportions shown below.
   (1) Using parts of a book. Include use of (three questions in all):
       a. Table of contents
       b. Index of titles
       c. Glossary   } If such sections are included in the
       d. Biographical data   textbook
       e. Introductory paragraph to story

(2) Vocabulary needs
    a. Meaning (seven to eight questions)
        1. General background of word meanings
           (a) select correct meanings from several dictionary meanings
           (b) antonyms, synonyms
        2. Contextual meanings
    b. Word recognition and attack (14–15 questions)
        1. Divide words into syllables
        2. Designate the accented syllable
        3. Note and give meaning of prefixes and suffixes
        4. Changing the part of speech of a word (i.e., noun to verb, adjective to adverb, etc.)
(3) Comprehension (11–12 questions)
    a. Noting the main idea
    b. Recalling pertinent supporting details
    c. Drawing conclusions, inferences
    d. Noting the sequence of ideas
(4) Reading rate—Have pupil note the time it takes for him to read the selection. Then figure his reading speed in words per minute. Example: Words in selection, 4000; Time to read: 10 minutes; 4000 ÷ 10 equals 400 words per minute. Time may be recorded by (1) pupil noting time by clock of starting and of stopping to get total number of minutes, or (2) teacher may record time on blackboard for each thirty seconds—1', 1'30'', 2', etc.
(5) Skimming to locate information (2–5 questions). Use a different selection that was not used for comprehension and speed purposes.

3. Choose a reading selection of not more than three or four pages.
4. In administering the inventory:
    (1) Explain to the pupils the purpose of the inventory and the reading skills the inventory is designed to measure. As the inventory is given, let the pupils know the skill being measured.
    (2) Read each question twice.
    (3) Questions on the use of the parts of the book are asked first. Pupils will use their books.
    (4) Introduce the reading selection, culling pupil background of experience on the topic and setting up purpose questions.
    (5) Selection read silently. Speed noted and figured.
    (6) Ask questions on vocabulary. Pupils will use books for questions measuring ability to determine meaning from context. They will not use books for other vocabulary questions. All other vocabulary questions need to be written on the blackboard.
    (7) Ask questions on comprehension. Pupils will not use books—books are to be closed.
    (8) Skimming, new selection used. Pupils will use books to find answers to questions.

5. A pupil is considered to be deficient in any one specific skill if he answers more than one out of three questions incorrectly, or more than two incorrectly when there are more than three questions measuring a specific skill.
6. This inventory, being administered to a group, does not establish a grade level. Nonetheless, any pupil scoring above 90 per cent may be considered as reading material that is too easy for him, and any pupil scoring below 65 per cent as reading material that is too difficult for him. If the material is suitable, the scores should range between 70–90 per cent.

Form of Inventory (Sample)

Parts of book

1. On what page does the unit (section) entitled "Exploring One World" begin? (shows use of table of contents)
2. What section of your book would you use to find out something about the author of a story in the book? (determines knowledge of section on biographical data)
3. In what part of the book can you find the meaning of a word that you might not know? (determines knowledge of glossary)

Introduce story: explore pupils' background of experiences on the subject of the story and set up purpose questions. Pupils read selection silently. Time for reading speed determined.

Vocabulary meaning

4. What is meant by the word *crab* as it is used in the story? (top line, second column, page 178)

Contextual meaning

5. What is meant by the word *eliminated*? (third line, second column, page 181)

Synonyms and antonyms

6. What word means the opposite of *temporary*?
7. Use another word to describe the coach when he looked *amazed*.

General knowledge of meaning

8. Select the proper meaning of the word *entice*.
   a. To lure, persuade
   b. To force
   c. To ask
   d. To caution
9. Select the proper meaning of the word *initial*.
   a. The last or end
   b. The first or beginning
   c. The middle
   d. A letter of the alphabet

10. Select the proper meaning of the word *rectify*.
    a. To do wrong
    b. To make right
    c. To destroy
    d. A priest's home

Word recognition, syllabication

11. Divide the following words into syllables and show which syllable is accented.
12. and 13. Eliminated
14. and 15. Amazed
16. and 17. Undemocratic
18. and 19. Fraternities

Prefixes and suffixes

20. What does the prefix *un* mean as used in *undemocratic?*
21. What is meant by *pre* in the word *prescription?*

Parts of speech

22. Change the verb *astonish* to a noun.
23. Change the adjective *democratic* to a noun.
24. Change the noun *boy* to an adjective.
25. Change the adjective *slow* to an adverb.

Comprehension, main ideas

26. What is a _____? What happened when _____?
27. Such questions as indicated here that ask for
28. only the main points of the story.

Details

29. Questions to ask for specific bits of information
30. about the principal characters or ideas of the
31. material.

Drawing conclusions, inferences

32. Questions, the answers of which are not completely found in the textbook.
33. Questions beginning with "Why," making comparisons, predicting what
34. may happen usually measure the drawing conclusions skill. Example: Why did Bottle imagine he could perform such astounding athletic feats as setting the State high school record in jumping?

Sequence

35. (May be omitted.) Questions asking what
36. happened as a result of _____, what steps
37. did the police use to solve the mystery, etc.

Skimming

38. Use a new reading selection. Questions
39. designed to have the pupil locate some
40. specific bit of information.

SOCIAL STUDIES: Group Reading Inventory

Directions for making a group reading inventory using the social studies textbook:

1. Use 26 to 30 questions.
2. Write questions designed to measure the following reading skills in the proportions as shown below:
   (1) Using parts of the book (5 questions)
   (2) Using resource (library) materials (4 questions)
   (3) Using maps, pictures, charts, etc. (4 questions)
   (4) Vocabulary (3 questions)
   (5) Noting the main idea (3 questions)
   (6) Noting pertinent supporting details (3 questions)
   (7) Drawing conclusions (3 questions)
   (8) Noting the organization of the material (1 question)
3. Choose a reading selection of not more than 3–4 pages in length.
4. Have questions of skills—(4) through (8)—vocabulary, main ideas, details, conclusions, and organization—based on the reading selection.
5. Explain to the pupils the purpose of the test and the reading skills the test is designed to measure. As the test is given, let the pupils know the skill being measured.
6. Read each question twice.
7. Write the page reference of each question on the blackboard as the question is read.
8. A pupil is considered to be deficient in any of the skills if he gets more than one question in any of the skills wrong. For example, if a pupil gets two vocabulary questions wrong, he will be considered deficient in vocabulary. If he gets only one vocabulary question wrong, he will not be considered deficient.

Form of Test (Sample)

Parts of book

1. On what page would you find the map that shows (name of map). (tests use of map table found in front of book)
2. On what page does Chapter _____ begin? What is the title of the unit of which it is a part? (use of table of contents)
3. How can the introduction on pages _____ help you in your study? (shows understanding of unit introduction)
4. Of what value are the questions, activities, and vocabulary shown on pages _____ to you for the understanding of the material of the textbook? (shows understanding of specific textbook study aids)

5. In what part of the book would you look to find the page references of this topic? _____ (purpose of index)

Use of resources

6. What library aid will tell you the library number of the book _____, so that you would be able to find it on the shelves? (knowledge of function of card catalogue)
7. What is a biography? (shows knowledge of a type of reference)
8. Name one set of encyclopedias. How are the topics in them arranged? (shows knowledge of a type of reference material)
9. Name a library guide that will help you to find a specific magazine article _____. If you were to give a report in class and you knew that most of your information would be in current magazines, what guide would you use that would tell you what magazine to use and what issue of it to use for information on your topic? (shows knowledge of a type of library guide to research)

Use of maps, charts, etc.

10. What does the map on page _____ show you? (shows an understanding of fundamental idea of map)
11. What do the black areas (or some other special feature) shown on the map on page _____ represent? (shows ability to read information from a map)
12. Turn to page _____. Ask for some specific bit of information that is shown by the chart. Example: "What are the three branches of our Federal Government?" (shows ability to understand diagrams)
13. Turn to page _____. Ask for some specific bit of information that is shown by the picture. Ask also for interpretation. Example: Picture showing sod house on the prairie: "What is the settler's house made of? Can you tell why that type of building material is used?" (shows ability to understand and interpret picture)

Vocabulary

Read pages _____.
14. Define _____ _____ _____.
15. What did "So and So" mean when he said _____ _____ (word or term to be defined from the comment must be pointed out to the pupils)? (contextual meanings)
16. What is a _____ _____?

Noting main ideas

17. Questions to ask for only the main points of
18. information—main ideas of the longer
19. important paragraphs.

Noting details

20. Questions to ask for specific bits of
21. information about the principal characters
22. or ideas of the material.

Drawing conclusions

23. Questions, the answers of which are not completely in the textbook. Ques-
24. tions beginning with "Why," making comparisons, predicting events,
25. usually measure drawing conclusions. Example: "Why did the pioneers brave the dangers to move westward?"
26. Each author follows an outline in writing the information in your textbook. In looking through the chapter (one from which the reading selection was taken) write down the author's first main topic.

or

If you were to outline the material that you have read, what would be the 1-2-3 main topics (headings) of your outline?

SCIENCE: Group Reading Inventory

Directions for making a diagnostic test using science textbook:

1. Use approximately 30 questions.
2. Write questions designed to measure the following reading skills in proportions as shown below:
   (1) Using parts of the book (4 questions)
   (2) Using resource (library) materials (3 questions)
   (3) Vocabulary (meaning from the context) (4 questions)
   (4) Noting the main idea (4 questions)
   (5) Noting pertinent supporting details (4 questions)
   (6) Following directions (3 questions)
   (7) Drawing conclusions (3 questions)
   (8) Applying theoretical information (3 questions)
   (9) Understanding formulas and equations (3 questions)
3. Choose a reading selection of not more than 3–4 pages in length.
4. Have questions on skills (3), (4), (5), (7), (8)—vocabulary, main ideas, details, conclusion, application—based on the reading selection. Items (6) and (9) may require student to refer to the textbook.
5. Explain to the pupils the purpose of the inventory and the reading skills the inventory is designed to measure. As the inventory is given, let the pupils know the skill being measured.
6. Read each question twice.
7. Write the page reference of each question as necessary on the blackboard as the question is read.
8. Have pupil score his own paper.

9. A pupil is considered to be deficient in any of the skills if he gets more than one question in any of the skills wrong. For example: If a pupil gets more than one question in any of the skills (two vocabulary questions) wrong, he will be considered deficient.

10. Form of Tabulation

Name of class_____Section_____Teacher_____

Name of pupil	Parts of book	Resource material	Vocabulary	etc.

_____ (state wherever the pupil is deficient) (See page 130.)

Form of Test (Sample)

Parts of book

1. On what page would you find the chapter called _____? (tests ability to use table of contents)
2. Of what value to you are the questions under the chapter section called _____? (shows understanding of specific textbook aids)
3. How are the chapters arranged or grouped? (shows knowledge of organization of textbook)
4. What sections of the book would you use to find the page reference of the topic _____? (shows knowledge of the purpose of the index)

Library

5. How are topics arranged in a "reference book"? (shows knowledge of organization of reference book under consideration)
6. What is a biography? (shows knowledge of a type of reference material)
7. Explain the difference between science fiction and science factual materials. (shows knowledge of important types of science reading materials)

Vocabulary

8. These questions test two ways of defining words:
9. One—through the context—turn to page _____.
10. How is the word used by the author?
11. Two—recall—what does the word mean? Use it in a sentence or give the definition and ask for the appropriate word.

Main ideas

12. Questions to ask
13. for main points of information—
14. for main ideas of the longer important paragraphs

15. (chapter headings, subheadings, marginal headings, introduction and summary).
16. Summary of an experiment.

Details

17. Questions to ask for specific bits of information about the principal
18. definitions and laws, aspect of a process, application of law, principal
19. steps in an experiment, a life cycle. Use words that select the relative
20. importance of details—how author shows the importance of specific details. All similar details are grouped around one main idea—each main idea has its qualifying details.

Following directions

21. Questions to show sequence of steps or ideas
22. for solving a problem or performing an
23. experiment. Chain of events.

Drawing conclusions

24. Questions, the answers to which are not completely found in the textbook.
25. Questions beginning with "Why," asking for the significance of a finding,
26. the value of the finding of an experiment, or the implication of a description of some species, or natural phenomena, cause and effect. What happens if certain natural conditions were present, comparing two or more types of living organisms or inanimates, etc.

Application

27. Questions asking for examples of how scientific laws and
28. principles can be put to practical use. Example: Explain the
29. relationship of photosynthesis to the conservation of plant life.

Formulas, symbols, etc.

30. Questions showing meanings attached to
31. symbols as given in the text.

The summary chart shown on page 130, with names of students to be listed along the left-hand side and types of reading difficulties enumerated across the top, summarizes the information for a class. When read horizontally, it describes the individual students; when read vertically, it shows which difficulties are common to the class. Thus the teacher sees the instruction needed by the whole class and the special help needed by individuals.

For students whose comprehension score is below 50 per

Summary Chart

Name of class _____   Diction _____   Teacher _____

Name	Use of parts of book	Vocabulary	Meaning	Contextual meanings	Synonyms and antonyms	General knowledge	Word recognition	Syllabication	Accent	Prefixes and suffixes	Part of speech	Comprehension	Main ideas	Supporting details	Drawing conclusions	Sequence of ideas	Skimming	Speed in wpm	Comments
John Jones	✓	✓	✓	✓	✓	✓	✓	✓	✓	✓	✓			✓	✓			194	(Check whenever pupil is deficient)
Robert Brown				✓	✓	✓									✓			150	

130

cent or above 95 per cent, Shepherd recommends administering the individual inventory (described in Chapter 10). Appropriate instruction should follow the giving of the inventory; this, indeed, is its main purpose. When the inventory is repeated at the middle and at the end of the semester, both teachers and students get a sense of accomplishment as they see improvement in reading skills.

Diagnostic Self-appraisal Teaching Procedure

The instructional value of these informal procedures is brought out more fully by the integrated procedure developed by Melnik (1960) for improving the reading of social studies in junior high school. This procedure

starts by asking students to state their aims or goals in reading a social studies assignment. Most students of this age are vague about their reasons for reading and about the reading method that would be most appropriate. They are then asked to read a selection from a social studies book that is typical of the material the students will be expected to read in their classes. After reading the passage they answer two types of questions—creative response or open-end: What did the author say? and a number of multiple-choice questions that are designed to furnish evidence of the student's ability to get the literal meaning, to see relations, draw inferences, make generalizations, and understand the meaning of key words.

As soon as the student has answered the questions, he has data before him for self-appraisal. He marks his own paper. He grades his free response on a ten-point scale, and analyzes the kinds of errors he has made in the multiple-choice questions (each choice represents a certain kind of error). Instruction immediately follows this self-appraisal, while the students are specifically motivated to learn how to get the right answers and to avoid the same errors next time.

There is a next time; the whole procedure is repeated with another similar selection. After the second exercise is completed and analyzed, the students are able to note the progress they have made. A third repetition of the procedure makes further improvement possible.

This testing-teaching-evaluating procedure bridges the gap between the hurriedly-made teacher test and the standardized test. It relieves the teacher of some of the burden of making instructional material; at the same time it gives him a concrete model for further testing-teaching-evaluating based on the text or reference books used by his particular class (Strang, 1961, pp. 386–387).

APPRAISAL BY STANDARDIZED TESTS

The standardized test is the most widely used instrument for appraising students' reading progress and for evaluating reading programs. However, its coverage is only partial; there are many aspects of reading achievement and many factors in reading success or failure that are not measured by standardized tests.

Before considering the uses of standardized reading tests and the weight that should be given them in the evaluation of students' reading proficiency, we should see what kinds of tests are available. Since complete lists of reading tests, together with descriptions and evaluations of those that are frequently used, are available in other sources (Bond and Hoyt, 1955; Buros, 1959; Strang and others, 1961, chap. 15 and pp. 386–387), we shall refer here only to certain tests needed for illustrative purposes.

Abilities Measured—and Not Measured—by Reading Tests

Standardized tests are mostly of the *survey* type. They give a general estimate of the reading level and the range of reading ability in a specific group. The abilities most often measured by survey tests are vocabulary and comprehension. Less frequently, they measure speed and study skills. The kind of information obtained varies with the test. In the past most standardized tests have measured a narrow range of reading abilities (see Table 1).

There are many important aspects of reading that standardized reading tests do not adequately measure at present, such as ability to (1) adapt rate and method of reading to one's purpose and to the kind of material that one is reading, (2) use context clues effectively, and (3) read critically and with appreciation. From standardized tests alone the teacher cannot distinguish between the slow learners and those who have potential mental ability to read better. Moreover, tests do not shed light on the student's reading process—how he arrived at the answers given or what difficulties he encountered in the reading tasks presented. Two students may get the same score on a test, but one may arrive at his comprehension of the passage by a much more mature thought process than the other.

We might also ask: What *do* reading tests measure—reading ability, intelligence, educational opportunity, industry, or family background? Or various linguistic abilities? Or the individual's

Table 1.   SKILLS MEASURED BY FIFTEEN SELECTED READING TESTS

Skill	1	2	3	4	5	6	7	8	9	10	11	12	13	14	15
Speed and comprehension															
Rate of comprehension			x	x			x				x	x		x	x
Speed of comprehension		x			x										
Level of comprehension		x		x	x	x									
Accuracy, efficiency					x										
Word meaning															
General vocabulary	x	x	x	x	x		x		x	x		x	x		x
Technical vocabulary												x			
Vocabulary in context			x			x									
Mathematics vocabulary	x														
Science vocabulary	x														
Social science vocabulary	x														
General comprehension															
Sentence meaning												x			
Paragraph meaning			x				x	x	x	x		x	x	x	x
Details			x					x							
Interpretations	x			x											
Perceptions of relations				x											
Integration of ideas				x											
Drawing inferences				x											
Poetry comprehension							x								
Work-study skills															
General reference	x														
Following directions	x														
Directed reading							x	x							
General information			x												
Use of index							x					x			
Selection of key words							x								
Directory reading												x			
Map-table-graph												x			
Advertisement															

1. California
2. Cooperative English
3. Diagnostic Examination
4. Diagnostic Reading
5. Gates Survey

6. Iowa Every-Pupil
7. Iowa Silent
8. Kelley-Greene
9. Metropolitan
10. Nelson-Denny

11. Schramnel Gray
12. SRA Reading Record
13. Stanford Achievement
14. Traxler High School
15. Traxler Silent Reading

SOURCE: Hunt, 1955.

values, purpose, or self-concept? All these factors enter into reading achievement in different degrees, for reading is a dynamic interaction of psychological forces. Anything as complex as this process of reading cannot be fully measured by standardized tests.

No one test can determine accurately the reading achievement of an individual student. Two tests are better than one, but all standardized test results should be supplemented by the teacher's informal tests and observation. The results for a particular student will vary with his familiarity with the field, with the similarity of the test selections to the reading he has been doing, with his understanding and interpretation of the directions, and with the kind of reading instruction he has had. Survey tests also fail to distinguish between deficiencies in word recognition skills and in higher levels of comprehension that depend on these basic skills. Some students would be able to comprehend the author's thought more fully if they were more proficient in the basic skills.

Tests of reading speed are probably the most unreliable because their results are especially dependent upon the instructions given and upon the way the individual interprets the instructions. The Iowa Silent Reading Tests and the Traxler Silent Reading Test for grades 7 to 10 instruct students to read so that they will be able to answer questions. Other tests give multiple-choice questions at the end of very brief paragraphs. The Michigan Speed of Reading Test includes in each two-sentence unit an irrelevant word to be crossed out. Such devices tend to interfere with the normal process of reading. One other disadvantage: On a speed test, the slow student is penalized. He may be able to comprehend on a high level if he has ample time. If he does not finish the test in the time allotted, he gets a low score on reading material that he could otherwise have understood well.

Diagnostic tests give a detailed picture of strengths and weaknesses. To obtain this picture, examine several diagnostic tests (Bond and Hoyt, 1955; Committee on Diagnostic Reading Tests, 1947–1960; Doren Diagnostic Reading Test, 1956; Roswell-Chall Diganostic Test of Word Analysis Skills, 1956–1958). Most recent is the Spache Diagnostic Reading Scales published in the Spring, 1963. These give interpretation as well as a valuable picture of a student's reading abilities and proficiencies. You will note that some tests provide more complete and adequate diagnostic clues than do others. These details may suggest hypotheses as to the causes of a student's reading difficulties. By following these leads the teacher can select appropriate procedures to improve the student's reading. If a test attempts to cover too many aspects of reading, its subtests are too short to be reliable.

A *learning methods test* has been developed to guide teachers in selecting the best methods to use with individual students. This unique Elementary Learning Test, devised by Mills (1954–55), consists of four trial lessons in word recognition, each taught by a different method. Comparable words are presented in each lesson, and the student's actual learning is tested both at the time of the lesson and one day later. Thus the teacher may discover the method by which an individual student learns best. Some students show a significantly superior learning aptitude for one method; others learn equally well by all methods.

Choice of Reading Tests

In choosing a reading test, the first questions to ask are the following:

What are my objectives—what specific reading abilities do I want my students to achieve?

Which of these objectives *can* be measured adequately?

Which of these objectives does *this test* measure adequately?

For which of the objectives must I use some nontest procedure?

For example, the vocabulary part of the Metropolitan Reading Test, Intermediate Level, Form R, directly measures the association of word forms with their correct meaning and, as a prerequisite, accurate discrimination of word forms. The paragraph reading section measures the ability to grasp the meaning of paragraphs and to cope with such factors as unusual word order, complexity of sentence structure, and abstract ideas. The students' test responses may be analyzed to show strengths and weaknesses in these important objectives.

Analysis of a Reading Test

The following form is a useful guide in careful test selection.

General facts: Title, author, publisher, designated function.

Reading abilities measured: Are they significant and suitable?

Validity: Does it measure what it purports to measure?

Reliability: Is it accurate and consistent?

Diagnostic value: Does it indicate the students' special difficulties and give clues as to why they are having these difficulties?

Norms: What types of norms are available? Are they representative of the total population or of certain groups?

Pupil performance: What does the pupil do?

Construction of test: How were the exercises selected?

Manual: Are the directions complete and easily intelligible? Are norms included, uses of the test described, and other data about test and teaching aids given?

Costs.

Mechanical considerations: Is it legible, etc.?

For brief analyses of widely used reading tests, see Appendix A.

Diagnostic Information from Standardized Reading Tests

In diagnosis the teacher tries to ascertain the reasons for, as well as the nature of, the reading difficulties. Even the so-called diagnostic tests do not yield much understanding of the causes of reading deficiencies. They give a certain amount of detail on the kinds of reading difficulty—lack of word attack skills, for example—but they do not explain why the individual is having this difficulty.

The amount of useful diagnostic insight that is actually extracted from standardized tests covers a range from practically none to a great deal. A single total score gives a basis for comparison with students of the same chronological age or grade. Subtests, while too short to be reliable, do suggest inequalities among reading abilities such as vocabulary knowledge and paragraph comprehension.

An analysis of the student's correct responses and errors on each reading item yields additional detailed information, depending upon the variety of responses that is called for in the test. Some of the test items call for merely knowing the common meaning of the words. Others test the ability to select the particular meaning that fits the context, to answer specific factual questions, to find the main ideas of the passage, to sense the author's mood and purpose, to recognize literary devices, to make generalizations, to draw inferences and conclusions, or to interpret character and motives. This kind of analysis has been worked out in detail in the reading section of the *STEP Manual for Interpreting Scores —Reading* (1959, p. 9). The Educational Testing Service Committee states that STEP Reading Test 1A measures five major reading-for-comprehension skills:

a. Ability to reproduce ideas

b. Ability to translate ideas and make inferences

c. Ability to analyze motivation

    d. Ability to analyze presentation

    e. Ability to criticize

The tables on pages 138–139 represent one method of identifying which of the five skills listed above are tested by each question in Part One and Part Two of the test. By checking incorrect responses in the blank columns, the student may more clearly identify those skill areas requiring further practice.

A similar analysis may be made of any test that consists of exercises that measure different skills.

From an analysis of a student's errors the teacher may recognize certain difficulties. For example, in a vocabulary test in which each mislead of the multiple-choice questions represents a different kind of error, he may note that a student frequently confuses two words that are similar in form or details. From this observation he may assume a tendency to give overpotency to the shape of a word or to certain prominent details in it. If the student gives a correct dictionary definition of a word but not the meaning that is called for by the context, the teacher may infer that the student is not sufficiently concerned with the meaning of what he reads. If he mentions only isolated details in a free-response question, he probably needs instruction and practice in organizing the author's thought. If he does much better on the factual multiple-choice questions than on those calling for inferences or interpretation, the teacher may assume that the reader has not been taught or has not learned the higher-level reading skills or that he is not mentally equipped to do the kind of reasoning that they require. There are, of course, any number of possible reasons for any type of error.

To check inferences based on an analysis of errors, the teacher needs another method: introspection. The examiner or teacher sits down with the student and invites him to try to explain how he made his errors and how he arrived at his correct responses. In this way both the examiner and the student will gain further insight into the reading process.

A depth analysis of a reading test has much educational value: It makes the student aware of his reading methods, motivates him to do better, and increases his receptivity to instruction on the specific skills in which he sees the need for improvement. What the teacher does with the diagnostic information thus obtained is, of course, of prime importance.

ANALYSIS OF SKILLS TESTED IN STEP READING TEST
PART ONE

No. of exercise	Skills measured				
	a	b	c	d	e
1		x			
2		x	x		
3		x	x		
4				x	
5		x			
6	x				
7			x		
8			x		
9		x	x		
10			x		
11	x				
12		x			
13			x		
14		x			
15				x	
16		x			
17		x			
18		x	x		
19	x				
20			x	x	
21	x				
22			x		
23	x				
24			x	x	
25		x			
26	x	x			
27	x				
28	x				
29				x	
30		x			
31			x	x	
32					
33		x			
34				x	
35				x	
Total	8	14	12	8	

PART TWO

No. of exercise	a	b	c	d	e
1	x				
2		x			
3			x		
4				x	
5		x			x
6		x	x		
7		x			
8			x		
9					x
10			x		
11				x	
12		x			
13	x	x			
14			x		
15					x
16				x	
17				x	
18		x			
19				x	x
20				x	
21		x			
22			x		
23			x		
24					x
25		x			
26	x				
27			x		
28		x			
29		x			
30		x			
31		x			
32			x		
33				x	
34		x			
35					x
Total	3	14	9	7	6
Total I	8	14	12	8	0
Total II	3	14	9	7	6
Total I and II	11	28	21	15	6
Percentage	14	34	26	19	7

Use and Misuse of Standardized Tests
(Traxler, 1959, pp. 18–20)

In Studying Groups. After studying the reading ability of groups, the teacher may merely divide the class into the lowest, second, third, and fourth quarters according to the test scores. This procedure gives him an estimate of the relative ability of the students as measured by the particular reading test. He will not be surprised if different tests produce different estimates of reading level.

By ranking all the students in order according to their standardized reading test scores, he will get an idea of the range of reading ability represented in the class. Such a list may be used to group students tentatively on reading levels and to provide suitable reading materials for each one.

The reading test results of a school or school district are often summarized in relation to intelligence and school achievement. Such a summary may call attention to the differences among schools as well as those among classes and individual students with respect to readiness for reading or reading achievement.

In Studying Reading Achievement in Relation to Intelligence Test Scores. Although the formerly rigid distinction between scholastic aptitude tests and achievement tests is breaking down, certain tests are composed chiefly of matter which children usually learn in school (achievement tests), while others mainly require answers that are not directly dependent upon school learning (scholastic aptitude tests).

The coefficients of correlation between group tests of intelligence and group tests of silent reading are normally substantial—between .50 and .80. However, the coefficients vary with the tests used. For example, between the Lee-Clark Reading Readiness Test and the Stanford-Binet Intelligence Test, the coefficients of correlation ranged from .25 to .48, too low to make confident predictions of IQ from the reading readiness test (Parsley and Powell, 1961, pp. 304–307). For intelligence tests that have both a verbal and a quantitative section, the correlation of the verbal scores with reading tests may be almost twice as high as the correlation with the quantitative scores. For example, the verbal score on the California Test of Mental Maturity correlated with scores on both the Thorndike-McCall and the Iowa Silent Reading Tests from .75 to .84; the quantitative score on the California correlated with the scores on the same two reading tests at .35 to .56. Similar results were obtained with college tests (Strang and others, 1961, pp. 276–277; 242–243).

A series of tests of achievement and intelligence such as the STEP and the SCAT tests (Alpert and others; Early and others; School and College Ability Tests), which have been standardized on the same population and whose scores have been converted into standard scores and percentile bands, may throw some light on a student's reading potential. For example, if he is in the highest quarter on SCAT and in a lower quarter on STEP, we have some indication that he has the mental potential to read better. But we must also take into consideration the facts that SCAT requires reading ability and that there is more than a chance difference between the two scores only if the student's percentile bands for the two tests do not overlap (see *STEP Manual,* 1959, pp. 16–17).

Another factor to consider is the influence of reading skills on scores of group tests of intelligence. Reading ability affects the predictive value of group intelligence tests. For example, in a study of 271 seventh-grade students (Mayer, 1958, pp. 117, 142), coefficients of correlation of .806 between SCAT total scores and STEP reading scores and of .624 between the WISC and STEP were reported. The difference between these two coefficients was statistically significant. Apparently the effective readers could score relatively higher on the group intelligence test than on the individual intelligence test that was less highly verbal in nature. If the reading ability required on an intelligence test is sufficiently above the student's reading efficiency to interfere with his rate and comprehension, it will lower his intelligence test score.

Much harm has been done by assuming that a student who makes a low score on a group intelligence test cannot learn to read. The test score may depend largely on the individual's lack of reading ability. Scores on group intelligence tests can safely be used as only one of several criteria for determining a student's need for special instruction in reading.

In Studying an Individual Student. In working with an individual, the teacher cannot rely on group averages; the individual may be one of the extreme deviates. The teacher is more concerned with the student's strengths and weakness and with inequalities among his performances on various reading tasks than with differences between his score and that of his classmates. For example, Ted may be able to answer specific factual questions better than he can get the main ideas of a selection. By analyzing Ted's test responses with him, the teacher may gain some indication of the boy's need for certain kinds of instruction.

A further understanding may be gained by the flexible use of standardized tests in individual cases. In 1937, Vernon (pp. 99–113) wrote a penetrating protest against the "rigid standardization of the testing procedure" and "the conception of traits or abilities as discrete variables, whose variations among different individuals are purely quantitative" (p. 100). Moreover, he said that the clinical psychologist

doubts the efficacy of standardizing the objective conditions of testing, since it may fail to standardize the "subjective situation," i.e., the meaning of the situation to the person tested; and it is this meaning which will determine the test response. . . . In our direct dealings with one another, qualitative distinctions appear to predominate, and single vectors of mind are seldom considered in isolation from the complex structure of the personality. . . . Only when such measures [of purely cognitive variables] are considered synthetically with other information about the personality can they tell him anything about the individual which will be of assistance in diagnosis and treatment (p. 101).

The Reading Profile shown on pages 144–145, developed by the Junior High School Division of the New York City Board of Education for the Remedial Reading Program and reproduced with the permission of Assistant Superintendent Max G. Rubinstein, relates test results to all other available information about the student.

In Promoting Self-evaluation and Independence. Tests may serve as a springboard for self-evaluation. By going over their own test exercises, students gain an understanding of their competencies and their difficulties. This understanding should lead to a clearer view of specific goals for improvement. Many students can raise their sights. Too often the reading task set serves as a ceiling, not a challenge. If students are free to set their own goals, they may surpass their previous performance and do more than teachers expect of them. They no longer aim simply to "get by." Instead of merely meeting the teacher's standards when he is present to enforce them, they will work on their own initiative.

Once they have determined to correct certain errors and to reinforce their correct responses, they are receptive to instruction. Parallel with and following instruction and practice, they keep their own records. Freedom of choice, accompanied by a sense of responsibility for their acts, accords with their desire to be independent.

Using tests to help students make a self-appraisal is a far cry from the common administrative use of tests. Though both uses share the common aim of promoting better reading, self-appraisal makes a more direct and effective approach because it evokes greater student motivation.

CONCLUDING STATEMENT

The most important use of reading tests is as an aid to teaching. If a test does not help a teacher, directly or indirectly, teach better, there is not much point in administering it. Much effort and money are wasted by giving tests that are not needed and by failing to use the results of tests that are given. The Cooperative Test Division of the Educational Testing Service is influential in helping teachers to make better use of tests.

To accomplish this purpose, informal reading tests based on selections from the books the students are expected to read may be most effective. Standardized tests can also be used for this purpose as well as for comparing the reading achievement of students of the same age and grade.

In making any decision or comparison, it is very important (1) to consider the error of measurement in a test score and (2) to use all other sources of information about the student's reading in conjunction with the test scores. No test score is infallible; it is not the student's true score because it includes an error of measurement. A difference between two scores, such as between a reading and an intelligence test score, may be canceled out by the errors of measurement of the two tests. We therefore should not hastily jump to the conclusion that an observed difference is a real difference.

Errors in judgment are often avoided by interpreting test scores in the light of other information about the student. A reading grade score of 3, for example, should be checked by asking the student to read a third-grade book. He often will not be able

SCHOOL _____ BORO _____

READING PROFILE

Date of Birth _____ Place of Birth _____ No. of Years in New York City _____

Date Admitted to Remedial Group _____ Reading Grade _____ Date Discharged _____ Reading Grade _____

Reason for Discharge _____ R.A. up to M.A. _____ Up to School Grade _____

Transferred to _____ Other Reasons _____

TEST RECORD
(Enter results of city-wide tests given in the 1st and 6th years; and individual B.C.G. results if available.)

INTELLIGENCE

DATE	NAME	FORM	I.Q.	COMMENTS

READING

DATE	NAME	FORM	READING GRADE	COMMENTS

HEALTH DATA

	BE SPECIFIC	CORRECTED	DATE OF CORRECTION
Vision			
Hearing			
Speech			

FAMILY HISTORY

Number of Children in Family _____

Languages Spoken in the Home _____

Parent Child Relationship _____

Parents' Cooperation with School _____

SCHOOL HISTORY

Attendance

			SCHOOL SUBJECTS	
			DOES WELL IN	NEEDS HELP IN
Elem. School				
J.H. School				
Remed. Read. Group				

PERSONALITY

A. Behavior   CHECK   COMMENTS (INCLUDE COMMENTS ON GROWTH OR CHANGES IN BEHAVIOR)

Dependent _____

Aggressive _____

Other Traits _____

B. Outstanding Problems _____

C. Referrals   DATE   DISPOSAL

Agency _____

School Nurse _____

School Doctor _____

Guidance Counselor _____

Confidential File in School _____ YES _____ NO _____

D. Outstanding Problems _____

GENERAL INTERESTS

A. Hobbies, Interests _____

B. Attitude toward

Reading _____

Remedial Group _____

CONTACT WITH SUBJECT TEACHER

DATE	REMARKS

NAME _____ ADDRESS _____ TEL. _____ CLASS _____

READING CHECK LIST
✓ To Indicate Area In Which Pupil Needs Help   Indicate Date Checked

SILENT READING								WORD RECOGNITION							
Pointing								Basic Sight Words							
Vocalization								Configuration Clues							
Rate								Context Clues							
Regressions								Structural Analysis							
ORAL READING								Phonic Analysis							
Word by word reading								Ability to Analyze							
Pointing								Ability to Blend							
Substitutions								Knowledge of Letter Names							
Reversals								Knowledge of Letter Sounds							
Omissions															
Insertions															
STUDY SKILLS								COMPREHENSION							
Organization								Understand concepts							
Parts of book - index contents								Understand general significance							
Dictionary, encyclopedias,								Remember important detail							
Maps, Globes								Follow directions							
								Draw conclusions							

DESCRIPTION OF REMEDIAL TREATMENT

A. Materials used in the Reading Program (list only those which have proved effective for this pupil)

  Devices _____

  _____

  _____

  Basal Reader (if any) _____

  Types of Books interested in _____

B. Procedures in remedial instruction (include changes made as work progresses)

  _____

  _____

  _____

COMMENTS AND RECOMMENDATIONS

  DATE

READING TEACHER _____

to do so. Facts about the student's background and experience often help to explain a low test score or a reading score higher than might be expected of a given student.

The cautious, flexible, purposeful, appropriate use of informal and standardized tests will yield much valuable diagnostic information.

Suggested Problems
Practice and Demonstration

1. Have the teacher-education class take a college-level reading test, such as the STEP, score it, analyze their responses, summarize it, and make recommendations for improving their own reading.

2. Summarize research on the relation between intelligence test scores and reading ability. A number of doctoral studies on this topic have been reported in *Dissertation Abstracts,* published yearly by the University of Michigan, Ann Arbor, Michigan. See especially vols. 19 to 23. Microfilm copies of all dissertations reported may be obtained from University Microfilms, Ann Arbor, Michigan.

3. Demonstrate the making, administering, and scoring of an informal group inventory in a given subject.

4. Using the form given in this chapter, make an analysis of a recent reading test.

5. Describe a class or school situation, state the objective for reading improvement, and select a test that would best meet all the criteria stated in this chapter.

6. Demonstrate the scoring, analysis, recording, and use of results of a reading test given to an elementary or high school class.

7. Demonstrate the discussion of his group test with an individual student.

References

Alpert, Harvey, and others: *Sequential Tests of Educational Progress: Reading,* Cooperative Test Division, Educational Testing Service, Princeton, N.J., 1956–1957. For Grades 13–14, Level 1; for Grades 10–12, Level 2; for Grades 7–9, Level 3; for Grades 4–6, Level 4. Forms A and B yield one over-all score.

Bond, Guy L., and C. J. Hoyt: *Silent Reading Diagnostic Tests,* Lyons and Carnahan, Chicago, 1955.

Committee on Diagnostic Reading Tests: Grades kindergarten–4, 4–6, 7–13, vocabulary, comprehension, rate, word attack, Committee on Diagnostic Reading Tests, Mountain Home, N. C., 1947–1960.

Doren Diagnostic Reading Test, Educational Test Bureau, Philadelphia, 1956.

Early, Margaret J., and others: *Sequential Tests of Educational Progress: Listening,* Cooperative Test Division, Educational Testing Service, Princeton, N.J., 1956–1957. For Grades 13–14, Level 1; for Grades 10–12, Level 2; for Grades 7–9, Level 3; for Grades 4–6, Level 4. Forms A and B yield one over-all score.

Hunt, J. T.: "Selecting a High School Reading Test," *High School Journal,* 39:49–52, October, 1955.

Mayer, Robert W.: "A Study of the STEP Reading, SCAT and WISC Tests, and School Grades," *The Reading Teacher,* 12:117–142, December, 1958.

Melnik, Amelia: *The Improvement of Reading through Self-appraisal: A Procedure for Teaching Reading in Junior High School Social Studies,* unpublished doctoral project, Teachers College, Columbia University, New York, 1960.

Mills, Robert E.: *Learning Methods Test,* Mills Center, Inc., Fort Lauderdale, Fla., 1954–1955.

Parsley, K. M., Jr., and Marvin Powell: "Relationships between the Lee-Clark Reading Readiness Test and the 1937 Revisions of the Stanford-Binet Intelligence Test, Form L," *Journal of Educational Research,* 54:304–307, 1961.

Roswell-Chall Diagnostic Test of Word Analysis Skills, Essay Press, New York, 1956–1958.

School and College Ability Tests, Educational Testing Service, Princeton, N.J. Levels 1–5 cover grades 4–14. Four forms of Level 1 and two forms each for other levels yield a verbal score, a quantitative score, and a total score, 1952.

Shepherd, David: *Effective Reading in the Social Studies,* 1961, and *Effective Reading in Science,* Harper & Row, Publishers, Incorporated, New York, 1960.

STEP Manual for Interpreting Scores—Reading, Cooperative Test Division, Educational Testing Service, Princeton, N.J., 1959.

Strang, Ruth: "Evaluation of Development in and through Reading," in *Development in and through Reading,* Sixtieth Yearbook of the National Society for the Study of Education, The University of Chicago Press, Chicago, 1961, chap. 21.

——— and others: *The Improvement of Reading,* 3d ed., McGraw-Hill Book Company, Inc., New York, 1961.

Traxler, Arthur E.: "Standardized Tests—What They Are, How They Are Used—and Misused," *NEA Journal,* 48:18–20, November, 1959.

Vernon, P. E.: "The Stanford-Binet Test as a Psychometric Method," *Character and Personality,* 6:99–113, December, 1937.

Suggested Readings

Boag, A. K., and M. Neild: "Influence of the Time Factor on the Scores of the Triggs Diagnostic Reading Test as Reflected in the Performance of Secondary School Pupils Grouped According to Ability," *Journal of Educational Research,* 55:181–183, December, 1961.

Buros, Oscar K. (ed.): *The Fifth Mental Measurements Yearbook,* The Gryphon Press, Highland Park, N.J., 1959.

Clymer, Theodore A.: "A Study of the Validity of the California Test of Mental Maturity, Elementary Language Section," in *The Eighteenth Yearbook of the National Council of Measurement Used in Education,* Ames, Iowa, 1961, pp. 125–128.

Conant, Margaret M.: *The Construction of a Diagnostic Reading Test,* Bureau of Publications, Teachers College, Columbia University, New York, 1942.

Lee, L. G.: "Evaluation of Standardized Tests Used in Diagnosis," *Conference on Reading,* The University of Pittsburgh Press, Pittsburgh, 1960, pp. 39–53.

McCullough, Constance M., and David H. Russell: *Reading Readiness Tests for Each Level* (prereading through the six grades), rev. ed., Ginn and Company, Boston, 1952–1957.

Nichols, Ralph, and Leonard Stevens: *Are You Listening?* McGraw-Hill Book Company, Inc., New York, 1957.

Swenson, Esther J.: "A Study of the Relationships among Various Types of Reading Scores on General and Science Materials," *Journal of Educational Research,* 36:81–90, October, 1942.

Tinker, Miles A., and Constance M. McCullough: *Teaching Elementary Reading,* 2d ed., Appleton-Century-Crofts, Inc., New York, 1962.

Triggs, Frances O.: "A Comparison of Auditory and Silent Presentations of Reading Comprehension Tests," in *The Fourteenth Yearbook of the National Council on Measurement Used in Education,* Educational Testing Service, Princeton, N.J., 1957, pp. 1–7.

Vernon, Philip E.: *The Measurement of Abilities,* Philosophical Library, Inc., New York, 1961.

Westover, Frederick L.: "A Comparison of Listening and Reading as a Means of Testing," *Journal of Educational Research,* 52:23–26, September, 1958.

Readings on Test Construction and Selection

Baron, D., and H. W. Bernard: *Evaluation Techniques for Classroom Teachers,* McGraw-Hill Book Company, Inc., New York, 1953.

Ebel, R. L.: "Writing the Test Item," in E. F. Lindquist (ed.), *Educational Measurement,* American Council on Education, Washington, 1951, chap. 7.

Furst, E. J.: *Constructing Evaluation Instruments,* Longmans, Green & Co., Inc., New York, 1958.

Graham, Grace: "Teachers Can Construct Better Achievement Tests," *Curriculum Bulletin,* University of Oregon, vol. 12, no. 170, December 10, 1956.

Making the Classroom Test, Evaluation and Advisory Service, series 4, Educational Testing Service, Princeton, N.J., 1959.

Odell, C. W.: *How to Improve Classroom Testing,* William C. Brown and Company, Dubuque, Iowa, 1953.

Selecting an Achievement Test, Evaluation and Advisory Service, series 3, Educational Testing Service, Princeton, N.J., 1958.

Wood, Dorothy Adkins: *Test Construction: Development and Interpretation of Achievement Tests,* Charles E. Merrill Books, Inc., Columbus, Ohio, 1960.

INDIVIDUAL METHODS

8

~~~~~~

INTRODUCTION

Although all the methods discussed in Part 1 may be used with individual cases, the procedures to be described in Part 2 must be applied individually. Some of these are relatively objective and standardized, such as visual and auditory screening tests, oral reading tests, the individual reading inventory, and the standardized individual diagnostic reading tests. On a higher level of psychological complexity are the individual intelligence tests and projective techniques which must be administered and interpreted by competent psychologists or clinicians. Apparently quite simple but actually requiring specialized clinical skill are the diagnostic interview, play therapy, and other kinds of therapy which may uncover the subtle factors that underlie severe reading disability. Since the reading process is so extremely complex, we need a diversity of methods for gaining understanding of it.

THE DYNAMIC VIEW (Strang, 1961)

The dynamic view seeks to ascertain the conditions that have caused or are now causing a given reading problem. It also seeks to detect "trigger reactions" that may release an individual's desire to improve his reading. The clinician may think of some serious reading problems as symptoms of an underlying personality disturbance or disorganization. He tries to create external conditions that may modify some of the psychological factors. He tries to discover the client's latent capacities for satisfaction in work, play, and creative activities. Success in learning to read often has a therapeutic influence.

CONDITIONS THAT LEAD TO READING DIFFICULTY

Because of the complexity of the reading process, the reading clinician needs a background knowledge of the wide variety of conditions that may prevent an individual from attaining his reading potential. Some of these conditions, described fully in references at the end of this chapter and in other chapters, will be briefly mentioned here.

Physical conditions, such as visual and auditory impairments, may aggravate or precipitate reading difficulty. Malnutrition, glandular disturbances, and prolonged illness interfere with the child's overall development and thus inevitably hinder his reading achievement. Illnesses or accidents that change the child's concept of himself often have disturbing secondary effects on his reading development. Maturational lag and disturbed patterns of mental and physical growth may especially affect a child's beginning reading progress and make it difficult for him to catch up with his classmates. However, other children with reading difficulty seem to be in excellent physical condition. Some of these try to compensate for their poor reading by achievement in athletics.

Among the possible organic causes of reading retardation are brain damage, confused laterality, and neurological disorganization. Many brain-damaged children are bright but so overactive and easily distracted that they have difficulty in focusing their attention on specific reading tasks. The relation of mixed laterality to reading is still a controversial issue (Vernon, 1957; see also Chapter 9). Neurological disorganization is considered by some to be a primary cause of severe reading difficulty but is extremely difficult to diagnose.

Educational deprivation of various kinds that may be due to prolonged absence from school, frequent change of schools, ineffective instruction, or dislike of the teacher is most serious in the primary grades. However, even in the upper grades serious consequences may ensue when there is insufficient basic instruction in reading for all students or neglect of special instruction and practice needed by retarded readers. The total curriculum and methods of instruction may have a pervasive effect on a child's reading development.

Unfavorable conditions in home and neighborhood background, such as an anti-intellectual attitude, are being increasingly recognized. Deprivation of cultural opportunities and intellectual stimulation may be found on all socioeconomic levels. On the lower levels, experiments in providing special guidance, instruction, and cultural advantages for the disadvantaged social groups are being conducted in a number of large cities.

Linguistic factors contribute largely to reading proficiency. Persons interested in structural linguistics emphasize the importance for success in beginning reading of a good foundation in spoken language. They say that a reader must go through a double perceptual process—look at the word and mentally hear its sound—before the printed page can have meaning for him. The mature reader depends on his word knowledge, word recognition skills, and sense of sentence and paragraph structure to get the author's thought.

Lack of mental ability to remember, to see relations, and to solve problems of word meaning obviously blocks progress in reading, since reading is a reasoning process.

Innumerable emotional difficulties may hinder progress in

reading. Secondary emotional difficulties may stem from initial failure in reading, from feelings of inferiority engendered by parental or peer attitudes toward the slow learner, or from physical disabilities. However, not all emotionally disturbed children are poor readers, nor are all poor readers emotionally disturbed.

Even children who have average or above average intelligence, who are not suffering from any organic limitations that can be detected, and who seem to come from economically secure homes where reading is encouraged may still lack sufficient drive to succeed in reading. They may be "lacking in spontaneity, enthusiasm and general outgoingness" (Vorhaus, 1946, p. 129). These deficiencies seem to originate in an unfortunate pattern of interpersonal relations, usually in the home environment. According to one theory, the child is unconsciously resisting demands that he conform to his parents' expectations of him—expectations that neglect his basic needs and interests. Therapy in these cases is directed toward helping the child gain "a better understanding of the growing-up process which will make it possible for him to substitute adjusted ways of fitting into his role for the repressive and destructive actions which had led to frustration and failure" (Vorhaus, 1946, p. 131). Another child may resent his parents' preference for a more able brother or sister or may feel guilty about the trouble and expense he feels he is causing his parents. Talking out these feelings with a sympathetic, understanding person may relieve the tension and anxiety that are interfering with the child's progress in reading.

Many kinds of anxiety and fear seem to be associated with reading difficulties. Some of these may originate in infancy or early childhood if the baby is seriously deprived of his mother's affection or of personal contact with his mother or mother substitute. The resultant anxiety and apathy, if extreme, seem to persist and to be quite resistant to therapy. It may be that some of our adolescent retarded readers who seem to be willing but unable to put forth the effort to improve their reading have suffered emotional deprivation of the kind described by René Spitz and others. Dealing with such cases requires a process of reeducation or reconditioning which involves overcoming fear and apathy by substituting feelings of security and adequacy. The reading teacher may relieve some of the individual's fears and conflicts incidentally as he works with him on his reading problem.

PARTICULARLY BAFFLING CASES

The most baffling cases are those who apparently have adequate ability and favorable home conditions but still do not learn to read. One of these extreme cases involves an adolescent boy from a well-to-do family. He has attended school up to the twelfth grade, has learned mathematics and science, but cannot read at all.

His parents have taken him to numerous clinics. He has had neurological, psychiatric, and psychological examinations and years of psychotherapy and remedial reading instruction. The parents, ever hopeful, wanted to take him to a new reading center. This possibility was discussed with the psychologist who last worked with the boy. Several courses of action were considered:

1. Refer the boy to the new reading center. This possibility was rejected because another futile referral would merely increase the boy's sense of hopelessness.

2. Ignore the reading problem for the present and focus on using the other avenues of learning with which he had been successful. This approach might remove some of the pressure from him, relieve his anxiety, help him to succeed in the things he can do, and build up his self-confidence. It is well established that although a certain degree of tension is a necessary condition for learning, intense anxiety disrupts learning. There are gradients of anxiety that should be recognized (Sullivan, 1953, pp. 151–154). Later, when his fear of reading has decreased, he may be accessible to instruction.

3. If, for some obscure reason, he seems to be incapable of learning to read, as a small fraction of one per cent apparently are, this social disability should be recognized. He should be taught by means of pictures, diagrams, films, discussions, recordings, and other instructional media and methods through which he can learn. The curriculum in high school and college should be adjusted to him. He should be permitted to sit in class and listen but should not be expected to read. He should have a congenial buddy who will read him the captions of pictures and diagrams. He should also have a reader and records, such as are available for the blind. All his teachers should be given an understanding of the case and be asked to cooperate in this highly specialized program.

These recommendations were based on the assumption that

the previous diagnosis was competent and would have uncovered any remediable physical, psychological, or educational factors that were blocking potential reading achievement. We should again emphasize that such cases of reading disability are very rare.

METHODS OF WORK WITH INDIVIDUALS

Any diagnostic procedure has possible influence on the individual—therapeutic or detrimental. For example, taking a standardized test may either bolster an individual's self-esteem or increase his feelings of inferiority or inadequacy. Composing a reading autobiography may give one student helpful perspective on his reading development but may leave another with an increased sense of hopelessness. Projective techniques may arouse vague feelings of anxiety. In most interviews, "relationship therapy" plays a part in varying degrees. The more intimate the procedure, the greater is its possible influence.

Personal Interview

The focus of the interview is on helping the individual with his reading problems; diagnosis is subordinate to this main purpose. In connection with every technique described, even when the focus is on diagnosis or appraisal, the interviewer may find opportunity to reinforce positive attitudes, to help the individual gain new insights, and even to impart instruction. Aid given at the moment of discovering an error or a need is of maximum effectiveness.

Interviews are held with reading cases for many purposes; some are primarily tutorial, others are exclusively therapeutic. If the student has had poor instruction in reading and is now eager to make up this deficiency, skillful instruction and ample practice in the reading skills he needs will have a therapeutic effect and will give him the stimulation of success. However, if the individual has inner conflicts that are making it impossible for him to concentrate on reading, then counseling procedures are necessary before he is receptive to reading instruction.

The interview with reading cases usually combines diagnosis, counseling, and instruction. After hearing the individual read a paragraph orally, the interviewer may give him instruction as to how he might have read it more effectively. While discussing the student's daily schedule, the interviewer may encourage him to suggest ways of using his time more efficiently. If conversation with the student suggests a disturbed father-son relationship, the interviewer may suggest that he read a story such as "My Father Doesn't Like Me" (Scott, 1959, pp. 208–230), which may help the child or adolescent to clarify this relationship and cope with the problem more effectively.

Neither developmental nor remedial reading can be compartmentalized; each is an integral part of the child's total development. Similarly, appraisal and diagnosis are integral parts of the complex process of understanding an individual and helping him to understand himself.

Working with Parents

Recognizing the role of the parent in helping the student take a new attitude toward his reading problem, reading clinicians are more and more involving parents in the reeducation process. For example, Studholme (1961) held a series of meetings with the mothers of six boys who had failed to improve after a year or more of remedial reading. These mothers were so eager to talk about their boys' reading problems that they practically took over most of the sessions. They seemed to profit most from being able to express their feelings of despair, hostility, and guilt; from knowing that other mothers have similar problems and feelings; and from hearing one another's concrete suggestions and those given by the discussion leader. They met over a period of several months. During that time the investigator noted marked changes in their expressed attitudes and reported behavior toward their children. Sympathy for the child began to replace resentment; there was less nagging and more appreciation of the child's progress. In discussions with groups and in interviews with individual parents, teachers and clinicians may gain much insight into parental attitudes and behavior toward their retarded children (Strang, 1962, chap. 1).

Usually the child is not present when the clinician interviews his parents or when professionally trained observers are present. However, some promising departures from this procedure have been made (Dreikurs, 1951). For over twenty-five years at the Chicago Community Child Guidance Centers, children have been counseled and diagnosed with no visible harm in family groups and in the presence of professionally trained persons. Even a few minutes' experience with this procedure in a strange situation seems to produce a deeper and more constructive impression on the child than does the usual individual counseling. The child expresses himself more accurately than in situations for which he has ready-made responses. He seems to be at ease and to feel free to talk with friendliness and frankness. One explanation of this positive response is that the child enjoys being the center of attention and is impressed by a setting in which adults are listening to him with interest, sympathy, and a desire to help. The parents are impressed with the child's insights into the nature of his problems and his understanding of adults. The discussion that takes place is enlightening to the adults. Obviously a procedure of this kind can be employed successfully only by a highly skilled, experienced person.

CONCLUDING STATEMENT

Any technique that is administered individually has many advantages. First and most important is the relationship with a person who is sincere, feels with the individual, is concerned about his welfare, and has a positive regard for him. Such a relationship may produce improvement in reading regardless of the methods of instruction used. A second advantage lies in avoiding any waste of time: The student has the teacher's undivided attention; he does not sit idle while other students are being helped. The third advantage is the opportunity the individual technique presents to adapt the procedure in accordance with the student's response. For these and other reasons, group methods should be supplemented by individual procedures so far as time permits.

Suggested Problems
Practice and Demonstration

1. Make a complete bibliography of case studies of reading difficulties by asking every member of the class to make a thorough canvass of sources of case studies in books, pamphlets, and articles for a given year from 1945 to the present.

2. If possible, have the class view over closed-circuit television a comprehensive diagnostic procedure with two cases of markedly different ages and reading problems.

3. Read several complete case studies in class, asking the students to interpret and synthesize the facts as the case is being presented. Also, list the diagnostic instruments used which seemed most appropriate for the particular case. What seemed to be the conditions giving rise to the individual's present reading development? What were the favorable factors in the individual and in his environment? What deficiencies or errors need the teacher's attention? Compare the causes of reading failure in these cases with the causes summarized in this chapter.

4. For information about each of the conditions that might lead to reading difficulties, read the pertinent references listed at the end of the chapter, for example, Cruickshank on methods of work with brain-injured or hyperactive children, Vernon on confused laterality, or Robinson on the reasons pupils fail in reading.

References

Dreikurs, Rudolf: "Family Group Therapy in the Chicago Community Child Guidance Centers," *Mental Hygiene,* 35:291–301, April, 1951.

Scott, William R.: "My Father Doesn't Like Me," in *Teen-age Tales,* D. C. Heath and Company, Boston, 1959, book 2, pp. 202–230.

Strang, Ruth: "A Dynamic Theory of the Reading Process," *Merrill Palmer Quarterly of Behavior and Development,* 7:239–245, October, 1961.

————: *Helping Your Child Improve His Reading,* E. P. Dutton & Co., Inc., New York, 1962.

Studholme, Janice: "Changes in Attitudes of Mothers of Retarded Readers during Group Guidance Sessions," unpublished doctoral project, Teachers College, Columbia University, New York, 1961.

Sullivan, Harry Stack: *The Interpersonal Theory of Psychiatry,* W. W. Norton & Company, Inc., New York, 1953.

Vernon, M. D.: *Backwardness in Reading,* Cambridge University Press, New York, 1957.

Vorhaus, Pauline G.: "Non-reading as an Expression of Resistance," in *Claremont College Reading Conference, Eleventh Yearbook,* Claremont, Calif., 1946, pp. 129–131.

Suggested Readings

Cruickshank, William: *A Teaching Method for Brain-injured and Hyperactive Children,* Syracuse University Press, Syracuse, N.Y., 1961.

Delacato, Carl H.: *The Treatment and Prevention of Reading Problems,* Charles C Thomas, Publisher, Springfield, Ill., 1959.

Ephron, Beulah: *Emotional Difficulties in Reading,* The Julian Press, Inc., New York, 1953.

Fernald, Grace M.: *Remedial Techniques in Basic School Subjects,* McGraw-Hill Book Company, Inc., New York, 1943.

Harris, Albert J.: *How to Increase Reading Ability,* 4th ed., David McKay Company, Inc., New York, 1961.

Robinson, Helen M.: *Why Pupils Fail in Reading,* The University of Chicago Press, Chicago, 1946.

————: *Clinical Studies in Reading I and II,* Supplementary Educational Monographs, nos. 68 and 77, The University of Chicago Press, Chicago, 1949 and 1953.

Smith, Donald E. P., and Patricia M. Carrigan: *The Nature of Reading Disability,* Harcourt, Brace & World, Inc., New York, 1959.

Strang, Ruth, and others: *The Improvement of Reading,* 3d ed., McGraw-Hill Book Company, Inc., New York, 1961.

Traxler, Arthur: *Research in Reading during Another Four Years,* Educational Research Bureau, New York, 1960.

Woolf, Maurice D., and Jeanne A. Woolf. *Remedial Reading: Teaching and Treatment,* McGraw-Hill Book Company, Inc., New York, 1957.

9

PHYSICAL FACTORS IN
READING DIAGNOSIS

Visual and auditory defects, malnutrition, glandular and other chemical disturbances, and illness may be primary or contributing causes of reading difficulty. Even if a physical defect—an eye defect, for example—is not severe enough to cause obvious interference with a child's reading, it may involve enough discomfort to make him reluctant to read. To learn to read and to

163

read with comfort, the child needs adequate vision. For this reason, physical factors should be checked for all children, not only retarded readers, in order that teachers may provide the optimum conditions for their education.

Among the machines in common use in the diagnosis and treatment of visual factors in reading difficulties are: vision screening and hearing testing machines, machines to photograph eye movements, tachistoscopic instruments, and pressure devices. Reading teachers and specialists are often confronted by the problem of whether to deplete a limited budget by buying machines or to spend the money on reading material. Administrators often ask advice on this question. We shall briefly consider the purpose for which each of these instruments is used and its value in the reading program in connection with the diagnosis of reading efficiency.

VISUAL FACTORS

The reading process starts with seeing—seeing dynamically, that is, coordinating the two eyes carefully and precisely along the lines of print. Unless there is a clear-cut retinal image, there will be confusion in perceiving letters of similar configuration. Words become blurred. Meaning becomes obscured. Perceiving and conceptualizing are basic to understanding and reflecting.

Seeing printed words is a learned process. It involves the making of many adjustments. The child beginning to learn to read must learn to change his focus from distant scenes to the page of the book in his hand. He has to hold this focus to prevent the print from blurring. At the same time he must use the six little muscles of each eye to turn the eye inward just enough to keep from seeing the print double. He must do all this while his eyes are moving from left to right across the page. To these physical adjustments he must add the ability to get meaning from the printed words.

Many children make all these adjustments. Others learn to suppress the vision in one eye when they have difficulty in fusing the images of both eyes. Some children learn to ignore distant vision and focus more and more on near distances, as one must do in reading. These children thus become myopic, but they are often good readers. The children who cannot adjust to the difficulties and discomforts of close seeing find the visual task so difficult that they give up trying to read.

Vision also has psychosomatic elements. The psychological factors in visual efficiency (Kelley, 1961, p. 349) are receiving increased recognition. For example, substantial temporary improvements in myopic conditions have been obtained by the skillful use of suggestion, which can produce actual changes in the retractive state of the eye. In interpreting the results of visual testing, we should recognize psychological factors as well as fatigue.

Relation of Vision to a Reading Difficulty

On this topic Robinson (1958, pp. 107–111) wrote a key article which will help teachers to understand and assist the poor reader. She and other investigators consider the following visual factors closely related to the reading process:

1. *Binocular coordination in visual performance*—seeing with both eyes at the same time and being able to fuse the two images in the brain. Fortunately this accommodative-convergence relationship is almost entirely a learned one and can be improved by training (Robinson, 1953, p. 127). Astigmatism, aniseikonia, and muscular imbalance may interfere with convergence and thus result in poor fusion.

2. *Far-sight or hyperopia* causes more difficulty in reading than nearsightedness. Eames (1959, pp. 2–35) in a study of 3,500 children, half of whom were reading failures, found farsightedness in 43 per cent of the reading failures as compared with 12 per cent in the unselected children. However, myopia should not be ignored; it is a handicap in seeing the board and in other activities that require distance vision.

Children who show these defects on a screening test should be referred to a competent eye specialist. At the University of Chicago Clinic, every third or fourth retarded reader needed referral. In view of the difficulty in interpreting visual screening tests and the possibility of missing some cases that could be helped by corrections, referral for any eye condition that might be related to reading is recommended for all seriously retarded readers.

The relationship between reading proficiency and visual difficulty has not been clearly established, although in individual cases investigators have found that visual defects are one cause of reading difficulty. The relationship may vary with different groups of students. It has been reported that functional visual difficulty has a more definite relationship to reading achievement in younger than in older children; the latter may have learned over the years to compensate for their visual defects. Even if an individual has learned to read effectively despite a visual handicap, he has done so at considerable cost. With the defect corrected and the necessary reading instruction provided, he could read with more efficiency and physical comfort and with less nervous tension and strain.

Since visual defects are important as part of the overall conditions that affect reading performance, every effort should be made to detect visual difficulties (Figurel, 1961). As a first step, the teacher's daily observation plays an important role. He can observe (1) the appearance of the eyes—watering of the eyes, frequent sties, redness; (2) behavior—bodily posture, position in which the book is held, signs of tension; and (3) complaints of headaches, nausea, blurring, seeing double. To assist teachers in becoming familiar with these symptoms of visual difficulties, Dr. Lois B. Bing and a committee on Visual Problems of Children and Youth of the American Optometric Association (St. Louis, Missouri) have prepared a set of materials comprising slides and a manual under the title "Children's Vision and School Success." The School Health Service of the Metropolitan Life Insurance Company (New York City) also has an exceptionally fine set of slides on "How Children See."

Older students may be asked to fill out a form such as the following:

Name_____ Date_____

1. Do you have any difficulty in seeing clearly at a distance?   At reading distance?

2. Do you have headaches from reading?

3. Do you often find it difficult to concentrate and sustain effort while reading or studying?

4. Do you sometimes see double (not blurred) when looking in the distance or reading?

5. Do you have a stiff neck or backache after you read or study for an extended time?

6. How long can you continue to read or study comfortably and effectively at one time?

The student's answers to these questions give clues to whether he needs a vision screening test, which would in turn show whether he needs a more thorough eye examination.

Visual Screening Tests

To detect the various visual difficulties that may affect an individual's reading, many tests are needed. Among these are tests of:

Visual acuity at far and near distance, ability to follow a moving object with each eye separately and with both eyes together

Ocular coordination at far and at near points, which is necessary for the formation of a single clear image

Other aspects of fusion

Movement of eyes too far inward or outward (known as phorias)

Ability to hold single monocular vision (known as ductions)

Uneven dominance of the two eyes (aniseidominance)

Unequal size and shape of images projected on the retina by the two eyes (aniseikonia)

Stereopsis or depth perception

Binocular skill indicated by speed of reading and number of errors when reading with one eye and with two

Facility of accommodation, changing focus from far to near and back again

Eye span—the number of letters or words one can see in one exposure

Other tests that may be more closely related to reading have not yet been developed. However, combinations of existing tests may show a relation of visual difficulties to reading ability when single tests do not. Accordingly, patterns or clusters of test results should be studied in relation to reading. Screening tests, though sometimes in error, are the most practical approach to the detection of visual deficiencies in children.

Comparative studies have been made of the results obtained with different screening instruments:

1. The illuminated Snellen Chart, supplemented by tests of farsightedness, muscular imbalance, and depth perception. This combination of procedures can be administered in about three to five minutes by a teacher or nurse who has been given instruction

in their use. The equipment is not expensive. A detailed description of this procedure is given by Sweeting (1959, pp. 715–722).

2. The School Vision Tester, originally the Ortho-Rater, now adapted for school use by Bausch and Lomb, Rochester, New York. This efficient visual screening machine measures at far point and at reading distance vertical and lateral phoria, acuity at right and left eyes separately and together, and depth perception.

3. The Massachusetts Vision Test, Welch-Allen, Auburn, New York, now included in the American Optical Company's AO Vision Screening Test. This test measures right and left eye acuity and vertical and lateral muscle balance.

4. The Keystone Visual Survey Telebinocular, Meadville, Pennsylvania. This device has the advantage of testing at both far point and reading distance. It is used in giving these important tests: (*a*) The long form of the vision test, (*b*) Spache Binocular Reading Test, (*c*) Gray Standardized Oral Reading Check Test.

These screening tests can be administered successfully by nurses and reading teachers who have been given training in their use. More experience is needed in testing first-grade than older children.

In an extensive survey (Crane and others, 1952), results of seven screening tests were compared with examinations by ophthalmologists. Of the 609 sixth-grade children examined by the ophthalmologists, 31 per cent were identified as having visual defects. The screening tests—Ortho-Rater, Sight Screener Test, and Telebinocular Test—administered by nurses and technicians referred correctly 20 to 25 per cent of the total group, that is, about three-fourths of the children identified by the ophthalmologists. However, these tests incorrectly referred about 30 per cent who did not need to be refracted. The percentage of incorrect referrals for first grade was still larger.

In general, referral standards depend upon the purpose of the testing. For retarded readers, one should use the procedure that refers the highest number correctly. Despite the expense involved in overreferral, it is better to refer some who do not need correction than to miss some who will be handicapped by an uncorrected visual defect.

The Chicago Reading Clinic supplements the Bausch and Lomb School Vision Tester with the Wirt Stereo Test as a near-depth measure and the Spache Binocular Reading Test. This combination is quite dependable. When the screening program does not include tests of binocular vision at the reading distance, many children handicapped in reading by visual difficulty are not discovered.

The following questions should be asked about visual screening:

1. What visual characteristics are important with respect to reading?

2. What visual characteristics do the screening tests evaluate?

3. How valid and reliable are visual screening tests?

4. How should the results of screening tests be interpreted for referral?

5. What are the problems and limitations in the use of visual screening tests?

6. To what extent is reported overreferral due to inadequate examination by the eye specialists to whom the children are referred? For example, it has been found that when children are referred because of failure on the muscle imbalance test or because of deficiencies in binocular functioning, more overreferrals are reported by ophthalmologists than by optometrists. To study this problem, workers in the field have suggested that the practitioners in a community meet together to determine (1) the tests to be included in the screening program, (2) the criteria or standards for referral, and (3) the items to be included in a complete clinical eye examination.

Following the vision screening tests, the first step in remedial reading procedure is referral to a broadly trained eye specialist who will cooperate with parents and teachers. A further step may be orthoptic or visual training which can relieve fusion difficulties caused by faulty muscle functioning. It is the responsibility of the reading specialist to check on the corrections made to see whether the student's discomfort in reading has been reduced.

Reading materials prepared for those of limited vision should be made available as needed (Matson and Larson, 1951; Galisdorfer, 1950). Students with visual handicaps may obtain mechanical aids, "talking books," certain types of training, and other items of assistance from the National Society for the Prevention of Blindness and the American Foundation for the Blind, New

York City. Extra training in visual discrimination, such as that described by Durrell and Sullivan (1941), will help to compensate for some irremediable visual defects.

Tachistoscopic Methods

A tachistoscope in its simplest form is a slide projector with a shutter. The shutter exposes pictures, numbers, words, phrases, or sentences for as short a time as 1/100 second. With practice, individuals can recognize many single characters and even sentences in this amazingly short exposure.

Researchers and educators do not agree as to the teaching value of this device. Some say tachistoscopic training per se cannot influence the reading process. Others believe that the tachistoscope is a remarkable device for improving reading abilities.

What is the evidence? Renshaw's report (1945) on the results of tachistoscopic training of various adult groups stimulated much interest. Four elementary school systems attributed large gains in the early grades to tachistoscopic training. However, all these studies contained too many uncontrolled factors to be conclusive. Goins (1958) on the other hand, in a carefully controlled experiment with first-grade children, found that "no positive effect was produced by the tachistoscopic training on the reading skill of the group as a whole" (p. 98). She added that her findings do not rule out the possible value of such training for selected older pupils who are having specific difficulties related to visual perception. One would assume that a certain familiarity with words and written materials would be prerequisite to tachistoscopic training.

The age of the pupils and the nature of the material used would affect the value of training in the recognition of visual forms. Leestma (1957, p. 94) studied 261 pupils who ranged in age from seven to seventeen and represented grades 2, 4, 6, 8, 10, and 12. He reported significant growth over the age range studied for all four kinds of material: digits, unrelated letters, unrelated words, and related words. Rate of growth was most rapid during the early years studied. Beyond ages nine or eleven the rate of growth slowed down. The amount of growth was directly related to the meaningfulness of the material. Although tachistoscopic span was more closely related to reading ability than to intelligence, the developmental level of the perceiver is one of the important factors in the success of tachistoscopic training.

Two Instruments for Tachistoscopic Training

The Flash-X

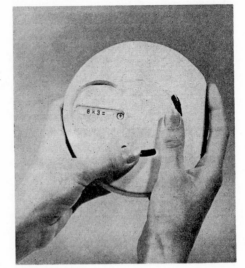

Tach-X

Pictures from Educational Development Laboratories, Inc., Huntington, New York. Similar illustrations and descriptions may be obtained from The Keystone View Company, Meadville, Pennsylvania.

Various instruments have been designed for giving training in quick word perception. A simple device for individual use is the Educational Development Laboratories' Flash-X. This instrument makes possible individual or team practice in quick recognition of words and phrases, either at home or in the classroom. Watching the exposure window carefully, the student flicks the tab, and the shutter opens for 1/25 second. To check the accuracy of his perception and recognition of the word, the student flicks another tab which gives a longer exposure of the word. With a turn of the card, the next exposure is ready. In addition to reinforcing the recognition of basic words, Flash-X training builds perceptual speed and accuracy. Each student may practice at his own pace for any length of time desired.

Other machines, such as the Keystone Reading Pacer (Keystone View Company, Meadville, Pennsylvania), may be used with a series of filmstrips for tachistoscopic training. The Tach-X illustrated on page 171 is another machine designed for the same purpose. According to the company's description (Educational Development Laboratories, Huntington, New York),

the Tach-X tachistoscope is a challenging and effective way to develop the ability to *see*.

All eyes watch the screen. At the touch of a button, a series of numbers, a word, or a phrase pops into view and then is gone. For a split second, perhaps only 1/100, the students reach out visually, learning to see rapidly. Through consistent practice, they develop in their ability to retain more visual material, more *accurately* and more rapidly than ever before. . . .

The Learning-through-Seeing Filmstrips may be used with this kind of tachistoscope.

Rather than exposing separate words and phrases for a fraction of a second, the reading film, such as the original Harvard Reading Films, uses connected sentences for training purposes. Since the film more closely resembles ordinary reading, its transfer value should be greater than that of the flash meter. It also has the advantage of giving the student practice in getting the author's thought at the first reading. The contents of the Harvard films are appropriate for college freshmen; comprehension is adequately tested by excellent multiple-choice questions. The Iowa Reading Films are more appropriate for high school students. Another

Instruments for Eye-movement
Measurement and Training

Controlled Reader

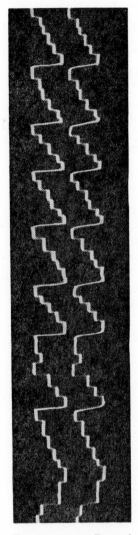

Eye-movement Record

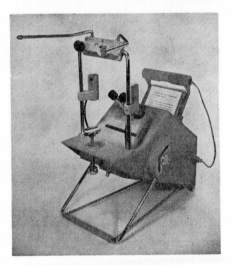

The Reading Eye

Pictures from Educational Development Laboratories, Inc., Huntington, New York.

machine of this kind is the Controlled Reader, which features a library of 330 filmstrips. It is described by its producers as follows. The Controlled Reader aims

to develop simultaneously the interpretive and the functional aspects of reading.

The students follow the story on the screen as it unfolds in a left-to-right fashion. The rate (0 to 1,000 words per minute) has been set so as to challenge them, and, because there is no chance to look back, they learn to organize their thoughts rapidly and remember well.

Many teachers who have used the tachistoscope in their classrooms have reported increased motivation and interest, better ability to concentrate, and greater willingness to put forth effort. As the student learns to recognize more words at a single quick exposure, he feels proud of his achievement. He has demonstrated to himself that he can read more efficiently than he thought possible.

The effectiveness of tachistoscopic training depends somewhat upon the manner in which it is introduced and used in the classroom. There may be some prestige value in mentioning to the students that it is used in business and in the armed forces. The goal of learning to recognize words and phrases in 1/100 second is specific, and success in doing so is impressive. The habit of alertness that the instrument requires may carry over to other reading and study tasks. Since research has shown its effectiveness, we should be receptive to the idea that the tachistoscope can be used in some situations to develop and extend the reading ability of children in grades beyond the first. But it is also recommended that such training be given in not more than ten- to twenty-minute periods and tied in with the development of a broad reading program.

Study of Eye Movements

It is well known that the eyes do not move smoothly along a line of print, but rather in a jerky sort of way in a series of stops and starts—fixations followed by swift movements. Sometimes they move backward, that is, make regressions over the line. Eye-movement records have given clues about the nature of the reading process. However, according to Tinker this type of research "has probably made its major contribution" (1958, pp. 215–231).

Conclusions from Studies. The results of research on eye movements have shown that:

1. The unit of word recognition is the word or group of words.

2. Rhythmic patterns are found in only a few good readers.

3. More difficult material is read with more fixations, other things being equal.

4. Eye movements also vary with the degree of the reader's familiarity with the material and the purpose for which he is reading it. Mature readers change their pace according to their purpose and the nature of the material; poor readers tend to be inflexible.

5. Eye movements reflect rather than produce reading efficiency.

6. Eye movements become more efficient with age; the most rapid growth is during the first four grades; there is very little change during the high school and college years. Progress seems to be related to the practice and instruction afforded by approved methods of teaching reading.

7. "The improvement obtained [by techniques that 'pace the eyes'] with or without elaborate apparatus is no greater than that resulting from well-motivated reading practice alone." [1]

Another conclusion to be drawn from Tinker's review of studies of eye movements relates to speed of reading. There is a physiological limit to actual eye span and the rapidity of reaction time. One investigator set this limit at 1,451 wpm. The psychophysiological limit, which allows for comprehension time, is probably not more than 800 or even 500 wpm. How, then, should we interpret the claims frequently made in popular articles that one can read 1,500 or more words a minute? The misunderstanding arises from a confusion between speed of steady reading, to which there is a definite physiological limit, and skimming speed. The latter has no limit and is determined much more by the reader's skill in finding what he is looking for than by physical factors.

Photographs of Eye Movements. The instrument used to study eye movements is a camera which photographs the pauses that the eyes make on each line of print as the person reads. One commercial form of the eye-movement camera is called "The

[1] Miles A. Tinker, "Eye Movements in Reading," reprinted from the May, 1959, issue of *Education*, p. 225, by special permission of The Bobbs-Merrill Company, Inc., Indianapolis, Ind.

Reading Eye." The makers of this instrument (Educational Development Laboratories, Huntington, New York) describe the process of eye-movement photography as follows:

As an individual reads a test selection appropriate for his level of reading achievement, small beads of light are reflected from his eyes and photographed on to moving film. After a comprehension check, the filmed record is analyzed and the reader's performance is compared with national norms in terms of fixations, regressions, span of recognition, duration of fixation, rate with comprehension, and relative efficiency. Also revealed are evidences of visual discomfort, nervousness, vocalization, perceptual confusion, etc. The vision specialist will be able to detect patterns of characteristics associated with myopia, hyperopia, nystagmus, suppression, and other visual anomalies.

The interpretation of eye-movement records is difficult. The subjects vary in their familiarity with the test material, in the purpose for which they are reading it, in the quality of their comprehension, and in other subjective factors. For example, one group of college freshmen made much poorer records than previous classes because some of the students who had previously taken the test warned the newcomers that they would have to answer specific comprehension questions. In another case a poor reader made a surprisingly good eye-movement record on difficult material. Later the examiner found that he had merely moved his eyes rhythmically across the lines without making any effort to comprehend. He made enough clever guesses on the easy comprehension test to get an acceptable score.

Informal Method. The eye-movement camera, or a more elaborate electrical method, is used for research purposes and in some reading clinics. There is also an informal method that may be used by the teacher, the so-called "peep-hole" method that has been described by Tinker as follows:

Upon a 9 × 12 inch cardboard attach two paragraphs of 6 to 10 lines of reading material of appropriate difficulty, one paragraph just above the center of the card and the other just below the center. In the middle of the cardboard cut a small hole, $\frac{1}{4}$ to $\frac{3}{8}$ inches in diameter. Hold the cardboard at the proper reading distance directly in front of a pupil and place your eye immediately behind the opening. You now have the most advantageous viewpoint from which to see the successive movements and fixation pauses of one of the pupil's eyes as he reads the material on the cardboard. The movements are seen most easily when you fixate your attention upon the dividing line between the colored zone and the white of the pupil's eye. The fact that the pupil sees only the reading material before him reduces the distraction that would occur if you were to attempt direct observation (as looking over the top of a book) without concealing your face behind the card.

This method may be used to determine the number of fixation pauses per line of print, to detect the presence of regressions, and confusions shown by detailed examination of a word or phrase. Even after practice, this method is not entirely accurate since some eye movements will be missed. Nevertheless, the technique is quite satisfactory in the classroom where the teacher wishes to detect signs of very good and very poor reading in comparison with the average, or wishes to find out what the eye movements of a particular pupil are like.

To insure a fair degree of accuracy, practice in counting the eye movements of another teacher for a few paragraphs should be undertaken before working with the children. Since there is a fixation pause at the end of each move, the number of pauses per line is easily obtained. Count the number of eye movements for the whole paragraph and divide by the number of lines. Do not attempt to note regressions and words that cause confusion while counting the interfixation movements. Look for these other things when a second or a third selection is read.[2]

This informal method of studying eye movements has one advantage over the machine methods. When the individual makes an unusually long pause, a regression, or a detailed examination of a word or phrase, the teacher can ask him what happened at that point. Perhaps the word was unfamiliar and he was trying to puzzle it out; perhaps his eyes had moved too far ahead of his mind, and he had to go back to get the meaning. From this kind of introspective information the teacher may gain insight into the factors that may be causing faulty or inefficient eye movements.

Training Eye Movements. Since eye-movement patterns often merely reflect the degree of difficulty that the reader is having with the reading material and "the clarity of perception and com-

[2] Miles A. Tinker, "Eye Movements in Reading," reprinted from the May, 1959, issue of *Education,* p. 576, by special permission of The Bobbs-Merrill Company, Inc., Indianapolis, Ind.

prehension taking place in the mind of the reader," [3] it is better to improve his vocabulary and comprehension skills than to focus on eye movements directly. We need not only to teach students how to read rapidly, but also to teach them when rapid reading is appropriate. We should also help them to acquire the skills that are needed for different kinds of comprehension.

Despite lack of experimental evidence that machines are capable of training eye movements more effectively than well-motivated instruction and practice in basic reading skills, a number of machines have been devised for this purpose. The tachistoscopic devices have already been mentioned. Other machines merely provide a mechanical stimulus to read faster.

These pressure methods may take the simple form of timing the student while he reads a selection. An informal method is to set a time limit, thirty minutes for example, and record the number of lines or words he reads in the given time. Pressure may also be exerted by a machine that has a lever or some other device by which one can set the pace for an individual reader. There are a number of these machines on the market, such as:

The Rateometer, Audio-Visual Research, Chicago, Illinois.

SRA Reading Accelerator, Science Research Associates, Chicago, Illinois.

The Franklin Reading Pacer, Franklin Research, Berkeley, California.

Shadowscope Reading Pacer, Psychotechnics, Inc., Chicago, Illinois.

Any pressure method merely urges the person to read faster; it gives little or no attention to his ability to vary his rate and method of reading different kinds of material for different purposes.

Although eye-movement patterns are good diagnostic signs of reading disability, specific training of eye movements is ordinarily not necessary to bring about improvement in reading. More efficient eye movements automatically appear as the reading is improved by other approved methods.[4]

[3] Miles A. Tinker, "Eye Movements in Reading," reprinted from the May, 1959, issue of *Education,* p. 578, by special permission of The Bobbs-Merrill Company, Inc., Indianapolis, Ind.

[4] Miles A. Tinker, "Eye Movements in Reading," reprinted from the May, 1959, issue of *Education,* p. 579, by special permission of The Bobbs-Merrill Company, Inc., Indianapolis, Ind.

EYE-HAND COORDINATION

The teacher can quite easily observe a child's difficulties in the motor aspects of learning. They may be shown by the reader's inability to keep his place. If he turns his eyes away from the page, he is unable to find the place again in the multitude of printed letters. Frequent skipping of lines may arise from inability to direct the eyes to the next line and maintain the motor adjustment as long as is necessary to comprehend the words. Poor hand control may interfere with the child's writing. He grips his pencil too tightly, exerts more pressure than necessary, and has difficulty in forming letters. Even though the slow, awkward child can manage to produce papers of acceptable legibility, he is unable to reach the standards set for his class. So much interest in the relation of motor coordination to reading achievement has been aroused that a specialist in physical education has been employed in several places to work with retarded readers.

The teacher may obtain indication of a child's eye-hand co-ordination by observing him in different situations: bouncing or throwing a ball, erasing the blackboard, driving a nail, cutting paper with scissors, tying his shoes, picking up a small object from the floor, replacing the cap on a pen, touching the end of his nose first with one eye shut, then with the other. Several tests give this kind of information with more precision. The Leavell Hand-Eye Dominance Test (Leavell, 1959) is quite widely used for this purpose. The Bender Visual Motor Gestalt Test (see Bender, 1956) is widely used in reading clinics to study eye-hand co-ordination and also to give to the clinically trained person, familiar with the test, clues of possible brain injury or neural disorganization.

Brain injury may occur as a result of minimal cerebral damage following abnormalities in the *pre* and *para* natal periods or it may accompany prenatal toxicity, birth trauma, anoxia, encephalitis, or head injury. The resulting disturbed pattern of neurological organization is often characterized by disability in dealing with words as symbols and is being recognized as a cause of primary reading retardation (Rabinovitch, 1962).

MIXED DOMINANCE

The effect of mixed dominance or incomplete lateralization on reading achievement is still a controversial issue. In a recent research project the investigator reported no significant relations between reversals and eye dominance and laterality in second-grade children (Beck, 1960, pp. 137–142). Another investigator found no significant differences between groups of college students who were right sided, left sided, ambidextrous, and functionally of mixed dominance (McConville, 1960, pp. 47–52). Although confused lateral dominance may result in reversals or mirror reading, many children experience directional imbalance or even brain injury without having reading problems.

Medical men are likely to attribute reversals and similar difficulties in word recognition to organic causes. Psychologists and educators more often give a psychological explanation. Educators take the view that, in many cases, laterality is learned. If this is true, parents and teachers can encourage the child to use the preferred hand in daily activities and can emphasize the left-right direction in reading and writing. Delacato (1959), who takes an extreme neurological view, advocates such measures as games that involve only the dominant eye and hand, choral speaking, and controlling the child's posture while he is sleeping.

After a thorough review of research on laterality as related to reading, Vernon concluded:

It is of course possible that incomplete lateralization is a sign of a general lack of maturation in the development of cortical functions, which also affects reading. . . . But clearly such cases form a small minority of all the cases of reading disability. . . . The investigations which have been cited give no clear evidence as to the existence of any innate organic condition which causes reading disability, except perhaps in a minority of cases; though certain innate factors may predispose the child towards difficulty in learning to read (1957, pp. 109, 115).

Tests of mixed dominance cover a range from casual observation to elaborate exercises for eyes, hands, and feet. Harris's test (see Harris, 1957) for handedness is one of the most comprehensive and widely used. Another test of ocular dominance was devised by Miles (1927–1946).

A device for correcting mixed dominance was described by Leavell (1959). It provides practice exercises in using eye and hand together, such as the following: The subject draws around a number of pictures, always from left to right. If in his initial attempts he spontaneously draws from left to right and points to the right, he is probably right handed. It has been estimated that thirty-two out of forty children are right handed.

AUDITORY AND SPEECH DIFFICULTIES

Loss of hearing may result in defective auditory discrimination, which in turn may prevent clear enunciation and which is likely to lead to difficulty in word recognition. However, many children are able to hear sounds perfectly but cannot distinguish different sounds in words, as for example the sounds of *care* and *car* or *boat* and *coat*. They apparently do not hear the sounds of letters and letter combinations clearly enough to remember them accurately enough to pronounce the printed words that they see. These children have normal hearing but are deficient in auditory discrimination. Of the four factors in success in beginning reading —auditory discrimination, visual discrimination, range of information, and mental age—auditory discrimination has been ranked first in importance by several investigators.

In view of the importance of auditory acuity and auditory discrimination, both should be tested. To test auditory acuity in an entire class simultaneously, the Western Electric Company's Model 4C audiometer may be used, except for young children who cannot make the necessary response of writing numbers.

If this quick and more accurate method of appraising auditory efficiency is not available, the teacher may use informal screening devices. In a quiet room he may hold a loudly ticking watch about 48 inches from the child's ear and then withdraw the watch slowly and record the distance at which the child fails to hear the ticking. Or he may use the whisper test with several children who stand 5 feet away with their backs to the examiner. The teacher gives a direction and notices the children who hesitate or fail to follow the directions. Other signs of possible hearing difficulty are inattention, misunderstanding of directions, frequent requests to repeat directions, a ringing or buzzing in the head, a blank expression, or posture indicating strain.

Children with auditory defects tend to learn better by visual than by auditory or phonic methods.

Deficiencies in auditory discrimination may be detected by asking the child to distinguish between words that sound alike and those that sound different. More definite tests of auditory discrimination require the child to name the beginning, middle, or final letter or letters of words that the examiner clearly pronounces. The Wepman Auditory Discrimination Test (1958, 1960) measures ability to recognize different phonemes of the spoken language, even when the sounds are highly similar. Many children from homes where English is spoken correctly will have learned to distinguish likenesses and differences in many words. Even these children may not be able to distinguish slight differences in sound such as the differences between *wear* and *where*. The initial digraph *wh,* according to competent linguists, may quite properly not be aspirated. When it is aspirated, the digraph is pronounced *hw* and is classified as one of the phonetic irregularities. To improve auditory discrimination, the teacher may use teaching materials such as those prepared by Durrell and Sullivan (1941).

The speaking vocabulary is more closely related to success in reading in elementary school than in high school or college. However, faulty pronunciation and inadequate speaking vocabulary may account for some of the errors in comprehension made by seriously retarded high school and college readers. Pronunciation, articulation, enunciation, pitch, and stress are all involved in the interpretation of language. Incorrect formation of speech sounds is more likely to be related to reading achievement than is stuttering. Moreover, any speech or auditory difficulty, insofar as it makes the individual feel less adequate as a person, may also make him less adequate in the reading situation.

MEDICAL TREATMENT OF READING PROBLEMS

More and more frequently, certain medicines are being advocated for use in the treatment of reading problems. Insofar as reading is an intellectual task, dependent upon the functioning of the nervous system, any drug that affects neural activity may be expected to be either detrimental or beneficial to reading.

Some experimentation along these lines has been reported (Park, 1959, pp. 213–218). Staiger (1961, pp. 48–51) studied the effect of a substance called *deanol* on sixty pairs of retarded readers in junior and senior high school. No significant differences in reading performance were reported. However, in all but one instance the differences favored the experimental group. The drug had some effect on perceptual speed and accuracy; on the more complex aspects of comprehension, its effect was negligible. Certainly no medication of this kind should be given by teachers or reading specialists. The disastrous effects of certain new drugs should emphasize the great caution to be exercised in the use of any new drug for any purpose.

CONCLUDING STATEMENT

The close relation between mind and body makes work with reading cases more than an intellectual task. Any one of a number of physical and physiological factors may affect a child's reading development directly or indirectly. To prevent such a detrimental effect, a physical examination including the features mentioned in this chapter should be given to every child at critical stages in his development.

Suggested Problems
Practice and Demonstration

1. Ask each member of the teacher education class to fill out the questionnaire on indications of visual difficulties given in this chapter. Also use whatever screening instrument is available to make a record of each student's visual efficiency. Compare the results of the visual screening test with the questionnaire and with an ophthalmological examination, if the screening test showed that one was needed.

2. Send for information on vision testing available from the National Committee for the Prevention of Blindness and from the National Foundation for the Blind.

3. Show American Optometric Association slides and the Metropolitan Life Insurance film describing visual difficulties of children.

4. Following directions in this chapter, make the peep-hole device to observe an individual's eye movements while he is reading, and ask him to explain the causes of excessive fixations or regressions he makes.

5. Summarize the facts about eye movements. What are your conclusions?

References

Beck, Harry S.: "The Relationship of Symbol Reversals to Monocular and Binocular Vision," *Peabody Journal of Education,* 38:137–142, November, 1960.

Bender Visual Motor Gestalt Test: see Lauretta Bender, *The Psychopathology of Children with Organic Brain Disorder,* Charles C Thomas, Publisher, Springfield, Ill., 1956. Also, Lauretta Bender, *A Visual Motor Gestalt Test and Its Clinical Use,* Research Monographs, no. 3, American Orthopsychiatric Association, New York, 1938.

Crane, Marian M., and others: *Study of Procedures Used for Screening Elementary School Children for Visual Defects,* National Society for the Prevention of Blindness, New York, 1952.

Delacato, Carl H.: *The Treatment and Prevention of Reading Problems,* Charles C Thomas, Publisher, Springfield, Ill., 1959.

Durrell, Donald D., and Helen Blair Sullivan: *Ready to Read,* Harcourt, Brace & World, Inc., New York, 1941.

Eames, Thomas H.: "Visual Handicaps to Reading," *Journal of Education,* 141:2–35, February, 1959.

Figurel, J. Allen (ed.): *Changing Concepts of Reading Instruction,* International Reading Association Conference Proceedings, vol. 6, Scholastic Magazines, Inc., New York, 1961, pp. 89–97.

Galisdorfer, Lorraine: *A New Annotated Reading Guide for Children with Partial Vision,* Henry Stewart, Incorporated, Buffalo, N.Y., 1950.

Goins, Jean Turner: *Visual Perceptual Abilities and Early Reading Progress,* Supplementary Educational Monographs, no. 87, The University of Chicago Press, Chicago, 1958, p. 98.

Harris, Albert J.: "Lateral Dominance, Directional Confusion, and Reading Disability," *Journal of Psychology,* 44:283–294, October, 1957.

Harris Tests of Lateral Dominance, rev. for ages 6 and up, The Psychological Corporation, New York, 1958.

Kelley, Charles R.: "Psychological Factors in Myopia," *American Psychologist,* 16:349, July, 1961.

Leavell, Ullin W.: "Ability of Retarded Readers to Recognize Symbols in Association with Lateral Dominance," *Peabody Journal of Education,* 37:7–14, July, 1959.

Leestma, Robert C.: "Age Changes in Tachistoscopic Span," *Dissertation Abstracts,* 17:94, 1957.

Matson, Charlotte, and Lola Larson: *Books for Tired Eyes,* American Library Association, Chicago, 1951.

McConville, Carolyn B.: "Handedness and Psychomotor Skills," *Journal of Developmental Reading,* 4:47–52, Autumn, 1960.

Miles A-B-C Vision Test of Ocular Dominance, The Psychological Corporation, New York, 1927–1946.

Park, G. E.: "Medical Aspects of Reading Failures in Intelligent Children," *The Sight Saving Review,* 29 (4):213–218, Winter, 1959.

Rabinovitch, Ralph D.: Recording just made for a conference of the Arizona Intermediate Counsel of the SRA, 1962. See also "Reading and Learning Disabilities," in Silvano Ariete (ed.), *American Handbook of Psychiatry*, Basic Books, Inc., Publishers, New York, 1959.

Renshaw, Samuel: "The Visual Perception and Reproduction of Forms by Tachistoscopic Methods," *Journal of Psychology*, 20: 217–232, 1945.

Robinson, Helen M.: "Vision and Reading Difficulties: The Findings of Research on Visual Difficulties and Reading," in *Reading for Effective Living*, International Reading Association Conference Proceedings, Scholastic Magazines, Inc., New York, 1958, pp. 107–111.

Staiger, Ralph C.: "Medicine for Reading Improvement," *Journal of Developmental Reading*, 5:48–51, Autumn, 1961.

Sweeting, Orville J.: "An Improved Vision Screening Program for the New Haven Schools: A Case History," *Journal of the American Optometric Association*, 30:715–722, May, 1959.

Tinker, Miles A.: "Recent Studies of Eye Movements in Reading," *Psychological Bulletin*, 55:215–231, July, 1958.

————: "Eye Movements in Reading," *Education*, 79:575–579, May, 1959.

Vernon, M. D.: *Backwardness in Reading, a Study of Its Nature and Origin*, Cambridge University Press, New York, 1957, pp. 109–115.

Wepman Auditory Discrimination Test, Joseph M. Wepman, Chicago, Ill. Copyright 1958.

Wepman, Joseph: "Auditory Discrimination, Speech, and Reading," *Elementary School Journal*, 60:325–333, March, 1960.

Suggested Readings

Bing, Lois B.: "A Critical Analysis of the Literature on Certain Visual Functions Which Seem to Be Related to Reading Achievement," *Journal of American Optometric Association*, 22:454–463, March, 1951.

Bond, Guy L., and Miles A. Tinker: *Reading Difficulties, Their Diagnosis and Correction*, Appleton-Century-Crofts, Inc., New York, 1957, part 3.

Buswell, Guy: *How Adults Read*, The University of Chicago Press, Chicago, 1937.

Carrigan, Patricia N.: "Broader Implications of a Chemical Theory of Reading Disability," *Journal of Developmental Reading*, 5:15–26, Autumn, 1961.

Eames, Thomas H.: "Visual Handicaps to Reading," *Journal of Education,* 141:2–35, February, 1959.

Ewalt, H. Ward: "Visual Performance and Its Relation to Reading Achievement," *Journal of the American Optometric Association,* 33:825–829, June, 1962.

Knox, G. E.: "Classroom Symptoms of Visual Difficulty," in *Clinical Studies in Reading: II,* Supplementary Educational Monographs, no. 77, The University of Chicago Press, Chicago, 1953, pp. 97–101.

Leestma, Robert C.: *Audio-visual Materials for Teaching Reading,* Slater's Book Store, Ann Arbor, Mich., 1954.

McCord, H.: "Note on the Use of the Psychogalvanometer as an Aid in the Diagnosis of Certain Persons with Reading Difficulties," *Journal of Developmental Reading,* 5:137–138, Winter, 1962.

Perry, William G., Jr., and Charles P. Whitlock: "The Right to Read Rapidly," *Atlantic Monthly,* 159:88–96, November, 1952.

Rabinovitch, Ralph D., and Winifred Ingram: "Neuropsychiatric Considerations in Reading Retardation," *The Reading Teacher,* 15:433–438, May, 1962.

Robinson, Helen M. (ed.): *Clinical Studies in Reading: II,* Supplementary Educational Monographs, no. 77, The University of Chicago Press, Chicago, 1953, pp. 1–183.

Spache, George D.: "Auditory and Visual Materials," in *Development in and through Reading,* Sixtieth Yearbook of the National Society for the Study of Education, The University of Chicago Press, Chicago, 1961, part I, pp. 206–225.

————: "Classroom Reading and the Visually Handicapped Child," in *Changing Concepts of Reading Instruction,* International Reading Association Conference Proceedings, vol. 6, Scholastic Magazines, Inc., New York, 1961, pp. 93–97.

———— and Lois B. Bing: *Children's Vision and School Success,* American Optometric Association, St. Louis, Mo., 1962.

———— and Chester E. Tillman: "A Comparison of the Visual Profiles of Retarded and Non-retarded Readers," *Journal of Developmental Reading,* 5:101–109, Winter, 1962.

Strauss, Alfred A., and Newell C. Kephart: *Psychopathology and Education of the Brain-injured Child,* vol. II, Progress in Theory and Clinic, Grune & Stratton, Inc., New York, 1955.

Taylor, Edith: *Psychological Appraisal of Children with Cerebral Defects,* Harvard University Press, Cambridge, Mass., 1959.

Tinker, Miles A., and Donald G. Patterson: "The Effect of Typographical Variations upon Eye Movement in Reading," *Journal of Educational Research,* 49:171–184, November, 1955.

10

~~~~~~

READING TESTS
ADMINISTERED
INDIVIDUALLY

Group reading tests yield information about students' vocabulary knowledge and certain comprehension skills. Incidental classroom observation of individual students, as they read aloud or silently, adds information about their reading interest and proficiency in different kinds of reading situations. The individual reading test or inventory gives more understanding of the student's reading process and indicates possible causes of his success or failure.

While administering the individual reading test, the teacher can observe the student more closely in standardized reading situations. His chance remarks, his facial expression, bodily positions, and expressive movements often give clues as to his attitudes toward himself and toward reading. His casual conversation may give insight into his early reading experiences and interests and his present family relationships. He will often tell how he thinks teachers have helped or hindered his progress in reading and what makes reading easy or difficult for him. The way in which he reads paragraphs on different levels of difficulty gives further information about his approach to reading, word recognition skills, and the quality of his comprehension. The individual reading inventory is, in effect, a more elaborate and systematic technique of observation to be used with individual students while the rest of the class is working independently. Given at the beginning of each school year, it furnishes both teacher and student diagnostic information that is needed to improve the student's reading.

THE INDIVIDUAL READING INVENTORY

The individual reading inventory is one of the most widely used techniques in the field of reading. In the Philadelphia reading program it is used on both elementary and secondary levels in the remedial, corrective, and developmental aspects of the program. It is basic to the selection of students for remedial classes. It is recommended as a technique to be used by the teachers of regular classes to answer many of their questions about students' reading. Every reading teacher should be prepared to use it.

As described here, the individual reading inventory is informal and flexible. The teacher may modify it in numerous ways to give him the kind of understanding he needs about an individual student.

Main Features

The individual reading inventory may include the following features:

Brief Preliminary Conversation. After explaining the inventory process briefly, the teacher may talk with the student to put him at ease. By asking casual questions, he gains some understanding of the student's interests, reading habits, attitudes toward himself, toward reading, and toward school. The following are examples of the areas of inquiry that might be covered in the course of this introductory conversation:

Of all the things you do outside of school, which do you like best? Which do you like least?

Of all the things you do in school, which do you like best? Which do you like least?

How far would you like to go in school?

What kind of work would you like to do? Why?

Have you had trouble with reading? For how long?

What seems hard about it?

Which seems harder, reading aloud or reading silently?

Have you had any special help in reading?

How is your spelling?

If the student talks freely, the teacher seldom has to ask direct questions. Instead, he simply follows upon leads that the student gives.

Test of Knowledge of Spoken Words, such as the Gates Oral Vocabulary Test (1953). This test is concerned with ascertaining the student's understanding of the meaning of spoken words; it does not involve reading. The teacher's purpose in giving an oral vocabulary test is to learn something about the student's oral language background and the level on which he may be expected to begin reading the oral paragraph. In introducing the test, the teacher may say in explanation, "First I am going to ask you about some words—the words you need in order to talk with people and to understand what they say and to listen to television." The students' responses—sometimes very meager and sometimes richly descriptive—tell much about the word meanings that they bring to their reading.

Test of Ability to Pronounce Printed Words. The vocabulary part of the Wide Range Achievement Test (Jastak, 1946) is an exercise in word recognition—the oral reading of words at sight; it does not involve word meanings. In introducing the Wide Range Achievement Test, the examiner says: "Look at each word carefully and read it out loud as well as you can. Begin here (point to the line) and read the words across the page, this line first, then the next, etc." (p. 5).

Use of Auditory-perception Technique. An exercise in the Gates Reading Diagnostic Tests (Gates, 1953) gives additional information about the range of the individual's speaking vocabulary and "divergent thinking," as well as about his ability to recognize and recall words that begin or end with the same sound. The following responses were made by a ten-year-old boy (Johnny, of course!) when he was asked for: (1) words that begin with the same sound as

>   *can*   king, cook
>   *saw*   see, so, salt, said

and (2) words that end with the same sound, that rhyme with

>   *can*   ban
>   *keep*   sleep, peep
>   *pig*   mig, lig

At this point the teacher said, "What does *lig* mean?" Johnny replied, "That gets me, too." Teacher: "You made it up, didn't you? We call it a nonsense syllable. It has no meaning. You have a very good ear for sounds."

A more elaborate phonetic inventory or word analysis test may also be used (Durrell, 1937–1955; Johnson).

Use of Oral Reading Paragraphs. For this important part of the individual reading inventory the teacher may use paragraphs from various sources: from the Durrell Analysis of Reading Difficulty Test (1937–1955), from a graded basal reading series that the student has not read, or from any other kind of graded reading material. One may also write paragraphs especially for this purpose and check them for reading difficulty. As in other testing situations involving achievement and capacity, it is desirable to elicit the optimum response from the individual. Since reading requires effort and since effort can be motivated by interest, the material selected should obviously be as interesting as possible. Otherwise lack of achievement is confused with lack of effort. Paragraphs from primary basal readers are often too childish in content for the bright child or the older retarded reader; he may resent being given such "baby stuff" and not even try to read it.

To be of practical value, a reading inventory for use by

teachers should be so designed that it can be administered and scored as simply and quickly as possible.

The comprehension questions should be of at least four kinds: questions of fact, questions requiring a grasp of the main idea, questions of inference, and questions of word meaning. Since the individual reading inventory is used as a clinical rather than as a psychometric device, the teacher may reword the question if he thinks the student knows the answer but is puzzled by the form in which it is asked.

Both teacher and student will find the administering of the test more convenient if each paragraph is printed on a separate card for the student and on a sheet for the teacher that contains space for recording the student's errors in oral reading and his answers to the questions on comprehension. The following is an example of an individual reading inventory such as any teacher might use:

INDIVIDUAL READING INVENTORY (Teacher's Record Form)

Some seeds travel
in the water.
Some seeds travel
in the air.
Some seeds travel
on animals.
Some seeds travel
on people's clothes.[1]

First Grade: "How Seeds Travel"
Questions:

1. What are these sentences about? (2 points)

2. In what ways do seeds travel? (4 points)

3. Why is it good for seeds to travel? (2 points)

4. What does *travel* mean? Give a sentence using the word *travel*. (4 points)

[1] *My Weekly Reader,* vol. 39, ed. 1, p. 3, Oct. 2–6, 1961.

Total no. words: 23   Accuracy:
    No. words correct: 90% (21)[2]
    No. errors: 95% (22)
Reading time (wpm):   Comprehension score:

> Autumn is a busy time
> in the north.
> Autumn is harvest time.
> Potatoes are dug in autumn.
> Corn is picked in autumn.
> Many crops are being harvested.[3]

Second Grade: "Autumn's Harvest Time"
Questions:
1. What are these sentences about? (2 points)

2. How is autumn described—what kind of a time is it? (1 point)

3. What happens in autumn? (3 points)

4. Why is autumn a busy time? (2 points)

5. What does *harvest* mean? Give a sentence using *harvest* or *harvested*. (2 points)

Total no. words: 27   Accuracy:
    No. words correct: 90% (24)
    No. errors: 95% (27)
Reading time (wpm):   Comprehension score:

> The U.S. Army has been buying
> dogs. The dogs are German shepherds.

[2] The figures in parentheses are the number of words correct to make 90 and 95 per cent accuracy.

[3] *My Weekly Reader,* vol. 31, ed. 2, p. 1, Sept. 18–22, 1961.

The Army needs 200 dogs. The dogs will help to guard top-secret Army camps.

The Army tests the dogs before buying them. Army dogs cannot be afraid of noise. They must be smart and able to obey orders.[4]

Third Grade: "Dogs Guard Army Camps"
Questions:

1. What are these paragraphs about? (2 points)

2. How many dogs does the Army need? (1 point)

3. What kind of dogs does the Army buy? (1 point)

4. What tests must the dogs pass? (2 points)

5. Why does the Army need dogs? (2 points)

6. What does *guard* mean? Give a sentence using the word *guard*. (1 point)

7. What does *top-secret* mean? Give a sentence using the word *top-secret*. (1 point)

Total no. words: 51	Accuracy:
No. words correct:	90% (46)
No. errors:	95% (48)
Reading time (wpm):	Comprehension score:

A giant, four-engine airplane swoops low over a burning forest in California. A "water bomb" drops from the plane. Soon, the roaring blaze is out.

A helicopter moves slowly over a

[4] *My Weekly Reader,* vol. 31, ed. 3, p. 13, Sept. 25–29, 1961.

newly cut forest in Minnesota. As the
helicopter moves, it leaves behind a
trail of small seeds.[5]

Fourth Grade: "How Airplanes Help"
Questions:
1. What are these paragraphs about? (2 points)

2. How do airplanes put out forest fires?

3. How do helicopters plant new forests?

4. What do you think a "water bomb" might be like? (2 points)

5. What does *swoop* mean? Give a sentence using the word *swoop*.
   (1 point)

6. How is a helicopter different from an airplane?

Total no. words: 49   Accuracy:
   No. words correct: 90% (44)
   No. errors: 95% (47)
Reading time (wpm):   Comprehension score:

The big jet screeches as its engines
turn. It takes off with a roar and climbs
swiftly into the sky.
   Inside the plane, the passengers hear
only a muffled sound of the jet's powerful
engines. The takeoff is so gentle that
travelers may not even know when the plane
lifts off the ground. The jets fly at from
450 to 600 miles an hour. Travelers can go

[5] *My Weekly Reader*, vol. 43, ed. 4, p. 1, Sept. 25–29, 1961.

from New York to Chicago in two hours. They
can travel from coast to coast in five to
six hours.[6]

Fifth Grade: "Facts about Jet Planes"
Questions:
  1. What are these paragraphs about? (2 points)

  2. How does a jet plane start? (2 points)

  3. How fast do jets fly? (1 point)

  4. How long do jets take to go from New York to Chicago? (1 point)

  5. From New York to Los Angeles? (coast to coast) (1 point)

  6. Why is it more pleasant to be a passenger inside the jet than a person
     standing outside it? (2 points)

  7. What is the difference between a *screech* and a *muffled* sound? Give
     an example of each. (1 point)

Total no. words: 87   Accuracy:
    No. words correct: 90% (78)
    No. errors: 95% (82)
Reading time (wpm):   Comprehension score:

Kruger Park is a wild animal
preserve. The fence around the park
will keep the animals in and unlicensed
hunters out. The fence is one of the
steps being taken to protect wild life
in African countries.
     Africa's wild life has been
disappearing at an alarming rate. One

[6] *My Weekly Reader*, vol. 44, ed. 5, p. 1, Nov. 27–Dec. 1, 1961.

wild-life expert says it is possible
that all large animals will be gone
from the continent within the next ten
to twenty years.[7]

Sixth Grade: "Protection of Wild Life in Africa"
Questions:
1. What are these paragraphs about? (2 points)

2. Where is Kruger Park? (2 points)

3. What use is the fence around the park? (2 points)

4. Are there more or fewer wild animals in Africa than there used to be?
   (1 point)

5. In how many years may all large wild animals be gone from Africa?
   (1 point)

6. Why are steps being taken to protect wild life in Africa? (2 points)

7. What is a wild animal preserve? Do you know of any wild animal
   preserves around here? (1 point)

8. What is a continent? (1 point)

Total no. words: 69	Accuracy:
No. words correct:	90% (62)
No. errors:	95% (66)
Reading time (wpm):	Comprehension score:

It is better to begin testing at too low than at too high a
level. The student's ability to read fluently and comprehend fully
on the easier passage gives him confidence. If he feels secure, he

[7] *My Weekly Reader*, vol. 16, ed. 6, p. 1, Oct. 2–6, 1961.

is likely to read the passages that are at grade level better than he otherwise would.

As the student reads each paragraph, the teacher indicates his errors and jots down his responses to the questions. Usually the teacher tells the student a word on which he pauses for about five seconds or asks for help. When the same word recurs in the paragraph, the teacher can see how the student attacks a word when he meets it the second time. His failure to recognize it a second time is counted as another error. The teacher may aid the student's comprehension by asking what the word might mean in the sentence, but he does not say whether the student's response is right or wrong. Inequality of response from paragraph to paragraph is to be expected. This may be owing partly to unequal interest in or degree of familiarity with the topics. When the paragraphs become very difficult, the examiner may ask the student just to pick out the words he knows. He stops before the situation has become too distressing.

If time permits, the teacher may learn more about the student's reading process by asking him about his method of reading, for example, how he got the meaning of some of the difficult words and why he had difficulty with others.

After the first oral reading the student may be asked to read the same paragraphs silently and then reread them orally. His improvement in pronunciation and comprehension is then noted. Improvement in comprehension may be due to his having the questions in mind as he rereads the paragraphs.

Looking over the record later, the teacher can note the errors in word recognition and the quality of the student's comprehension —whether he answers questions briefly or at length, in his own words or in the words of the book; whether he reports accurately what the author says or makes up stories of his own and inserts information that was not in the paragraphs.

In a reading diagnosis the teacher usually wants to determine a student's upper and lower levels of reading ability. From the information recorded in the individual reading inventory, the teacher may estimate the student's reading level and capacity. The characteristics of these levels have been described by Betts (1954) and others.

Use of Silent Reading Paragraphs. Different paragraphs on the same levels of difficulty may be used for this purpose. The

Durrell Analysis of Reading Difficulty Test (1937–1955) includes a set of both oral and silent reading paragraphs. The individual continues with the graded series of paragraphs until he reaches his frustration level. With stories, the teacher may orient the reader to the story as he does in teaching story material. For example, he may say, "This story is about a boy. It tells what happened on a weekend trip. Let's see what happened."

In testing comprehension the teacher may ask the pupil to tell in his own words what the author said: "You read the story to yourself. When you've finished it, put your book down and then, instead of asking you questions, I'll ask you to tell the story." Many students can answer questions better than they can tell the story. This may be because they have had more practice in answering questions than in organizing the ideas they gain from reading. They need the clues that questions give. Inability to organize ideas is a poor prognostic sign.

When a student recognizes his specific limitations, this is an encouraging sign of "learner literacy."

Test of Listening Comprehension. The teacher begins by reading paragraphs a little above the level on which the student has failed to read orally or silently. From there he continues to the highest level on which the student can answer the comprehension questions.

The oral comprehension of retarded readers of normal mental ability is usually higher than their reading comprehension. The relatively higher it is, the better is the prognosis for improvement in reading. The difference between capacity of auditory comprehension level and instructional level is one useful measure of reading potential.

Recording of Student's Responses. When a series of graded paragraphs is used with each student, the teacher may indicate the errors and other kinds of responses made at various levels of reading difficulty. The student may make no errors on the easiest paragraph but may make certain kinds of errors as the paragraphs become more difficult. The following is a checklist for recording a student's oral and silent reading performance on a series of paragraphs.

CHECKLIST FOR RECORDING PERFORMANCE
ON ORAL READING PARAGRAPHS

Name_____Grade_____Date_____

Paragraphs	Rating on given paragraph level						General impressions
	I	II	III	IV	V	VI	
Word attack:							
Refuses to attempt unknown words							
Omits words or parts of words							
Inserts words							
Guesses at words:							
Makes sense							
Does not make sense							
Repeats words or parts of words							
Reverses letters or words							
Spells out words							
Sounds out words laboriously							
Recognizes beginning sound							
Mispronounces the whole word							
Recognizes other sounds and tries pronunciation							
Checks pronunciation with meaning in sentence							
Uses structural parts							
Uses combination of methods							
Phrasing:							
Reads in thought units							
Poor grouping							
Word-by-word reading							
Monotone							
Ignores punctuation							
Posture:							
Good							
Book too close							
Book too far							
Finger pointing							
Speed, wpm:							
Comprehension:							
Main ideas identified							
Details							
Inference							
Vocabulary							
Comparison between oral and silent reading comprehension:							
Little or no difference							
Silent reading slightly superior							
Silent reading twice as good as oral							
Little or no improvement in oral reading							
Grade levels:							
Independent							
Instructional							
Frustrational							
Capacity 75% comprehension or better							
Listening comprehension:							
No better than reading							
Slightly better							
Much better							

Summary of Instructions for Administering the Individual Reading Inventory

1. Have a brief talk with student in a friendly, interested way.
2. Give short tests of oral vocabulary, ability to pronounce printed words, and auditory perception.
3. Use reading paragraphs as follows:
    a. Give pupil first paragraph card.
    b. Ask him to read it orally.
    c. Record errors as he reads.
    d. Ask comprehension questions; write answers as he gives them.
    e. To obtain supplementary information, ask child to read paragraph silently, then orally again. Record changes in comprehension and increase or decrease in errors.
    f. Continue with next paragraphs until frustration level is reached:
        (1) Comprehension less than 50 per cent
        (2) Inability to pronounce 10 per cent of running words
        (3) Inability to anticipate meaning
        (4) Inability to get facts
        (5) Evidence of distraction
        (6) Evidence of withdrawal
    g. Read aloud to the student other paragraphs beginning at his frustration level; ask comprehension questions.
    h. Record on form for each paragraph the number and percentage of errors in word recognition and comprehension. Summarize results on checklist, profile, or description of student's specific abilities.
4. Administer a timed silent reading test using similar paragraphs.

The teacher may select from the procedures suggested as many as are appropriate to the situation. Even a recording of a child's response to one or two paragraphs is of value.

Values

In the primary grades, oral reading makes possible an appraisal of the child's basic vocabulary and word recognition skills. It offers a natural transition from spoken language to silent reading. By checking on the child's comprehension of the selection read, the teacher avoids overemphasis on pronunciation per se. Dramatized reading of conversation gives further indication as to whether the student is reading for meaning with proper phrasing and expression.

The values of the individual reading inventory may be summarized as follows:

1. It is a quick and easy way to see how a student is functioning in reading.

2. It informs us about his range of reading levels, i.e., what kind of book he can read independently, what kind he can read with some degree of instruction, and what kinds cause him nothing but tension and frustration. The student's independent reading level, as observed in the individual reading inventory, is generally about two years below his standardized test grade score.

3. It shows the extent of the pupil's reading problem and his specific difficulties, such as his method of word attack, his verbal fluency (the ease with which he thinks of words), and his phonetic ability.

4. It aids the teacher in grouping students for instruction and in selecting suitable reading material.

5. It makes possible a comparison between the pupil's oral and silent reading ability.

6. It makes it easy for the teacher to base instruction directly on the inventory results, since the material in the test is similar to the contents of the books that the students are reading in class.

7. It gives some indication of how a pupil can handle an oral reading situation.

Apart from these specific values, the individual inventory is useful in helping the teacher establish a good relationship with the student. It also helps the student to see his reading difficulties objectively. If the teacher suggests exercises to correct difficulties as they are discovered, the student is immediately motivated to work on them.

Areas of Interpretation

In the individual reading inventory, many kinds of information may be obtained either systematically or incidentally. The following are a few suggestions for interpreting this information:

Vocalization and Word Calling. The examiner notes students who are seen to vocalize the words while reading. He is alert to detect "word callers" who read with apparent fluency but no comprehension. He may also detect individuals who have visual memory but lack the ability to read with comprehension. These and other students are sometimes able to use clues provided by the questions to answer them without reading the paragraph.

Word Recognition Skills. Since phonics is first of all a matter of hearing sounds, the examiner informally checks on the individual's auditory acuity. He may say something in a low voice when the individual is not looking at him. A phonics inventory indicates the student's ability to associate letters with sounds. However, he may be able to recognize the sounds of letters in words and to give all the consonants in a word but be unable to pronounce the word correctly. Many students are able to recognize only the initial sound of a word. The ability to use letter-sound associations in solving unfamiliar words seems to be related to a general organizational ability as measured by the WISC.

Word Meaning. In recording substitutions, it is important to note what kinds of words are substituted. The student who substitutes *scurried* for *scampered* in the sentence "The squirrel scampered" shows that he is reading for meaning, whereas the student who reads "a bowl of soap" for "a bowl of soup" shows lack of concern for content.

Mental Ability. The individual inventory situation, if supplemented, as it usually is, by the teacher's information about the children in his class whom he already knows very well, yields clues that help the teacher interpret a student's mental ability. For example, the following information was obtained about Andy:

His mother had always worked, at least as long as he could remember.

Neither mother nor father had completed high school.

His skull was fractured in an accident before he came to school.

Despite unfavorable home conditions, his speaking vocabulary was superior for a boy of his age.

He understood directions quickly.

He enjoyed any humorous references in the story or in conversation.

He profited immediately by the instruction he was given.

Some of these clues indicated that the boy had superior mental ability, which may have been suppressed by his deprivation of close contact with his mother in infancy, by an anti-intellectual environment, and perhaps by the secondary anxiety or fear caused by the skull injury.

Attitudes and Emotions. From observation of the individual's personal appearance and behavior, his friendliness or unfriendliness, his social poise or embarrassment, his enthusiasm or indifference, the teacher may gather something about his attitudes. John had experienced several failures and was resentful about them. In his words, the art teacher was "crazy"; the shop teacher was "an old guy, quite crazy, too." In a class for slow learners, the other boys called him "the genius" because his mother had insisted on his going into the high school academic course and was determined that he would eventually go to college. He stopped going to church and Sunday school because he was called upon to read aloud. His subsurface hostility came out in many ways, directly or indirectly.

Another boy, who gave many indications of anxiety and apathy, was asked what was his favorite activity; he replied, "Going to bed." The fact that he was blocked on the easiest paragraph but later read a harder one fairly fluently showed that he could perform more efficiently after he realized that the situation was nonthreatening.

Signs of tension such as nail biting or twisting and turning in the seat may be readily observed. It is also interesting to see how an individual responds to increased difficulty and what happens when he moves from a satisfying to an unsuccessful experience.

Interests. Students usually express their interests freely in the individual reading situation. For example, one boy spoke with enthusiasm of the wonderful time he had had on a New England farm during the summer. During the winter he spent much time watching TV; "Gunsmoke" and "The Whirly Birds" were his favorite programs. It was significant that he had given up going to the YMCA because it was no fun to go alone.

Recommendations

Recommendations based on the individual reading inventory plus all the other information available about the individual should accentuate the positive. They should include references to all the assets on which the student may build.

Among general recommendations frequently growing out of an individual inventory are the following:

1. Continued efforts in school to give the student the experience of success in reading. In every class skillful instruction along the specific lines indicated by the diagnosis can lead to improvement.

2. Provision of suitable reading material; even "baby books" are sometimes recommended. Some emotionally disturbed children have a need to live again through the baby stage; these books may help to meet that need. In such cases, these books have therapeutic value as well as that of increasing the child's reading fluency. Older students who are eager to read better will often accept beginner books if they are convinced that this is the path to improvement.

3. Referral to a counselor, who can find resources for widening the individual's school activities and interests, provide supporting counseling, and adjust the school program to meet the student's need. Sometimes it is desirable that the student be given a change of class or course. If the parents refuse to consent to the change, they must assume responsibility if the student continues to fail in his present course, if his reading problem becomes aggravated or if, as may happen, he undergoes a psychoneurotic breakdown.

4. Work with parents when there is clear evidence that home conditions are continuing to prevent reading improvement. With adolescents whose parents have confirmed unrealistic attitudes and ambitions, it is sometimes possible to help the child change his attitude toward the home situation so that it does not continue to interfere with his progress.

5. Referral to a child guidance or mental hygiene clinic if the problem is primarily emotional.

STANDARDIZED ORAL READING TESTS

As suggested in Chapter 4, oral reading tests, informal or standardized, are the core of appraisal procedures in the primary grades. One of these tests is included in any thorough diagnosis of reading difficulties.

Several standardized oral reading tests are available, such as:

1. Gray Oral Reading Test by William S. Gray, for grades

1 to 8, two forms. The Bobbs-Merrill Company, Inc., Indianapolis, Indiana, 1963. The original oral reading test was a pioneer in the field. It has been widely used and recently revised to include questions to check the student's comprehension of each paragraph.

2. Leavell Analytical Oral Reading Test by Ullin W. Leavell, for grades 1 to 10, Forms A and B, time fifteen to twenty minutes. Educational Test Bureau, Minneapolis, 1952–1953.

3. Gilmore Oral Reading Test by John U. Gilmore, for grades 1 to 8, Forms A and B, time fifteen to twenty minutes. Harcourt, Brace & World, Inc., New York, 1952.

It is important not only to know the response a student makes, but also to know how he arrives at it, e.g., how he tries to identify a certain word, why he substitutes one word for another, etc. Such understanding may be gained by asking him occasionally to think aloud as he attacks an unfamiliar word.

COMPREHENSIVE READING ANALYSIS TESTS

Oral reading paragraphs are an important feature of the more elaborate diagnostic tests developed by Durrell (1937–1955), Gates (1953), and by Bond, Clymer and Hoyt (1955). More recently Botel (1961) has devised an informal, "streamlined" reading inventory including reading placement tests and a phonics mastery test. Its purpose is (1) to ascertain the books that students can read with profit and (2) to determine each student's need for instruction and practice on specific word attack skills. The test accomplishes this purpose through "a Word Recognition Test, which is a measure of oral reading, and a Word Opposites Test, which gives an estimate of comprehension. The Phonics Mastery Test determines the word attack skills of each pupil" (Botel, 1961, p. 3). Much emphasis is placed on reading levels and on finding "the right book for each child." The Word Opposites Test (Listening) covers a range from first grade through senior high school. "Instead of running words, or continuous reading matter, the Word Recognition Test consists of graded lists of words through the fourth grade level" (p. 5). Detailed scoring sheets and charts for recording and summarizing results are suggested. The *Illinois Test of Psycholinguistic Abilities* includes tests of auditory and visual reception, association, vocal expressive and motor expressive abilities, sound blending, perceptual speed, visual closure, and visual discrimination. These are important mental abilities related to language and reading. Deficiency in any one of them may block the reading process.

The most adequate individual reading tests combine (1) an analysis of visual and auditory perception and discrimination, (2) specific word recognition skills, (3) spelling, and (4) oral and silent comprehension of paragraphs of graded difficulty. Many tests of this kind are described in books on reading evaluation and reading instruction (see references at end of chapter).

The best way to become acquainted with any of these tests is to send for a sample set. Before giving the test, one must study the test manual thoroughly and practice the procedure described.

RELATIVE CONTRIBUTION OF STANDARDIZED TESTS AND INFORMAL PROCEDURES

One wonders, however, whether the purpose of determining a student's reading level might not be served as well by having him read sample passages from books of different levels of difficulty. The most direct way of seeing whether a child can read a given book on the independent, instructional, or frustrational level is to give him a chance to read a short passage from it. In observing a child read aloud, the teacher sees errors as they occur. Each hesitation, each omission, each reversal raises questions as to their causes.

During an instructional period also, much diagnostic information may be obtained. The most valuable diagnostic contribution of such a period is the insight that the teacher can gain into the student's learning capacity. After he has been given instruction in paragraph comprehension, for example, the teacher can note how quickly he "catches on." One boy who was unable to get the main idea of the first paragraph he read could give the main idea and supporting details of comparable paragraphs after he had had instruction in how paragraphs are built. The surest test of a student's learning ability is whether he learns when he has been given the best possible instruction.

CONCLUDING STATEMENT

The individual reading inventory is an elaboration of the simple procedure of asking a student to read a paragraph or two aloud. The inventory may consist simply of series of graded paragraphs to be read aloud. If time permits, the analysis of the student's oral reading may be supplemented by any or all of the other techniques suggested in this chapter.

Interpretation may be based on fairly objective evidence of proficiency in word meaning and word recognition or it may involve inferences derived from subtle clues of mental abilities, attitudes, and emotions.

Diagnostic information obtained from the individual reading inventory may be used immediately to help an individual student; it may be tabulated for the whole class as a guide to group instruction; it may be used to show trends in the development of a student's reading over a period of time. The important thing is that such information should be *used*.

Suggested Problems
Practice and Demonstration

1. Build up a file of reading tests, including samples of each, the accompanying manual, and the articles and pamphlets describing its construction and use. Include also a copy of the appraisals of the test from Buros's latest *Mental Measurement Yearbook* and from other sources.

2. Select one standardized oral reading test and one diagnostic test and demonstrate with a child in the teacher-education class. Have members of the class record, score, interpret, and make tentative recommendations on the basis of the information thus obtained.

3. Give a similar demonstration of the individual reading inventory.

4. Ask teachers to construct an individual reading inventory using paragraphs from the books they will be expecting the pupils in their elementary or secondary school classes to read.

5. Use the McCullough Word Analysis Tests, grade 4 through college (Ginn and Company), to obtain information on each type of word recognition skill.

6. How might the individual reading inventory be adapted for use by classroom teachers? When would they have the time to give it to each pupil individually?

7. What should a teacher do with a fourth-grade pupil who reads silently with adequate comprehension but makes many errors in pronunciation when reading orally?

References

Austin, Mary C., and others: *Reading Evaluation,* The Ronald Press Company, New York, 1961.

Betts, Emmett Albert: *Foundations of Reading Instruction,* American Book Company, New York, 1954, chap. 21.

Bond, Clymer-Hoyt Silent Reading Diagnostic Tests, Lyons and Carnahan, Chicago, 1955.

Botel Reading Inventory, Follett Publishing Company, Chicago, 1961. *Guide to the Botel Reading Inventory,* Follett Publishing Company, Chicago, 1961.

Durrell, Donald D.: *Durrell Analysis of Reading Difficulty,* grades 1–6, one form for individual administration in grades 1–6, time 30–90 minutes, Harcourt, Brace & World, Inc., New York, 1937–1955.

————: *Improving Reading Instruction,* Harcourt, Brace & World, Inc., New York, 1956.

Gates, Arthur I.: *Gates Reading Diagnostic Tests,* rev. ed., grades 1–8, time 60–90 minutes, Bureau of Publications, Teachers College, Columbia University, New York, 1953.

Jastak, Joseph: *Wide Range Achievement Test* and *Manual,* Wilmington, Delaware, 1946.

Johnson, Eleanor: *Phonics Inventories,* published periodically in *My Weekly Reader.*

Kirk, Samuel A., and James J. McCarthy: "The Illinois Test of Psycholinguistic Abilities: An Approach to Differential Diagnosis," *American Journal of Mental Deficiency,* 56:399–412, November, 1961.

Suggested Readings

Bond, Guy L., and Miles A. Tinker: *Reading Difficulties: Their Diagnosis and Correction,* Appleton-Century-Crofts, Inc., New York, 1957.

Brueckner, Leo J., and Guy L. Bond: *The Diagnosis and Treatment of Learning Difficulties,* Appleton-Century-Crofts, Inc., New York, 1955.

Buros, Oscar: *The Fifth Mental Measurement Yearbook,* The Gryphon Press, Highland Park, N.J., 1959.

Fernald, Grace M.: *Remedial Techniques in Basic School Subjects,* McGraw-Hill Book Company, Inc., New York, 1943.

Gates, Arthur I., and Eloise B. Cason: "An Evaluation of Tests for Diagnosis of Ability to Read by Phrases or Thought Units," *Elementary School Journal,* 46:23–32, September, 1945.

Harris, Albert J.: *How to Increase Reading Ability,* 4th ed., David McKay Company, Inc., New York, 1961.

Hildreth, Gertrude: *Teaching Reading,* Holt, Rinehart and Winston, Inc., New York, 1958.

Monroe, Marian: *Growing into Reading,* Scott, Foresman and Company, Chicago, 1951.

Schonell, F. J.: *The Psychology of Reading,* Oliver & Boyd, Ltd., London, 1961.

Smith, Henry P., and E. V. Dechant: *Psychology in Teaching Reading,* Prentice-Hall, Inc., Englewood Cliffs, N.J., 1961.

~~~~~~

11

INDICATORS OF
READING POTENTIAL

For many years the oral reading test, the silent diagnostic reading test, and the individual intelligence test formed the backbone of diagnostic procedure. As the complexity of the reading process has received increasing recognition, the need for teachers' observation and a combination of other diagnostic instruments has become apparent. But no entirely satisfactory method of diagnosing reading potential has yet been found.

INDIVIDUAL INTELLIGENCE TESTS

Intelligence tests have been the most important instrument used in predicting an individual's ability to make progress in reading. They have been used to answer the teacher's question: Can we expect more of this student, or should we accept his present reading performance as the best he can achieve?

However, skepticism about the value of intelligence tests in the diagnosis of reading difficulty has been growing. As mentioned in Chapter 7, the group intelligence test has been discredited as a measure of reading potential. The total score or mental age obtained from individual intelligence tests is also being used more cautiously. Experts in testing are constantly warning us against the "overinterpretation" of test scores.

Causes for Caution

There are many reasons why we should be cautious in using intelligence tests to predict reading potentiality.

Intelligence tests are not a sure measure of innate ability to learn. They measure "developed ability," not innate or potential intelligence. Previous achievement affects the test results. The poor reader is penalized on the verbal parts of the test. The fact that his store of information is limited by the small amount of reading he has done also works against him.

Intelligence tests, such as the Davis-Eells games (1953), which require no reading may be more effective than other tests in measuring certain kinds of intelligence but less effective in predicting academic success. Other intelligence tests that involve little or no reading are:

Full-range Picture Vocabulary Test by Robert Bruce Ammons, Southern University Press, Louisville, Kentucky.

Nonlanguage section of the California Mental Maturity Tests, California Test Bureau, Los Angeles.

Revised Beta Examination, Psychological Corporation, New York.

Chicago Non-verbal Examination, Psychological Corporation, New York.

Portions of SRA Primary Mental Abilities Test, Science Research Associates, Chicago.

We should also remember that our intelligence tests show how an individual is functioning at present; they measure the result of the interaction between his heredity and his environment at the time he takes the test.

An individual's intelligence test scores fluctuate from test to test. They vary with the type of test used and with the interval that has elapsed between testing. Children may change more than fifteen IQ points between the ages of three and ten. During the elementary school years only about half the children tested may maintain the same score; half of the remainder may show a rising IQ trend, a few may show a falling trend, and about a third will show irregular growth curves. IQs have been reported to fluctuate by as much as forty points for one reason or another.

It must also be recognized that intelligence tests may have a serious lack of both validity and reliability. After all, any test is bound to be a fairly crude measure of something as complex as intelligence. At best it can only sample a small portion of the abilities that constitute intelligence broadly defined. It is known, for example, that group intelligence tests given below the fourth grade are unreliable and that mental ages are not valid above age thirteen.

A given IQ should not be taken at face value as indicating one specific figure. It should be interpreted as a range or band, not as a point. For example, a reported IQ of 90 may actually mean anywhere from 80 to 100, or even from 75 to 105. If a student gets an IQ of 125 on the California Test of Mental Maturity, his IQ is somewhere between 115 and 135. A difference of at least fifteen IQ points is necessary before one can generalize about the comparative intelligence of individuals. When several successive IQ scores *on the same test* are available, an average of the scores is generally more reliable than a single score; one should never average IQ scores from different tests.

In view of the unreliability of tests and the probable error of the difference between the results of two tests, we must question the assumption that an individual whose mental age is a year higher than his reading age will be able to read better. On the Stanford-Binet test the error of estimate ranges from one to eight months. It varies with both age and intelligence but is greatest for the bright older children. The error of estimate is comparably large on most reading tests. Consequently, at some intelligence levels we cannot be sure that a difference of less than sixteen months between mental age and reading age is significant.

We may also make errors in interpretation if we fail to take into account the student's cultural background and home environment. In some cases, the same conditions that are causing the reading difficulty may also be depressing the intelligence test score. In other words, some underlying cultural or emotional factor may be responsible for both the low reading performance and the low intelligence rating.

Vocabulary plays a large role in determining a total intelligence test score. It is well known that children from non-English-speaking homes and other environments in which they have little stimulation to explore, listen, talk, and ask questions and small likelihood of having their questions answered are likely to be retarded in language development. Moreover, as stated earlier, tasks presented even on individual intelligence tests may be of such a nature that they are more familiar to urban than to rural students or to students from upper rather than lower socioeconomic levels. For all these reasons, test results should always be interpreted in the light of the student's particular cultural background and educational experience.

Practice and coaching may raise intelligence test scores (Vernon, 1954). However, it is one thing for a student to score high because he has had stimulating teachers and curricula and quite another thing for a student to score high because he has had specific practice or coaching. The latter has strictly limited effects. Nevertheless, a student who has had no previous experience in taking standardized tests is penalized in comparison with a student of equal ability who has become "test wise."

In view of all these limitations, it is obvious that mental age as measured by tests is not an adequate guide to an individual's reading potential. Some children read better than could be expected from their mental test scores; others fail to read up to expectation even under the best instruction.

RELATION BETWEEN READING AND INTELLIGENCE

Since reading, broadly defined, and intelligence have so much in common, intelligence tests cannot be counted on to predict reading potential. According to Guilford's analysis of intelligence (1959), the processes characteristic of intellectual activity are also characteristic of reading: (1) "cognition"—recognition or discovery of units, classes, relationships, systems; (2) memory of what is recognized; (3) "divergent thinking," which involves fluency and originality in dealing with words, ideas, and relations; (4) "convergent thinking," which leads to the right or best answer; and (5) evaluation, which includes critical thinking, the making of inferences, and the drawing of generalizations and conclusions.

These processes may be applied alike to concrete material or content perceived through the senses, to symbolic content such as the alphabet or number system, to semantic content in the form of verbal meanings, and to behavioral content which relates to what has been called social intelligence. It would seem possible to measure both intelligence and reading ability with two complementary tests, one dealing with symbolic and semantic content and the other dealing with concrete and behavioral aspects. This combination has been partially made in the intelligence tests that give both a quantitative and a verbal score.

Both the intelligence and the reading tests that are now available measure reading ability. The curves of intelligence and of reading as measured by tests are usually quite similar for students with average IQs of 90 to 110. Students with IQs above 110 may have mental ages from one to two years above their reading ages. The reading of less able learners with IQs below 90 is likely to be from one-half to two years above their tested intelligence. These relationships, of course, would vary according to the characteristics of the student and the quality of his previous education.

The relation between reading achievement and intelligence test scores also varies according to the child's stage of reading development. In beginning reading, Durrell and his associates (1958) reported that a "high mental age does not assure a high learning rate in beginning reading. . . . It is apparently the letter knowledge rather than the mental age which produces the high learning rate (p. 24)." It is quite understandable that skill in such a relatively simple process as associating the visual perception of a word with the spoken word may be determined more by previous experience in visual and auditory discrimination than by intelligence. As making sound-symbol associations becomes subordinate to comprehending sentences and paragraphs, the need for intelligence becomes greater.

The relation between intelligence test scores and reading achievement also depends greatly on the tests used. The two most widely used individual intelligence tests—the Stanford-Binet and the Wechsler Intelligence Test for Children (WISC)—are not entirely comparable. In general, the WISC scores seem to be lower than those obtained on the Stanford-Binet for the same individuals. The highest IQ obtainable on the WISC is 155; on the Stanford-Binet it is over 200. More than the WISC, the Stanford-Binet, which includes many verbal tasks, tends to underestimate the intelligence of poor readers.

Despite the limitations of these tests, some reading teachers, on the basis of individual intelligence test scores, have made a reading expectancy chart for each student which sets specific reading goals that he seems capable of attaining. This reading expectancy chart is based on the relation between the student's mental age as determined by an intelligence test and his initial reading grade. For example, if J.B.'s chronological age is 15 years 7 months, his IQ 71, his mental age 11 years 1 month, and his present reading grade score 2.8, his reading expectancy would be 4.5, i.e., he may be expected to learn to read fourth-grade books. These expectancy figures are supplemented by information about other circumstances that may affect his reading expectancy, such as bilingual background, emotional disturbance, and physical defects. Although such an expectancy chart is delightfully definite, its value is impaired by the difficulty of obtaining an accurate measure of mental ability.

The same caution should be shown in using any table of reading expectancy for the mentally slow child. However, a table such as that on page 217 is useful because it calls attention to the reading performance that might be expected of a slow-learning or mentally deficient child and the difficulty which he might have with beginning reading.

With respect to the interpretation of intelligence test scores

Table 2.   ACADEMIC EXPECTANCY: READING GRADE LEVELS

CA	IQ 50–59	IQ 60–69	IQ 70–75	IQ 76–85
6.0–6.6	Readiness	Reading	Readiness	Reading
7.0–7.6	Readiness	Reading	Readiness	Reading
8.0–8.6	Readiness	Reading	1	1
9.0–9.6	Readiness	1	1	1, 2
10.0–10.6	Readiness	1	2	2
11.0–11.6	1	2	2	3
12.0–12.6	1	2	3	3, 4
13.0–13.6	1	3	3	4
14.0–14.6	2	3	4	5
15.0–15.6	2	4	4, 5	5, 6
16.0–16.6	2	4	5	6

in relation to reading, Kirk (1962), who has worked extensively with mentally deficient children, has become very cautious in predicting reading achievement from mental age. Two children with the same mental age may have very different mental abilities.

Concept formation ability has recently been reported as a better predictor of reading potential than intelligence test scores. In addition to a test of listening comprehension, a concept formation test would be useful, especially for pupils above the first grade. Different kinds of mental ability are required for success at different grade levels.

A low IQ indicates that the individual has difficulty in orienting himself to the symbolism expressed in language. It has also been suggested that an extremely high verbal IQ may be a danger signal indicating too great a preoccupation with words and a neglect of the learning that should accrue from life experiences.

RELATION OF OBSERVATION TO TEST RESULTS

Tests cannot supplant the perceptive teacher or clinician. In a series of interviews, the teacher can obtain a fairly accurate impression of the student's ability to remember and to see relations; his use of words; and his quickness to learn, to follow directions, and to solve practical and theoretical problems. In his daily contacts with the teacher, the student reveals these and other indications of mental ability. The teacher also has the advantage of possessing background information that helps him to interpret his observations.

If the prospect of taking an intelligence test looms as a threat to the individual, perhaps it had better not be given. There is danger in damaging the student's self-esteem, which is so important a factor in the effort he puts forth to improve his reading.

DIAGNOSTIC VALUE OF SUBTESTS

The diagnostic value of the individual intelligence test has been greatly increased by its clinical use as advocated by Vernon (1937, pp. 99–113), Wechsler (1958), Rappaport (1950), and others.

In intelligence tests as well as in reading tests, the strong may balance out the weak points in an IQ or a total reading test score. The profile of subtests, showing the ups and downs in performance on different tasks, has much more diagnostic significance. Study of the subtest responses of poor readers on the WISC gives clues to some of the hidden factors that may be hindering their achievement:

Women consistently do better than men on the language tests, whereas men are superior on the arithmetic tests.

High subtest variation is often related to low learning proficiency.

The block design test may indicate disturbances in the higher perceptual processes, especially when there is organic impairment. According to Wechsler, the object assembly test may have special diagnostic value since it is the one test where a low score is consistently associated with pathology.

A possible explanation of unequal performance on the subtests is individual differences in the ability to handle abstractions or remember associations—abilities indispensable to reading success. The poor reader tends to approach a reading situation as though it were a matter of manipulating concrete entities. The good readers have the ability to use abstractions and to retain what they have learned (Brooks and Bruce, 1955). This ability is needed more in some subtests than in others.

The use of these tentative interpretations of the possible significance of the subtests of the WISC is illustrated (on pages 220–

221) in the detailed analysis of this test in connection with the scores achieved by one reading case.

None of these interpretations has been definitely established. At present they are merely diagnostic clues to be considered along with the accumulated information from all relevant sources.

However, some important studies have been made of the WISC as a diagnostic instrument in reading disability (Neville, 1961; Graham, 1952). In general, retarded readers score higher on the performance section of the scale than on the verbal section. This may be due to an inherent lack of verbal ability; to environmental, emotional, or other factors that have interfered with verbal ability; or simply to failure to learn to read. We should remember, however, that on the WISC, the nonverbal IQ generally runs higher than the verbal.

In the verbal section, the poor readers tend to score lowest on the subtests related to school learning, namely, information, arithmetic, and digit span. The digit symbol subtest is often the lowest subscore within the performance group. A low score on this test may reflect inability to concentrate, fluctuations in attention, and moodiness—characteristics often observed in poor readers and intensified, perhaps, by anxiety in the test situation.

The unsuccessful reader's highest scores were in tests not directly related to school instruction, namely, picture arrangement, block design, and object assembly. An analysis of items in the picture completion test of the Wechsler Adult Intelligence Scale (WAIS) suggests that three factors may be operating here which observation has shown enter into serious reading problems. One is inability to make contact with the reading task or "impaired contact with reality." The second is "maintenance of perspective," and the third is "awareness of uncertainty," a mental state in which the individual "may suspect a correct answer without having the confidence to guess it overtly" (Saunders, 1960, pp. 146–147). Factors such as these sometimes partially explain an individual's puzzling success or failure in a reading situation.

Further analysis of the individual's responses on the vocabulary tests may have diagnostic value. In addition to his fluency and the extent of his vocabulary, the way in which he defines a word is also significant. The new vocabulary section of the Wechsler Adult Intelligence Scale is designed especially to elicit responses colored by personal factors.

WECHSLER INTELLIGENCE SCALE FOR CHILDREN*

Verbal IQ: 108   Classification: Average, Superior, Bright,
Performance IQ: 122   Normal (Wide range in subtests makes
Full-scale IQ: 116   general classification misleading.)

IQ range, verbal scale: 75 (information) to 138 (comprehension)
IQ range, performance scale: 100 (object assembly) to 135 (picture arrangement)†

Subtest	IQ level	Classification	General significance of subtest
Subtest Scores, Verbal Scale			
Information	75	Borderline	Measures background of general information; memory development and functioning; "intellectual ambitiousness." Reflects educational and cultural environment and background. Score will suffer from educational and cultural deprivation.
Comprehension	138	Very superior	Measures practical common sense; good judgment; understanding of everyday social situations; acceptance of conventional standards of behavior; stable emotional balance.
Arithmetic	100	Average	Measures powers of arithmetical reasoning; concentration; attention. Reflects reaction to time pressure.
Similarities	131	Very superior	Measures logical thought processes; intellectual maturity; ability to handle abstract ideas, to see relationships, to form concepts, to generalize.
Vocabulary	106	Average	Measures many of same mental processes that are measured by information and similarities. Also serves to suggest level of auditory comprehension. Score not likely to be depressed by emotional disturbance, but will reflect educational and cultural deprivation.
Digit span	94	Average	Measures powers of attention; concentration; retention for immediate recall when stimulus is auditory. Reflects behavior during a learning situation.

* Analysis reported by Dr. Dorothy Withrow, psychologist, Philadelphia Reading Clinic.
† Measurements are approximate and relative, rather than exact and

WECHSLER INTELLIGENCE SCALE FOR CHILDREN* (Continued)

Subtest	IQ level	Classification	General significance of subtest
Subtest Scores, Performance Scale			
Picture completion	128	Superior	Measures alertness to environment; ability to note detail and to distinguish essential from nonessential detail. Involves visual perception; minimum of verbalization.
Picture arrangement	135	Very superior	Measures "social good sense"; ability to see cause and effect relationships, to figure out chronological sequence, and to note significant detail. Involves visual perception; minimum of verbalization.
Block design	121	Superior	Measures ability to analyze, to synthesize, and to copy, using abstract designs as patterns. Involves visual perception, visual-motor coordination, no verbalization.‡
Object assembly	100	Average	Measures ability to analyze and to synthesize, using concrete, relatively familiar material; also reflects ability to see relationship of whole to part of whole, to visualize or "anticipate" whole from part. Involves visual perception, visual-motor coordination, no verbalization. An "easy" subtest; low correlation with general mental ability. Subjects with reading disability often have trouble.
Coding	128	Superior	Measures ability to associate meaning with symbol; to "learn" when stimuli are visual and kinesthetic. Furnishes clues to subject's ability to use left-to-right progression in reading and writing. Subjects with reading disability often have low score. Involves visual perception, visual-motor coordination, no verbalization.

absolute. The last five subtests, constituting the performance scale, show reaction to time pressure and practice effect of previous testing, as well as the impaired functioning sometimes caused by emotional disturbance. This is less true of the verbal subtests.

‡ (Block design score correlates highly with general mental ability.)

RORSCHACH INDICATIONS OF INTELLIGENCE

It seems paradoxical that tests designed to measure intelligence should sometimes be used to give indications of emotional difficulties and that the Rorschach, a measure of personality, should sometimes be used to detect potential mental ability. Although a test should be used for the purpose for which it is primarily designed, we are justified in making use of any supplementary clues that it may yield. A Rorschach given by an adequately trained Rorschach clinician to a retarded reader sometimes yields valuable information about potential intelligence that is not revealed by the usual intelligence test, which measures *functioning* intelligence (see Chapter 13).

The following types of response to the Rorschach ink blots may indicate potentially adequate mental ability: the tendency to see wholes rather than parts or trivialities; and the tendency to see precise, relevant, and reasonable resemblances in the forms suggested by the ink blots. Using a predictive formula with a group of 400 veterans, Abrams (1955, pp. 81–83) found that the derived mean Rorschach IQ was almost identical with the full-scale IQ obtained on the Wechsler Adult Intelligence Scale. However, results from a special group of adults cannot be applied to adolescents, whose Rorschach responses are especially unstable and whose backgrounds are so different.

INTERPRETATION AND USE OF INTELLIGENCE TESTS

Despite criticism, the intelligence test remains a useful tool in the appraisal and diagnosis of reading. The mental age is a measure of mental maturity; the IQ, an indication of rate of mental development. The total score is useful in indicating the individual's present overall capacity to think, to act, and to deal purposely and effectively with his environment. The subtest scores and the observations made during the individual testing give clues to the nature, and sometimes the causes, of the person's reading difficulties.

To the extent that the reader must mobilize his entire self to read, reading techniques and skills would seem to be almost constantly affected by personality factors. For this reason, the personality clues obtained from a study of individual intelligence test responses may prove increasingly valuable in the exploratory diagnosis of reading.

In general, an individual intelligence test should be given when (1) the individual's group test scores seem inconsistent with his performance or with the teacher's estimate of his intelligence and achievement and (2) when a teacher is uncertain about whether an individual student has unrealized potential reading ability or is doing the best he can.

The teacher may request an individual test on a form such as the following:

Name of pupil_____Date of birth_____Grade_____

Previous test results:
  Name of test   Date given   Results

Health record:

Teacher observations:
  Pupil's attitude toward himself and toward reading
  Social relations
  Books he can read independently
  Books he cannot read without frustration

Teacher's questions about pupil:

The examiner should return the teacher's report with this additional information:

Name of test_____Date given_____By_____

Observation of pupil during test:

Interpretation of test results in detail:
  General level of ability
  Mental abilities in which pupil scored relatively high _____
_____, relatively low _____
_____, significance of these results
  for reading _____

Answers to teacher's specific questions:

Suggestions for helping pupil improve his reading:

The examiner should have a conference with the teacher in which they jointly discuss the findings and make recommendations. At least a conference should be held to supplement the written report. If we take the time to give individual tests, we should take enough additional time to see that their results are used to help both teacher and student.

When a parent asks point blank what his child's IQ is, what should the reading teacher say? If the teacher is trained in test interpretation, he can point out to the parent the implications of the test and describe the different kinds of learning ability it measures.

The teacher can also use the test results to help the student think about his strengths and limitations, emphasizing what he *can* rather than what he *cannot* do. He can suggest books that the student can read independently with enjoyment and outline the progress in reading that he may be expected to make. In this discussion the teacher avoids labels and tries to correct wrong impressions which the student may have previously acquired. The teacher need not mention specific scores in order to help the student arrive at a realistic concept of his ability. We must remember that an intelligence test is not just a test of the student's ability to learn; it also indicates something about what he has already learned.

The amount of interpreted information that the teacher gives would differ with different parents in the same way as a physician may give detailed facts to one patient but not to another; it is an individual matter. The only blanket rule is this: Give only as much information as you feel sure will be used for the good of the student.

TESTS OF LISTENING COMPREHENSION

The degree of comprehension that the individual shows in answering questions on paragraphs of graded difficulty that are read to him is a useful measure of his potential for further reading development. There are several standardized listening comprehension tests:

1. Brown-Carlsen Listening Comprehension Test, grades 9 to 13, two forms, time about 50 minutes, Harcourt, Brace & World, Inc., New York, 1953–1955.

2. Diagnostic Reading Tests, Section II, Comprehension: Silent and Auditory, Forms A, B, C, D, rev. 1957, The Committee on Diagnostic Reading Tests, Mountain Home, North Carolina.

3. Listening comprehension section of the STEP tests, two forms on each of four levels, Educational Testing Service, Princeton, New Jersey, 1956–1959.

Using these standardized tests, the teacher can compare the individual's ability to comprehend when he listens and when he reads similar material silently. The teacher may also learn much by the simple procedure of reading a selection aloud and having the student answer significant comprehension questions on it.

Listening comprehension tests also have faults. The relationship between comprehension when listening and when reading varies with the difficulty of the material. As reading material becomes more difficult, individuals tend to do better in reading than in listening. Moreover, listening skills can be improved by instruction. This fact makes them less valuable for prediction because some individuals will have had more incidental instruction than others.

The correlations between tests of reading and of listening comprehension are substantial but still low enough to indicate deviations in many individual cases (Cleland and Toussaint, 1962, pp. 228–231). The following correlations show the relation of listening to reading and to intelligence, as measured by certain tests:

Test	Correlation
STEP Listening Comprehension with Gates Reading Survey	.6679
STEP Listening Comprehension with Stanford-Binet	.6349
STEP Listening Comprehension with Durrell-Sullivan Reading Capacity	.7030
SRA Primary Mental Abilities (PMA) with Stanford-Binet	.7239
STEP and PMA with reading	.7564
STEP and PMA with American School Arithmetic, the highest correlation	.7852

If the student's STEP reading percentiles and his listening comprehension percentiles show a difference as great as three stanines in favor of listening comprehension, we may assume that he would have the ability to comprehend verbal material if he did not have a reading difficulty. Students with relatively high listening comprehension scores are most likely to profit from reading instruction. In general, prognosis for improvement in reading is good (1) when a student's listening comprehension is 75 per cent or better, (2) when he is able to relate to his life experiences the information he gains through listening, and (3) when he can use in his conversation vocabulary and language structure that are as mature as those in the passage that is read to him.

PERSONALITY AND SOCIAL INSIGHT TESTS

Many studies have been made of the relation between personality tests or inventories and reading achievement. The results have been inconclusive. Instead of identifying the dynamics in the reading process, most of the studies merely report correlations, which represent only a crude step in this direction.

A recent example involves the application of a "select personality and social insight test" to 400 high school students referred for the purposes of psychological study and consultation. Three-fifths of these referrals scored significantly below grade on reading scores. In this study (Cassel and Haddox, 1961, pp. 27–30), the total scores of both the Group Personality Projective Test and the Test of Social Insight were reported to be "significantly related to (1) level of reading competency, (2) total educational development, and (3) grade point average" (p. 29).

It is also quite possible that high scores on intelligence tests may in some cases be related to what are generally considered undesirable or unsocial personality characteristics. For example, at age six it was found that children who were rated high in aggressiveness and competitiveness tended later to increase in IQ. Both personality and cultural factors are related to the nature of the individual's mental development.

CONCLUDING STATEMENT

The diagnostic value of observation and individual intelligence and personality tests lies in the indications they give of the causes and conditions that are affecting reading development. Affectivity and intelligence are interwoven; together they influence reading achievement. According to Piaget

There are no acts of intelligence, even of practical intelligence, without interest at the point of departure and affective regulation during the entire course of action; without joy at success or sorrow at failure. Likewise, at the perceptual level we have affective motivations. What we perceive is a function of attention regulation, which is pretty much motivation by needs and interests (1962, p. 130).

Other factors, too, offer some indications of success in reading: age of school entrance, physical development, listening comprehension, and social and cultural factors. Reading, like intelligence, may be considered an expression of individuality.

Suggested Problems
Practice and Demonstration

1. Give a demonstration of the WISC or the Stanford-Binet test with a dull and with a bright child. Have the students observe the differences in the two children's responses to the same mental tasks. Have the observers also record their impressions of the children's attitudes and personality traits.

2. Have individual students write a thorough review of the literature on each of the specific topics indicated by the main headings of this chapter.

3. If detailed scattergrams of WAIS or WISC are available, repeat Graham's study of unsuccessful readers.

4. On the basis of all the information available about students in one of your classes, make a prediction of each student's reading scores at the beginning of the year. Compare your predictions with the actual scores obtained at the end of the year, and try to ascertain reasons for marked discrepancies between your predictions and the students' achievements.

5. Appraise various methods that have been proposed for predicting potential reading ability.

6. On what bases could students in a class set realistic reading goals for themselves?

7. What are some of the factors that might cause a discrepancy in predictions of reading potential based on individual intelligence tests? On listening comprehension tests?

References

Abrams, Elias N.: "Prediction of Intelligence from Certain Rorschach Factors," *Journal of Clinical Psychology,* 11:81–83, January, 1955.

Brooks, Harold F., and Paul Bruce: "The Characteristics of Good and Poor Readers as Disclosed by the Wechsler Intelligence Scale for Children," *Journal of Educational Psychology,* 46:488–493, December, 1955.

Cassel, Russell N., and Genevieve Haddox: "Comparing Reading Competency with Personality and Social Insight Test Scores," *California Journal of Educational Research,* 12:27–30, January, 1961.

Cleland, Donald L., and Isabella H. Toussaint: "The Interrelationships of Reading, Listening, Arithmetic Computation, and Intelligence," *The Reading Teacher,* 15:228–231, January, 1962.

Davis-Eells Test of General Intelligence or Problem-solving Ability, grades 1, 2, 3–6, one form, time 30–35 minutes, Harcourt, Brace & World, Inc., New York, 1953.

Durrell, Donald D. (ed.): "Success in First Grade Reading," *Journal of Education,* 140:1–48, February, 1958.

Graham, Ellis E.: "W-B and WISC Scattergrams of Unsuccessful Readers," *Journal of Consulting Psychology,* 16:268–271, August, 1952.

Guilford, J. P.: "Three Faces of Intellect," *American Psychologist,* 14:469–479, August, 1959.

Kirk, Samuel A.: *Educating Exceptional Children,* Houghton Mifflin Company, Boston, 1962.

Neville, Donald: "Comparison of WISC Patterns of Male Retarded and Non-retarded Readers," *Journal of Educational Research,* 54:195–197, January, 1961.

Piaget, Jean: "Affectivity and Intelligence," *Bulletin of the Menninger Clinic,* 26:130, May, 1962.

Rappaport, David: "The Studies of Diagnostic Psychological Testing," *Journal of Consulting Psychology,* 12:1–3, January–February, 1948; also "Diagnostic Testing in Psychiatric Practice," *Bulletin of New York Academy of Medicine,* 26:115–125, 1950.

Saunders, David R.: "A Factor Analysis of the Picture Completion Items of the WAIS," *Journal of Clinical Psychology,* 16:146–147, April, 1960.

Vernon, P. E.: "The Stanford-Binet Test as a Psychometric Method," *Character and Personality,* 6:99–113, December, 1937.

———: "Practice and Coaching Effects in Intelligence Tests," *The Educational Forum,* 18:269–280, March, 1954.

Wechsler, David: *The Measurement and Appraisal of Adult Intelligence,* 4th ed., The Williams & Wilkins Company, Baltimore, 1958.

Suggested Readings

Burt, Cyril: "The Gifted Child," General Introduction in *The Gifted Child, The Yearbook of Education,* Harcourt, Brace & World, Inc., New York, 1962.

Clymer, Theodore: "The Utility of Phonic Generalizations in the Primary Grades," in *Changing Concepts of Reading Instruction,* International Reading Association Conference Proceedings, vol. 6, Scholastic Magazines, Inc., New York, 1961, pp. 156–159.

Durkin, Dolores: "Children Who Learned to Read at Home," *Elementary School Journal*, 62:15–18, October, 1961.

Goins, Jean Turner: *Visual Perceptual Abilities and Early Reading Progress*, Supplementary Educational Monographs, no. 87, The University of Chicago Press, Chicago, 1958.

Strang, Ruth: "Relationships Between Certain Aspects of Intelligence and Certain Aspects of Reading." *Educational and Psychological Measurement*, 3:355–359, 1943.

————: "A Dynamic Theory of the Reading Process," *Merrill-Palmer Quarterly*, 7:239–245, October, 1961.

Thurstone, Thelma Gwinn: *Your Child's Intelligence: A Briefing for Parents*, National Education Association, Washington, n.d.

Vernon, Philip E.: *Intelligence and Attainment Tests*, University of London Press, Ltd., London, 1960.

————: "The Determinants of Reading Comprehension," *Educational and Psychological Measurement*, 22:269–286, Summer, 1962.

12

‹‹‹

INTERVIEW TECHNIQUES

The interviewer has this advantage over the physical scientist: He can obtain information from the person as well as about him. Furthermore, the student's analysis of his reading problem is often sound; the parents' comments, often enlightening. A skillful interview is the surest means of gaining information and insights from both parents and students.

Interviews with parents give glimpses of parent-child relations and specific information about the student's characteristics, habits, and home environment. Interviews with children and young people may be primarily exploratory or for the purpose of establishing a good relationship, definitely diagnostic or essentially therapeutic. Most often they are for the purpose of giving individual instruction in reading, although every interview combines, in varying proportions, diagnostic, instructional, and therapeutic elements. Insights gained by the student and put immediately to work have a beneficial effect on his interest and effort, his self-confidence and self-esteem.

INTERVIEW TECHNIQUES IN GENERAL

There is no substitute for experience in interviewing; we learn from our successes and our mistakes. Experience helps us to recognize characteristic responses, to distinguish antecedents from consequences. By comparing the individual's responses with behavior that he has previously observed in other students, the experienced interviewer is able to interpret what he sees and hears.

Research has shown that it is more important for the interviewer to have a rich background of experience and a positive regard for the interviewee than to employ any particular technique. The least successful interviewers tend to be those who are aloof and impersonal.

Within limits, the interviewer uses the method that is most congenial to him. This gives some interviewers a feeling of confidence that is lacking when they use a technique with which they do not feel competent. Some interviewers are insecure unless they feel that they are in control of the situation; they prefer to be directive. Others prefer to let the interviewee take the lead, to listen and to respond appropriately. These interviewers are relaxed. They are not disturbed by silences.

Actually the interviewer who maintains a sensitivity to the way the interviewee is thinking and feeling may find himself using the best features of several different approaches. On the directive-nondirective continuum, he may move toward one extreme or the other in response to indications in the behavior of the person whom he is interviewing. For example, with a compulsive talker, he may listen and make notes about questions to be asked later.

However, if the parent or student is so wound up that he is just going around in circles, the interviewer may have to assert control by interrupting the reiterated grievances.

An interview differs from a conversation in that it is purposeful; it is a conversation with a purpose (Strang, 1949). The interviewer should have some goals or objectives in mind to guide his thinking. Otherwise his questioning will be random and may have a desultory effect that is disappointing to the parent or student. One mother said indignantly, "I made a real effort to come for this interview and went to the expense of hiring a babysitter. And all I've learned is that 'Jimmy is a nice boy.' "

Interviewing is two-way communication; it requires mutual understanding. Sometimes language is a barrier; words have different meanings to different persons, depending upon their experience. As one boy said to his counselor, "Miss S, when my generation uses certain words they don't mean what your generation means." To one parent a "reading problem" may mean a serious handicap; to another it may indicate a minor inconvenience. To one parent an IQ may mean predetermined success or failure in life; to another it may be merely "another one of those school ratings."

It is often hard for children and parents to understand the interviewer's language, especially if he talks psychological jargon or "pedagese." In talking with parents, the interviewer should avoid technical words unless they are clearly explained. On the other hand, he should not talk down to parents or children, nor should he use slang or other expressions that might cast doubt on his professional competency.

The interviewer should also avoid wordiness—a rather common fault. The listener gets lost in a morass of unnecessary words. We should all cultivate the art of not saying everything.

The interviewee will not make the effort to communicate his thoughts and feelings unless he expects them to be understood. Unless he believes that whatever he confides will be accepted and held in confidence, he is not likely to speak frankly.

Listening is both an art and a skill. It is perhaps the most neglected aspect of interviewing. Listening is not just keeping still. It is giving wholehearted attention to what the other person is saying—and feeling, insofar as feelings can be inferred. Some interviewers have the art to make the interviewee feel as though he were the most important person in the world for the moment; this manner assures him that what he is saying is worthy of the closest attention.

To be sure that he has heard correctly, the interviewer may from time to time reflect the person's thoughts or feelings. He may ask, "Is this what you meant?" "Am I seeing it your way?" "Am I right about this?" "You feel . . . ?" In this way the interviewer checks his understanding of what the person is trying to communicate. The person may correct, confirm, or modify the interviewer's initial impression.

Inexperienced interviewers who have become enthusiastic about the so-called nondirective approach often try to gain a nondirective effect by merely parroting what the person has just said. This practice may annoy or otherwise disturb the interviewee. He may think, "What's wrong with the way I said it?" Skillful, accurate reflection of feeling, on the other hand, helps the person to understand himself better and gives him confidence in the interviewer's insight.

Unless the interviewer can put himself in the place of the parent or the child and look at things from his point of view, unless he can enter the interviewee's psychological world, he will not be able to understand fully what he is saying and feeling.

The interviewer must be cautious and tentative in his interpretations. He must learn to suspend judgment, to refrain from jumping to conclusions. The effect of excessive or premature interpretation may be to put the other person on his guard. He may feel, "This fellow knows too much about me." One emotionally disturbed boy said that the person he hated most was the psychologist because "he knows so much about me." It is sometimes enlightening to ask the person how he would interpret some thought or feeling that he has expressed.

By showing compassion for the ordeal that the child or parent is undergoing and respect for the resources that each person has within himself, the interviewer encourages the subject to respond as fully and frankly as possible.

At the end of any interview, the person should have a feeling of satisfaction; he should feel that he has profited in some way from the experience.

The time element has important implications for both the interviewer and the person interviewed. Both should be on time. If the student is late, he loses part of his allotted time. Habitually coming late often has diagnostic significance. If the interviewee comes early, he may be expressing anxiety or eagerness; if late, reluctance; if he is invariably on the dot, this may indicate some compulsive tendency.

Some interviewers take no notes but write up the important points immediately after the interview. Others will jot down key words and phrases during the interview to aid them in writing a fuller report later. Still others make a tape recording; this practice frees the interviewer to give his full attention to the client. It is extremely difficult for the interviewer to respond to the person whom he is interviewing and take notes at the same time. Later he will play back the interview to study what the client said, what he himself said, and what he might have said. He will also catch important points that may have slipped his memory. Recording also gives the interviewer the advantage of being able to say to the client later on, "You said this some time ago; how do you feel about it now?" As the interviewer studies the recording, he may note changing patterns or trends in attitudes and performance.

The practice of recording interviews is of special value to persons while they are learning the technique of the interview. They make tape recordings which they can play back, analyze, and discuss with their supervisor. In a reading clinic or center, however, where the purpose is to serve as many clients as possible, it is not feasible to keep verbatim records on each interview; there must be a balance between the time spent in appraising a client and the time spent in helping him.

The interviewer always asks the client's permission to make a recording or to take notes. At first, either form of record keeping may make the interviewee a little self-conscious; however, he soon learns to ignore it. Note taking stimulates some persons to think better; they may even ask, "Why don't you take notes? You may be missing important points." A response of this kind may indicate that the client is genuinely working on his problem with the interviewer.

Any notes or recordings are, of course, to be considered confidential; this fact should be made clear to the client.

SPECIAL PROBLEMS IN INTERVIEWING

If the person has difficulty talking, the interviewer may reflect his feeling by saying, "It's hard to know where to begin." Or he may ask if a few questions would help him to get started. If he gives only the barest answers to these questions, the interviewer may ask him to tell more or to explain a statement more fully. A nod or an expression of interest, such as "Yes, I see" or "That must have been difficult for you," conveys the idea that the interviewer accepts him and encourages him to continue. If he pauses, it is well to give him time to think the matter through. The interviewer should not get impatient or panicky if there is a silence. The interview time is the client's time to use as he wishes.

When the person interviewed talks about irrelevant things, it is usually better not to interrupt him. During the course of his random remarks he may contribute important diagnostic information. However, as already suggested, there are some parents and students who are compulsive talkers. They have rehearsed a sequence trend of thought many times and repeat it over and over like a broken record. Unless the interviewer breaks the circuit, they will make no progress in the interview.

When parents or students complain about other teachers, they create a situation that is hard to handle. When a student complains about a teacher, he may be encouraged to understand the teacher, to put himself in the teacher's place just as a teacher should do with a student.

Parents, too, have to realize that teachers are different; some are more skillful than others and have better personal relations with their students. The interviewer may point out that some teachers are better for certain students than for others. The very sensitive, overconscientious child needs a lenient teacher. The child of ability who is slipping into lazy habits needs a firm teacher who will hold him to appropriate standards of excellence. In the end, such a child will usually appreciate people who make him do what he ought to do.

It is usually better not to take sides with or against the student or parent about a person or an institution. If a mother complains about her husband's treatment of the child, the interviewer should not take sides with either wife or husband. The role of the interviewer is to show a sympathetic understanding of the situation, emphasize any positive aspect of it, and change the subject if necessary by asking a question about another problem. Contradicting the person or arguing with him defeats the purpose of the interview.

In working with emotionally disturbed children, one must set limits and hold them firmly. The interviewer should remember that the child may be frightened by his own aggressiveness. Like other persons, the emotionally disturbed child needs to obtain an image of his most acceptable self, of the kind of person he can become. This goal is best achieved as the interviewer reflects his positive feelings and thoughts. For example, one child who was worried by the thought of being an adopted child made this comment at one point in the interview: "It [being an adopted child] doesn't matter." The reading teacher immediately picked up this positive insight and said, "You're right. It really doesn't matter. Your foster mother loves you very much."

One of the most difficult persons to interview is the student who conceives of himself as a person who cannot learn to read. He comes to the interview with a strong negative evaluation of himself. When asked about his previous instruction in reading, he insists that he "didn't learn nothing." He works halfheartedly on any method suggested or demonstrated by the teacher, almost as though he were trying to prove that he cannot learn to read. Later he may begin to think that he is as good as some others; as one nonreader said, "The other kids can't read neither." When he begins to take a more positive view of himself, the interviewer feels he is making progress.

INTERVIEWS WITH PARENTS

In interviews with parents the general goals are to help them and to get help from them in a mutual effort to understand the child and the conditions that are preventing him from realizing his potential reading ability.

Parents of children who are not realizing their reading potentialities are a valuable source of diagnostic information. Their contribution will supplement the school's factual information on how the child reads. They will give valuable clues about the causes of the child's retardation. Some of these causes lie in the reading habits of the family: there may be few books or magazines in the home or the parents may take a dim view of education in general and reading in particular. Skillful interviews elicit valuable understanding of parent-child relations as well as showing whether the parental attitude toward the child's reading is one of solicitude, anxiety, indifference, or annoyance.

Parents who write readily may give some of this information on a special record form prior to the interview. Reading centers and clinics have their own application blanks that ask for information on family background, education, reading history, and present interests and activities.

The parent fills out the blank if the child is not able to do so. Sometimes parent and child fill it out together. When the child or young person himself writes the information requested, one gains additional information about his writing, spelling, vocabulary, and sentence structure as well as about his attitudes toward himself, toward school, and toward reading.

It is desirable to hold at least two parent conferences while working with a child. The first, at the beginning of a series of interviews, will give much understanding helpful in working with the child. Another conference at the end of the series offers valuable opportunities to review progress and to work out the next steps. For example, in one windup conference the mother asked, "Do you think Helen had better stay in the eighth grade than go ahead to the ninth?" The interviewer did not fall into the trap of giving the mother advice when she was not really ready for it. Instead, he asked such questions as, "Why do you think it might be best for Helen to repeat the eighth grade?" "How do you think Helen would feel about staying in the eighth grade another year?" "What is her relationship with the teacher that she would have if she repeated the grade?" "Does she have many friends in her present class or are most of her friends neighborhood children?" "Is Helen more or less mature physically and socially than other children of her age?" These and other questions helped the mother think through the problem herself.

Some parents come to the school voluntarily to talk with the teacher about their child's reading, usually to complain, sometimes to express appreciation. It was for the latter purpose that Mrs. L came to the school to see her son's young third-grade teacher, who was new to the school. Mrs. L first expressed her dissatisfaction that Billy had not made more progress in reading in the first two grades and criticized the teaching methods that had been used there. She then told Miss J how pleased she was with his progress this year.

The role of the teacher in this interview was:

To show appreciation of the mother's interest in visiting the school

To listen intently to the mother's comments

To explain briefly her methods of work with Billy and give information the mother wanted

To reinforce the mother's positive feelings about Billy's progress and the school situation

To leave the way open for the mother to come in for another conference, if she wanted to come

Quite different was Miss J's role in the telephone conversation with Johnny's mother, who had been annoyed by reports of Johnny's bad behavior. Miss J permitted the mother to express her negative feelings about the school and the teachers. Then she tried several approaches which are usually effective:

She assured the mother that she had not singled out Johnny for exceptional treatment but was having conferences with all the parents and that she had not been influenced by the other teachers' unfavorable comments about Johnny.

As a new teacher she appealed to the mother for help and expressed respect for the mother's superior knowledge of her own child.

She showed consideration for the mother by offering to have the conference at a time convenient to her, either at home or at school.

She pointed out that they were both concerned primarily with helping Johnny.

Despite the teacher's efforts to establish a friendly relationship, the mother persisted in her attitude and refused to make a definite appointment for a conference. In view of the intensity of the mother's attitude, Miss J should have accepted her feeling for the time being and ended the phone call sooner than she did. At another time the mother might have been in a more receptive mood. Then, Miss J and the mother could explore various possible causes of the child's reading difficulty: his physical condition, his social relations, parental attitudes toward the child and toward reading, family conditions such as methods of discipline that might be related to the child's reading development, competing interests and activities, and previous special instruction in reading or other individual help.

This information is best not elicited by a series of staccato questions. The interviewer should start with an unstructured question that invites the parent to present the problem or explain the situation in his own way. From then on, the role of the interviewer is to:

Encourage the parent to continue thinking about the problem.

Ask for clarification of the parent's remarks, e.g., "Can you tell me how he shows his shyness?" "What is it that worries you when he is out?" "How long have you been helping him at home?"

Express sympathetic understanding and appreciation of the parent's efforts, e.g., "That must have been very difficult for you." "You've tried very hard to be helpful to him."

Skillfully conducted interviews with parents develop a great variety of significant information, as shown in the following brief illustrative quotations from interview reports:

PHYSICAL CONDITIONS. M became very ill when in grade 2 with nephritis. He was in a children's hospital for ten weeks and home for quite a while before getting back to school.

In elementary school, B was often ill and his attendance was necessarily poor. Thus, an initial lack of reading skills may have affected his whole history and contributed to the personality difficulty which seems to have blocked any remedial efforts.

PARENT-CHILD AND FAMILY RELATIONS. The father is extremely interested in his girls and fond of them. He claims he practically raised C in the early years, even changing her diapers, etc., because his wife worked even then. He also claims that even now Mrs. M is away from home altogether too much for the good of the girls.

Trouble between the parents began when this girl was a baby, when the father first came home from the army from overseas experience. The parents are now separated.

T's father has very little use for him and associates with him very seldom. T has to go elsewhere for adult male companionship. T's brother is a very fine student and very ambitious. He goes to high school and holds down two jobs. T is very proud of him. T's brother has always called him stupid because he has not been able to do his work. Mother has stopped this though. Mother has great concern for T and wants to do all she can to help him.

A twin brother gives D much competition. The brother is capable, enthusiastic. D has always "let brother do it." Brother reads well. D was retained in first grade while brother passed.

PARENT'S DESCRIPTION OF THE CHILD. The mother feels quite strongly that O is capable of better work at school than she is doing. She characterized her daughter as "boy crazy" and not very willing to study at all. She does no free reading, has poor concentration span, and did not want to come to the clinic for help.

ATTITUDE OF PARENT TOWARD CHILD. The mother indicated her fears for the boy, and stated that regardless of how hard she worked to support him, he did not appreciate it. She added that both she and the older sister tried to help him with his reading, but that he was so stupid they lost patience with him. She said that he was a healthy child who suffered from occasional colds, that he had many personal friends, and that he was satisfied to go through junior high school accumulating a report card full of Fs, "just like in the lower grades."

She brought up the subject of his irresponsible attitude at home, his laziness when asked to help around the house, his constant bickering with the older sister. She added that it was her plan to "get him through ninth grade" so he could enter the auto mechanics course in a nearby senior high school, but she was afraid he was "too dumb to make it."

SCHOOL RELATIONS. E never liked school, even when very little. She completed the third grade at public school without being held back, even after the illness of the previous year. Did well that year although she was behind in reading. Got good school reports, liked the teacher that year.

Fourth grade was at a different school, this time in another borough because she went to live with an aunt while the sister, three years older, remained with the mother through a family crisis. She remained in the fifth and sixth grades at the same school, although she commuted to school when she went back to live with the mother. In the seventh grade she changed to the present school because her mother considered it superior to the one in their own neighborhood.

P suffered from going to a part-time school when the schools were overcrowded. She went only half days in the early grades. She freezes on tests.

Interviewer's Responsibility for Referral. If the child seems to be in need of special help in reading, the interviewer should, first of all, be sure that referral is desirable and necessary. Referral to a clinic or a psychologist often causes anxiety on the part of child and parent. If additional services are clearly needed, it is part of the interviewer's responsibility to give the parent an idea of the treatment process and suggestions about the best way to prepare the child for it.

INTERVIEWS WITH STUDENTS

There are many ways of conducting first interviews with students. With some, a visual screening test may be a good initial approach; with others, it may be better to try an informal conversation, a basic vocabulary test, a chance to choose books on different levels of difficulty, or a reading game. Whatever the approach, the interviewer will be sensitive to the individual's response.

The interviewer will have certain objectives for the interview but will not insist on cramming it into a preconceived frame. During the course of the interview he will obtain information about the student's attitudes toward reading, his ability to learn, his word attack skills, and other factors.

In each interview it is important to give the student some experience of success and then ask him to summarize the procedures by which he reached it. If instruction is given, as indicated by some difficulty detected in the diagnostic procedure, the student will feel he has learned something and the interviewer can see how well the student profits by instruction.

After the interview, the interviewer may ask himself such questions as these:

Did I achieve my objectives?

What information did I obtain that will help me understand the individual's reading capacity, achievement, and difficulties?

How did the individual feel at the end of the interview—did he have a feeling that something had been accomplished?

What were the best features of the interview?

In a similar situation in the future, what might I do differently?

Exploratory Interview

In the first contact, exploration is mutual. It is natural for a student to be reticent at the beginning of the first interview. He wants to find out what kind of person the interviewer is, whether he can be trusted, and whether the interviewer is willing to work with a person like him. The reputation that the interviewer has built up with other students helps this student decide whether he can talk frankly, freely, and easily to him.

The interviewer should always know the person's name and something about his present dissatisfaction with his reading. The application blank or cumulative record often gives clues to the best approach to use and to areas to explore or avoid. The interviewer does not begin by asking "What's your name?" and "What is your problem?" A good approach is to let the person start any way or anywhere he desires—let him present himself and his problem in his own way.

In addition to establishing a mutual relation of trust and respect, the exploratory interview should also give some idea of the individual's reading difficulty and the factors that are contributing to it. For example, in one case the child got off to a poor start in the primary grades. His first instruction in phonics did not "take." In the second grade he had some instruction in sounding out words, with special emphasis on initial sounds. He read better in the third and fourth grades but did not have the help he needed in the fifth. The sixth-grade teacher taught him to use the dictionary. In the seventh grade he learned to divide words into syllables, studied vocabulary, and did appropriate exercises in the SRA reading laboratories. In his present grade, the eighth, he has a period of reading each day.

Despite all the special help he had received, he was unable to meet the reading requirements of his grade. In the exploratory interview, the interviewer obtained several indications of an unwillingness to grow up. His father treated him as though he were a much younger child; the boy showed no initiative in volunteering information or suggestions; he insisted that none of the remedial work had improved his reading.

An exploratory interview with a nonreading student was described in some detail by Bullock:

Interview with Charles

This boy was an unprepossessing client of a welfare agency with a long record of truancy, referred to the worker for help in reading. Half an hour after the time for the scheduled interview, the worker had almost given up hope of seeing the boy when the secretary ushered in a sullen-looking boy of fourteen and a determined-looking girl of about seventeen.

Worker: Are you Charles?
Client: Yeah.
Sister: And I'm his sister. He wasn't going to come, so I brought him.
C: I was too (savagely).
W: Well, anyway, thanks for bringing him. How old are you, Charles?
C: Thirteen.
S: He'll be fourteen next month.
W: I see. Well, tell me, why did you come here?
C: Oh, Mr. _____. What's his name?
W: Simpson?
C: He told me to come here for reading.
S: Every Monday he told him to come here. (Sister leaves.)
W: Well, now, why did Mr. Simpson tell you to come here?
C: I dunno. He told me to come here to learn, you know, both speaking and how to read.
W: I see. Have you been having trouble with both speech and reading?
C: Yeah. I have like hoarse, like a hoarse voice.
W: Yes? How did it happen?
C: I don't know.
W: Has it always been that way?
C: I have it for three years or four.
W: Three years or four. . . . Did you have a cold or get sick or something? Did that bring it on?
C: I had a cold and every time I talk I get a hoarse voice.
W: Well, how about reading?
C: I don't know how to read big words; I just know how to read four letters, three letter words.
W: Always had trouble?
C: Yeah. Since I started school.
W: What grade are you in now?

C: Seventh.

W: Seventh. Let's see, thirteen. . . . You missed one year somewhere. Which year was that?

C: Last year I was in the seventh, you know, I didn't go to school and I used to play hooky and then I got back to the seventh again.

W: I see, last year. And how's your attendance been this year? A little better, or about the same?

C: Same.

W: About the same. Is it because you don't like school? Or are there things outside that you'd rather do?

C: School.

W: Tell me about school.

C: Like I don't know how to read, so the teacher gives us a test and I don't like to go when they give a test. Sometimes they give you a reading test and I don't know how to do it, I just sit there.

W: I can see why you wouldn't like that. . . . Tell me some more about school.

C: I like to do arithmetic, but sometimes like when they give a test on arithmetic, they give like fractions and I don't know how to do that and I sit down, and then the teacher comes around and sometimes he hits me and sometimes scolds me.

W: Does that happen often?

C: Like sometimes when the class is reading, so the teacher tells me to read, and like I don't know how to read, he tells me, "What was you doing, playing?" And then he hits me. . . .

W: You like arithmetic. (C nods.) Because you can do it. Now, let's see. How do you feel about English?

C: No, I don't like that.

W: Why?

C: The teacher doesn't show you how to read. They just give you the book and then they tell you to read.

W: They just tell you to read. What sort of books do they give you?

C: Like fifth year books, you know, but they have big words, nine, eight letters, like that.

W: Some of the words are hard. Do they tell you what they are?

C: No.

W: Do you ask the teacher what the words are?

C: No. He says, "You should know."

W: Do your friends tell you?

C: Yeah, like if the teacher sees my friends tell me, the teacher comes over, you know, hits my friend.

W: Oh, for talking. That's too bad. . . . Well, how about social studies?

C: I don't like that either.
W: What is it about?
C: Anything like, you know, about Christopher Columbus and explorers and all that.
W: And what do you have to do in that class?
C: The teacher takes the book and writes, you know, on the board and then we take and copy it in the notebook.
W: You don't mind that as much as the other?
C: No, that I like, you know. I like to write. . . . (Bullock, 1956, pp. 45–49)

In this initial contact the interviewer presented himself as a sympathetic, understanding person and obtained a vivid impression of the boy's school experiences and extreme difficulty in reading. He did nothing to increase the boy's sense of failure. To nonreading students, tests are almost always a threat. To obtain some idea of their reading ability, one may start with familiar signs and directions and then proceed to paragraphs of gradually increasing difficulty. Instead of continuing to test up to the individual's frustration level, it is better to stop at the instructional level and teach the student how to overcome some specific difficulty that he recognizes at that level.

More able learners may be encouraged to analyze their reading problem and suggest procedures that they think may be helpful. It is naturally difficult for them to detect emotional factors or personality traits that may interfere with their reading achievement.

Diagnostic Interview

Although also somewhat exploratory in nature, the definitely diagnostic interview tries to assess more systematically many aspects of a student's reading. The interview may be presented to the student as an opportunity for him to explore his reading. An individual who talks freely will often answer many of the questions that the interviewer has in mind. If he does not mention them directly, the interviewer can often follow up on some clue the student has given and thus avoid abruptly asking for the information he wants. In this informal way, the interviewer may learn about intellectual, social, and emotional conditions that may be related to the student's reading and note any obvious visual or auditory difficulties (see Chapter 9).

By giving the student a book from which he can select a passage to read silently, the interviewer will gain information such as the following:

How does the student explore a book?
What kind of article or story does he select?
Does he pause to think after reading the title?
Does he vary his rate of reading with the kind of material and with his purpose?
Does he stop to think while reading it?
What did he get out of it? How well did he organize the ideas?
How accurate was his report? Was it appropriate to the nature of the article or story?
Did he relate it to other books he has read or to his experiences?

Questions about his reading interests grow naturally out of the article or story he selected.

If he is asked how he spent his time during the previous school day and over the last weekend, he may reveal much about his recreational interests, study methods, voluntary reading, friends, etc. (see the section on Daily Schedule in Chapter 5).

While the student is reading a short selection aloud or silently, the interviewer may elicit such comments as the following:

I used to read good, but now I don't know what's happened to me. I used to like arithmetic, but now I'm lousy at it.

I know what the words are but I just can't get them out. When I run across words like that, I think of all kinds of words it might be but reject them immediately when I know they are incorrect.

Therapeutic Interview (Ephron, 1953)

When an individual is not receptive to reading instruction, counseling or psychotherapy is indicated. This is the province of the specially trained person. Sometimes a reading teacher or specialist who is also trained in clinical psychology or a psychologist who has had additional training in reading can handle certain of these cases, using whatever technique seems appropriate at a given stage in the treatment.

EVALUATION OF STUDENT PROGRESS

In a series of interviews one should be able to observe movement in desirable directions. More expansive voluntary contributions on the part of an initially unresponsive person or an increase in initiative on the part of an immature youngster is usually a sign of progress. Greater enjoyment of reading, a growing list of words recognized at sight, and increased skill in comprehension are other indications of improvement. In one case, for example, during a semester in which the boy was interviewed once a week, the following changes were noted:

On the Iowa Silent Reading Test, an increase from the 26th percentile to the 61st percentile

Observed changes in attitude—less anxiety, greater composure, less self-depreciation, more confidence in several areas

Changes in approach to reading situations, greater eagerness to read, more voluntary reading

Day-by-day improvement in comprehension on reading exercises such as those in the Science Research Reading Laboratories

Extension of the areas in which the student is able to concentrate

Increasing ability to analyze the reading methods that brought him success and to use them in new situations

More ability to perceive the reasons for the mistakes he was making

Changes in the parents' understanding of and attitudes toward the boy

CONCLUDING STATEMENT

Desirable changes in the student may be due to many factors, some of them related to the interview situation. The atmosphere of the interview is more permissive than the classroom atmosphere. Too often teachers have been critical, indifferent, or too persistent in their efforts to help. In a secure interview relationship, the student may obtain emotional release from anxiety and tension. By accepting him without criticism, the interviewer helps him to accept himself. In a successful counseling relationship, the student tends to become more hopeful and positive in his thinking.

Increasingly, cultural influences, the personality of the interviewer, the interaction between interviewer and interviewee, and their purposes and values are being recognized in guidance ("Guidance," 1962). These factors are equally important in working with reading cases.

Suggested Problems
Practice and Demonstration

1. Read several application blanks and cumulative records from a school. Discuss the possible significance of each item from the standpoint of the student's reading performance. Show how the initial impression thus gained might be used in the first interview.

2. Read several recorded initial interviews, one student reading the counselor's part, another reading the student's responses. Begin with an interview with an inexperienced teacher and work up to more expert interviews. Discuss each dramatized reading from the standpoint of the student being interviewed, the understanding gained by the interviewer, and the specific points of interview techniques.

3. Have a panel of parents discuss before a group of teachers or prospective teachers the kind of interviews they would like to have with teachers.

4. Read several different kinds of interviews, stopping at certain points to let the students suggest responses they think the interviewer might have made at that point. Then compare the suggested responses with the responses the expert interviewer actually made.

5. What might be the purposes of the initial interview?

6. What approaches might be most effective with different kinds of students and parents?

7. When and how might tests or inventories be introduced in a series of interviews?

8. Observe the following characteristics of an individual during an interview or individual testing situation:

   a. Personal appearance—signs of neglect of cleanliness, grooming; clothes extremely different from other people's of same age, old-fashioned, bizarre, etc.

   b. Posture and expressive movements—how he walks, stands, sits; fidgets, moves hands nervously, has nervous tics, mannerisms, etc.

c. Habitual facial expression—sad, anxious, tense, cheerful, fatigued, etc.

d. Ways of talking—rapid or slow, hesitant or fluent, long pauses, uncommunicative, etc.

e. Quality of verbal expression and response—vivid, apt, picturesque or incoherent, dull; good vocabulary, meager vocabulary, etc.

f. Attitude toward examiner or counselor—overdependent or hostile, suspicious, uncooperative or cooperative, self-centered or considerate, impatient, etc.

g. Reaction to difficulty—immediate reaction to difficulty, effect of failure on some items of subsequent performance, rationalization or other mechanisms used to explain failure

h. Reaction to success

References

Bullock, Harrison: *The Non-reading Pupil in High School,* Bureau of Publications, Teachers College, Columbia University, New York, 1956.

Ephron, Beulah K.: *Emotional Difficulties in Reading,* The Julian Press, New York, 1953.

"Guidance—An Examination," a special issue, *Harvard Educational Review,* 32:373–501, Fall, 1962.

Strang, Ruth: *Counseling Techniques in College and Secondary School,* 2d ed., Harper & Row, Publishers, Incorporated, New York, 1949, chap. 5.

Suggested Readings

Frank, George H., and Anders Sweetland: "A Study of the Process of Psychotherapy: The Verbal Interaction," *Journal of Consulting Psychology,* 26:135–138, April, 1962.

Howe, Edmond S., and Benjamin Pope: "Therapist Verbal Activity Level and Diagnostic Utility of Patient Verbal Responses," *Journal of Consulting Psychology,* 26:149–155, April, 1962.

Lowrance, Robert Bruce: *The Development and Application of a Method of Analyzing the Reading Interview,* unpublished doctoral dissertation, Teachers College, Columbia University, New York, 1960.

Moore, Mary R., and W. James Popham: "Effect of Two Interview

Techniques on Academic Achievement," *Journal of Counseling Psychology,* 7:176–179, Fall, 1960.

Quast, Wentworth: "The Bender Gestalt: A Clinical Study of Children's Records," *Journal of Consulting Psychology,* 25:405–408, October, 1961.

Roby, D. L.: "Learning about Pupils: Non-test Tools and Their Uses," *Teachers College Record,* 31:65–66, December, 1959.

~~~~~~

13

PROJECTIVE METHODS

Projective methods furnish keys to some of the deeper determinants of reading development. They may give glimpses of potential mental ability, of a personality structure capable either of preventing or of promoting reading achievement, and of personal relationships that are influencing the individual's behavior for the better or for the worse. Projective methods are primarily concerned with the psychodynamics of personality. This is the unique contribution of projective techniques to the diagnosis of reading difficulties.

The special feature of projective methods is that they present an unstructured situation, i.e., a situation for which the individual has no ready-made or habitual response (Sargent, 1945; Shaffer and Shoben, 1956, pp. 334, 342). The stimulus may take the form of clay or some other plastic material to be manipulated, cloud pictures, ink blots, pictures of people in ambiguous situations, incomplete sentences or stories, or other media. To these unstructured materials the individual makes his own unique response and thus reveals himself.

The results of projective techniques can be used in planning remedial work, in the day-by-day contacts with the individual, and in the evaluation of changes that have taken place in his attitudes and personal relationships. As with all the other techniques described in this book, the impressions gained from projective methods should be checked against all the other available information about the student.

PROJECTIVE METHODS ON THREE LEVELS

Projective methods may be classified on three levels according to the degree of specific clinical training required. The first involves life situations. Whenever an individual is confronted with a new problem, he reveals himself to some extent through his behavior. Observations such as a teacher might make over a period of time will show the individual's characteristic ways of coping with life situations. One child will be eager and curious, another suspicious and hostile, still another apathetic and withdrawn. Their casual comments may give some clues as to the motivations that lie behind their behavior and their relations with parents, brothers, and sisters.

The second level is more technical. On this level the reading teacher may use certain projective techniques with individuals or with groups. Examples are the incomplete sentence or story; the ambiguous picture; the draw-a-person, house, and tree technique; the three-wishes question; the question "Who are you?" The teacher interprets the student's responses to any of these stimuli as he would interpret any other significant observed word or action. An experienced psychologist or psychiatrist might find deeper meaning in the responses.

The third and most technical level includes projective techniques such as the Rorschach (Rorschach, 1942; Sargent, 1945) and the Thematic Apperception Test (TAT) (Bellak and Bellak, 1949; Murray, 1943; Schneidman, 1949; Symonds, 1948). These tests must be administered and interpreted by persons with a clinical background and special training in projective techniques. The reading teacher may request a clinical examination, including these projective methods, to elucidate questions such as these:

Is there a discrepancy between the individual's potential and his functioning capacity?

What possible personality factors may be interfering with better functioning?

How strong is his achievement motivation? Does he desire achievement to strengthen his self-esteem, to win approval and love, to compete successfully with a rival, or for some other reason?

If he shows little ambition, what values have replaced a desire for success?

Why does he lack creative energy? Is his creative energy being shunted off into blind alleys?

Are conflicts and tensions making it impossible for him to function effectively?

Is he insecure and depressed about his relations to others?

What treatment is indicated by the report on the projective methods?

The Rorschach is said to throw light on the personality structure and on the adaptations that the individual has made as a result of his interaction with his environment. The TAT supplements the Rorschach by showing the specific ways in which the individual's personality expresses itself in a number of imagined situations. By studying and comparing the individual's total responses to the Rorschach and the TAT, a perceptive clinician may arrive at a personality picture that suggests promising ways of dealing with the case.

EXAMPLES OF INFORMAL PROJECTIVE METHODS

The reading teacher may use a number of informal projective methods to supplement his observation of the student in groups and in interviews. Recognizing that he must have the student's interest and cooperation in order to get authentic results, he will present any of these stimulus situations on a voluntary basis. He will also be cautious in using any of these techniques in communities where parents object to the school's collecting any kind of personal data. In interpreting an individual's responses to these techniques, the teacher will also avoid delving into deeply hidden meanings.

Incomplete Sentences

The following form of the incomplete sentence technique was prepared especially for reading cases (Strang and others, 1961, pp. 322–323):

Date_____Grade_____Name_____

Directions: Complete the following sentences to express how you really feel. There are no right answers or wrong answers. Put down what first comes into your mind. Work as quickly as you can.

1. Today I feel _____
2. When I have to read, I _____
3. I get angry when _____
4. To be grown up _____
5. My idea of a good time _____
6. I wish my parents knew _____
7. School is_____
8. I can't understand why _____
9. I feel bad when _____
10. I wish teachers _____
11. I wish my mother_____
12. Going to college _____
13. To me, books_____
14. People think I _____
15. I like to read about_____
16. On weekends, I _____
17. I don't know how _____
18. To me, homework _____
19. I hope I'll never _____
20. I wish people wouldn't _____
21. When I finish high school_____
22. I'm afraid_____
23. Comic books _____
24. When I take my report card home _____

25. I am at my best when _____
26. Most brothers and sisters _____
27. I'd rather read than _____
28. When I read math _____
29. The future looks _____
30. I feel proud when _____
31. I wish my father _____
32. I like to read when _____
33. I would like to be _____
34. For me, studying _____
35. I often worry about_____
36. I wish I could _____
37. Reading science _____
38. I look forward to _____
39. I wish someone would help me _____
40. I'd read more if _____
41. Special help in reading_____
42. Every single word is _____
43. My eyes _____
44. The last book I read _____
45. My mother helps _____
46. Reading in junior high school _____
47. My father thinks reading _____
48. I read better than _____
49. My father helps _____
50. I would like to read better than _____

These incomplete sentences have elicited from young adolescents responses such as the following:

Today I feel (good because we don't have any homework) (tired).

When I have to read, I (do something else instead) (make myself comfortable) (don't mind it).

I get angry when (my father insults me).

My idea of a good time (is going to a school dance) (is to do just what you want).

I wish my parents knew (me better) (I wasn't smart) (that I really love them) (that I try to do my best of everything) (what I really think about things).

I feel bad when (people make fun of me) (I'm not being noticed) (my mother goes away for a long time) (my mother makes me dance in front of her guests) (my mother hits me) (I get a low mark on a test).

I wish teachers (would keep their word more often) (had more sense of humor) (would make things just a little clearer) (were stricter, some of them).

To me, books (are O.K., though school books aren't as interesting as free reading books) (are a source of pleasure) (are fascinating) (carry me into places and relax me).

On weekends, I (hate to read) (like to play with my friends) (like to stay in bed) (like to go out with my family).

I wish people wouldn't (think I am stupid) (blame me for things I don't do) (start war) (prosecute me so) (make fun of me).

I'm afraid (of poison spiders) (of high places) (of reading new words).

Comic books (are fun to read) (are fun but noneducational) (set me in a much happier mood) (are getting worse and worse every day).

I'd rather read than (write) (watch TV sometimes) (do math) (jump off Brooklyn Bridge) (go to bed) (go to the dentist).

I like to read when (I have around two hours spare time) (I have knowbody to play with on a hot day) (I am board) (the book is interesting).

I'd read more if (I had more free time) (my eyes were better) (the books were ones I picked) (I didn't watch television) (I was smarter) (I made myself read) (I wasn't made to read) (I could find better books).

In reading through an individual's responses, the teacher becomes aware of certain recurring themes. Sometimes these relate to physical conditions such as feeling tired, "like to stay in bed," and would read more "if my eyes were better." Many responses relate to family relations: "My father insults me"; "I wish my parents knew that I really love them"; "My mother hits me"; "My mother goes away for a long time." The sentences relating specifically to reading often give insight into the individual's attitude toward books and reading and reveal some of the difficulties he is having. Information of this kind, in conjunction with classroom observation and the analysis of test results, helps the teacher to individualize his program of reading instruction.

Informal Projective Picture Stories

Any picture that portrays some person with whom the individual can identify or some situation into which he can project himself is suitable for this purpose. Advertisements and cover pictures of popular magazines can be used effectively. The directions for responding may be as follows:

What do you think is happening in this picture? Who are the people? What are they thinking? How are they feeling? What do you think will happen next?

A seventh-grade teacher, Carrie E. Hammil, reported a response made by an Indian boy to this technique. The picture was a photograph of the Golden Gate Bridge in the fog, with a subdued sun like an immense full moon shining through the suspension cables. The class discussed the picture and suggested several topic sentences for a paragraph about it. Then each student wrote a paragraph about the picture. The Indian boy who wrote the following paragraph seemed rather dull in most of his work; he is much larger and somewhat older than his classmates. He speaks seldom; when he does, his voice is so low as to be almost inaudible. He sits hunched over his desk as though afraid of missing a word. Yet, at other times, he is apt to lose interest in what is going on and begin disturbing his classmates. In this paragraph, unchanged in spelling and grammar, he revealed a previously unsuspected creativity and depth of thought:

> The fog maks the bridge look like it starts nowere and goes nowhere. It is almost like life wich ends and starts agen and we do not no wer it was befor it come to us or wat we was befor we come to live this time. If it was no foggie we culd no look at the sun. But wen it is fogie we can look at the sun and no burn our eyes maybe life is like that too. When we die is it fogie and we get to see wat the sun is?

This response to the picture has an almost Biblical, poetic rhythm and quality, and the analogy between something seen and something spiritual is unusual for a boy of this age. The philosophy of life, expressed spontaneously, is also unusual.

Children's Own Drawings and Paintings

In another projective approach, the student draws his own pictures. The freest and most tension-releasing medium is finger painting. In finger painting the child freely applies pastelike colors with his fingers, hands, and even his arms to make any designs he fancies. From both finger painting and the more conventional spontaneous drawings and paintings of children, the teacher may gain clues of personality traits from the choice of subject, the colors, the size of the figures, the lines and outlines (faint and weak or bold and strong), and other combinations of elements in the drawing.

In interpreting children's drawings, one must know about the situation in which the drawing was made and the child's own interpretation of it. The teacher must resist the temptation to read into them far more than is warranted. To safeguard against over-interpretation, he should check his ideas about the drawings with all the available information about the child.

The Machover draw-a-figure test (Machover, 1950) is a useful source of diagnostic information. In this test the child is asked to draw a picture of a person. In a modified form of the test, he may also be asked to answer such questions as these about the person he has drawn:

1. What is the person doing?
2. How old is the person?
3. What grade is this person in?
4. Is the person good looking?
5. What are this person's worst physical features?
6. What are this person's best physical features?
7. What are this person's best personal characteristics?
8. What are this person's worst traits?
9. What makes this person angry?
10. What makes this person happy?
11. Will this person marry?
12. What type of person will this person marry?
13. If this person were given three wishes, what would he wish?

In using this technique with nonreaders, the teacher can ask the questions orally and write the answers each student gives. One emotionally disturbed child drew a robot whose appearance was quite sinister. The fact that the child gave his own age as the robot's age suggests that he might be identifying with his drawing. His response to the question about three wishes indicated a type of emotional disturbance whose presence the interviewer was able to confirm after further work with him. The child's three wishes were (1) to rule the earth, (2) to be master on his planet, and (3) to have everything he ever wanted.

The draw-a-person technique has been extended to include drawing a family, a house, a tree. In the drawing of the family, primitive stick figures may suggest immaturity; aimless activity, such as figures shooting in all directions, may suggest personal or family disorganization; a mighty woman who towers over a puny father and a still more diminutive child may suggest a domineering mother—or rather a mother whom the child perceives as domineering. In drawing a house, some children carefully build a fence all around it, perhaps as an expression of a desire to be let alone. These and other interpretations are made *very* tentatively. They are valuable in alerting the teacher to watch for certain kinds of behavior as he observes the child in his daily contacts with him.

A quite different type of test which has proved very useful in reading diagnosis is the Revised Bender Visual Motor Gestalt Test (Pascal and Luttell, 1944–1960). It tells much to the skilled clinician. In the drawing of the forms the child may show reversal tendencies, figures that suggest neurological disorganization, wavy lines that help to convince an unsympathetic teacher of the child's lack of visual-motor coordination and control.

CONCLUDING STATEMENT

Used as part of a clinical procedure or as one of many techniques of observation in the classroom, the projective methods contribute to the understanding of the more subtle factors that are involved in reading cases. The contribution of these techniques is limited by an absence of norms; we cannot compare the individual's responses with average behavior for other students of the same age and similar background. Inferences should not be drawn from separate items but from patterns of test responses interpreted in the light of all the available background knowledge about the individual.

Suggested Problems
Practice and Demonstration

1. Have the teacher-education class take one or more of the simple projective tests. This will give the students a feeling for the way individuals may be thinking when they are responding to such non-structured or slightly structured tests.

2. Present to the class several of the results of projective tests obtained from children of different ages. Ask the class to write their

interpretations and compare them with those made by a clinical psychologist with special background in projective techniques.

3. Present a reading case in which results of the Rorschach and TAT tests were included. Discuss the contribution of the projective tests to the understanding of the case. To what extent did the projective techniques reinforce impressions gained from other sources or add new understanding?

4. Examine a number of children's drawings, preferably in crayon, paint, or finger painting. Ask the class to speculate about the characteristics suggested by the paintings. Compare their descriptions with known characteristics of the children.

5. Summarize pros and cons about the validity and reliability of projective techniques.

6. Make a study of the three-wishes technique or paintings by the same children over a period of years; compare these findings with their reading development.

7. Give the draw-a-figure test as described by Machover to a class of children and study its usefulness in understanding their reading problems.

References

Bellak, L., and Sonya S. Bellak: *Children's Apperception Test,* C.P.S. Company, New York, 1949.

Machover, Karen: *Personality Projection in the Drawing of the Human Figure; A Method of Personality Investigation,* Charles C. Thomas, Publisher, Springfield, Ill., 1950.

Murray, H. A.: *Thematic Apperception Test,* Harvard University Press, Cambridge, Mass., 1943.

Pascal, Gerald R., and Barbara J. Luttell: *Visual Motor Gestalt Test,* for ages 4 and over; commonly called *Bender Motor Gestalt Test,* Grune & Stratton, Inc., New York, 1944–1960.

Rorschach, H.: *Psychodiagnostics,* 2d ed., Verlag Hans Huber, Berne, Switzerland, 1942.

Sargent, Helen: "Projective Methods: Their Origins, Theory, and Application in Personality Research," *Psychological Bulletin,* 42: 275–293, May, 1945.

Schneidman, E. S.: *Make a Picture Story (MAPS) Test,* Psychological Corporation, New York, 1949.

Shaffer, Laurance F., and Edward J. Shoben: *The Psychology of Adjustment,* 2d ed., Houghton Mifflin Company, Boston, 1956.

Strang, Ruth, and others: *The Improvement of Reading,* 3d ed., McGraw-Hill Book Company, Inc., New York, 1961.

Symonds, P. M.: *Symonds Picture-story Test,* Bureau of Publications, Teachers College, Columbia University, New York, 1948.

Suggested Readings

Abet, L. E., and L. Bellak (eds.): *Projective Psychology,* Grove Press, Inc., New York, 1959.

Alexander, Theron: "The Adult-Child Interaction Test: A Projective Test for Use in Research," *Monographs of the Society for Research in Child Development,* series 55, vol. 17, no. 2, 1952, Child Development Publications, Champaign, Ill., 1955.

Eiserer, Paul E.: "Group Psychotherapy," *Journal of the National Association of Deans of Women,* 19:113–122, March, 1956.

Moustakas, Clark E.: "Frequency and Intensity of Negative Attitudes Expressed in Play Therapy: A Comparison of Well-adjusted and Disturbed Young Children," *Journal of Genetic Psychology,* 86: 309, June, 1955.

14

<hr>

INTERPRETATION AND
SYNTHESIS OF INFORMATION

The process of interpreting and synthesizing case data goes on continuously as one works with an individual, as well as at the end of a formal diagnostic study. As the teacher works with the student or the clinician works with the client, he gains increasing understanding of the reading process and sensitivity to the individual case. As he learns more and more about the case, he constantly evaluates and reevaluates his diagnostic formulation. The process is somewhat comparable to making an oil painting: The initial sketchy outline is gradually filled in with details which are often painted over as the artist gains fresh insights.

SUGGESTIONS FROM COUNSELING, PSYCHOTHERAPY, AND MEDICINE

Some suggestions for diagnosis of reading development have come from research on counseling procedures. Koester (1951, pp. 473–486) asked counselors to "think out loud" before a microphone while they read case materials and made diagnoses. He found that diagnostic understanding emerged slowly rather than suddenly. It seemed to proceed in an orderly way from examination of the available data to interpretation of it to formulation of hypotheses and finally to the evaluation of these hypotheses in the light of the data available. He implied that his counselors performed least well when they adopted a particular "set" toward a given case—when they attempted to make the person fit into a particular category or a preconceived theory.

Dressel (1954, pp. 4–7), after listening to tape recordings of professional counselors working with college freshmen, concluded that the counselor should be less concerned with understanding the client and more concerned with helping him understand himself. The goal of counseling is not to give the counselor more information about the client, but rather to give the client more understanding of himself. Self-understanding and self-acceptance will ultimately give him greater self-sufficiency in handling his problems with his own resources. The Self-appraisal Program of Guidance in the Philadelphia schools is an attempt to carry out this philosophy of self-appraisal. Both Koester's and Dressel's suggestions for counselors are equally applicable to reading teachers.

The psychotherapist seeks to ascertain both the nature of the client's difficulties and the general state of his health; he tries to identify potential strength. In using his diagnosis in treatment, he often finds that by strengthening and integrating the ego, the individual will be better able to meet his difficulties. In his treatment, the psychotherapist capitalizes on the client's innate striving for wholeness. At the same time, he is concerned with whatever is causing an interruption of the normal learning process and with removing these blocks so that the client may resume learning.

Another parallel may be found in medicine. In making a medical diagnosis a physician first obtains the facts about the patient from his history, from physical examination, and from laboratory tests. Second, he evaluates the relative importance of the signs and symptoms that he has noted. Third, he tries to see what disease, if any, the signs and symptoms indicate. He considers combinations of symptoms in conjunction with combinations of diseases, not just separate symptoms in relation to separate diseases. In addition, the physician also has a "feeling about the case" based on intuition and general impressions. A complex combination of reasoning and "educated guessing" is involved both in the diagnosing of the case and in determining the optimum therapy.

Ledley and Lusted (1959, pp. 9–21) describe how symbolic logic, "probabilistic concepts," and value theory may enter into a medical diagnosis. An important difference between the medical case and the counseling case is that in the former the responsibility for understanding rests much more heavily on the doctor than on the patient; in counseling, it is self-understanding that is therapeutic. Reading diagnosis may lie somewhere between counseling and medical practice. Although the procedures used in counseling and medicine may seem too complicated to apply to reading cases, the fact remains that reading clinicians should put more emphasis on understanding patterns of signs and symptoms in relation to the individual's total reading development and possible difficulties.

SIGNIFICANCE OF ITEMS OF INFORMATION

Interpretation involves knowledge of the possible significance of each kind of diagnostic information.

Parents' Name and Residence

The parents' name often suggests a particular racial, religious, or national background which may be associated with certain cultural characteristics. However, the teacher or counselor should avoid jumping to the conclusion that any particular individual has the common attitude or characteristics of the group.

To one who is familiar with the community, the student's address is significant; it gives a clue as to the family's socioeconomic status and the cultural level of the neighborhood. Some children live in environments that not only fail to stimulate worthwhile reading interests but actually discourage intellectual pursuits.

Facts about the Family

The marital status of the parents and the composition of the family raise questions that can only be answered by further study. For example, there is no conclusive evidence about the influence of a broken home. Its effect on the child depends upon a number of factors, such as the degree of antagonism between the parents and, in the case of death, whether the deceased parent suffered a prolonged illness. The low economic status of the family and certain parent-child relationships may markedly affect a child's reading development (see Chapter 12).

Similarly, in cases where the mother is employed outside the home, the effect of this circumstance depends on such factors as the age of the child, the financial need of the family, whether the child has been able to secure a satisfactory mother substitute, the parent-child relationships, the family's health, the attitude of the father toward the mother's working, and the mother's satisfaction in her work. Any disturbing family conditions may inhibit a child's desire to learn to read or decrease his interest in reading at a strategic time.

School Marks

The cumulative record of the student's marks lends itself to various kinds of interpretation. Ups and downs suggest a degree of sensitivity to conditions in school or outside. High marks in mathematics and science and low marks in English and social studies often suggest a reading problem. The trend in marks is also important; is the student doing better or worse each year? The relation of the teacher's marks to the standardized test scores in the same subject is also enlightening. If the mark is higher than the score, this may indicate a personality that is pleasing to the teacher or a great deal of home study. If the score is higher, this may indicate exactly the reverse.

Intelligence Test Scores

As we have already noted in Chapter 11, a poor reader's scores on group intelligence tests that require much reading ability do not give an accurate prediction of his learning capacity or reading potentiality. We must not, therefore, overemphasize the relation between low group intelligence test scores and reading potential. As presently constituted, group intelligence test scores largely reflect the individual's present attainment. Recognizing this, the teacher will not take a fatalistic attitude toward a low IQ. He will reserve judgment until he sees what progress the student makes under the best possible instruction. If he learns, fine; if he does not learn, the teacher tries other methods and instructional materials.

Within the same IQ range, pupils show much variation in performance. Too often the teacher either expects these "slow-learning" pupils to do the impossible or does not expect them to do as much as they can. He needs (1) to know what they can learn and the methods by which they can learn, (2) to set appropriate curricular goals, and (3) to provide suitable instructional materials.

With children who show extreme distractibility, overactivity, general disorganization, and other signs of possible brain injury, the simple draw-a-person test and the Bender Visual Motor Gestalt Test in addition to the Stanford-Binet Individual Intelligence Test give much insight to the skilled clinician who has used this same combination of methods with many children.

Listening Comprehension

The student's score on a listening comprehension test contributes much to the interpretation of his potential reading ability. If his listening comprehension is significantly higher than his reading comprehension of similar material, the prognosis for improvement in reading is favorable (see section on Tests of Listening Comprehension in Chapter 11).

Results of Reading Tests

An analysis of the student's performance on reading tests, both standardized and informal, can be used to answer such questions as these: How does his reading achievement compare with his mental ability? What books can he read independently; which would only frustrate his attempts to read them? Where does his difficulty lie—in inability to recognize instantly the Dolch basic vocabulary, to apply word recognition skills in solving unfamiliar words, to comprehend the author's literal meaning, to interpret, to make inferences and generalizations, to appreciate and use the material he reads?

DIAGNOSTIC SUMMARY OF A READING CASE

The following is an example of a traditional detailed diagnosis, analysis, and interpretation of the reading skills of a twelve-year-old boy (Tanyzer, 1956):

John entered kindergarten at the age of four years nine months. His teacher described him as "of average size, left-handed, right-eyed, babyish in speech, nervous during testing." His responses suggested immaturity. During this first year of school he was absent about one-third of the time.

His parents were of Irish descent. His father was foreman in a factory; his mother, a housewife. He had a brother thirteen years old in the eighth grade and a sister four years old. English was spoken in the home.

On the Monroe Reading Aptitude Test, which he took during the spring of his year in kindergarten, he scored high on the language part of the test, almost average on the visual section, and very low in auditory, motor, and articulation abilities:

Part of test	Percentile
Language	85
Visual	42
Auditory	4
Motor	13
Articulation	19

Since auditory and visual discrimination are prerequisite to phonic instruction, a child who is deficient in these two skills is likely to have difficulty when the visual-auditory approach to beginning reading is used.

The Keystone Visual Screening Test showed good visual acuity and revealed no eye defects. The speech consultant reported no hearing loss in either ear but a functional lisp and some difficulty with s and with blends such as thr and str. However, he could produce sounds correctly if he observed and imitated the way the teacher produced them. He needed to learn the difference between related voiced and voiceless sounds, i.e., s-z, b-d, k-g; to recognize long and short vowel sounds and diphthongs; and to learn how to use organs of articulation in producing these sounds.

On the Iowa Silent Reading Test (elementary form) given when John was in the sixth grade, his grade scores were:

Reading comprehension	3.0
Vocabulary	2.8
Total	2.9

At the same time his grade level on the Gray Oral Reading Paragraphs was 3.1. On the Durrell-Sullivan Reading Capacity Test (Intermediate), which is composed entirely of pictures and uses the child's ability to understand spoken language as a measure of his capacity to read, his scores were as follows:

Word meaning—understanding of spoken words:

Grade equivalent	7–8 plus
Age equivalent	13–4 plus

Paragraph meaning:

Grade equivalent	8–6
Age equivalent	14–4

Total:

Grade equivalent	8–3
Age equivalent	13–9

These results definitely indicate superior ability and high reading capacity. The gap between his reading level and his capacity level —the degree of retardation—is great. This discrepancy is confirmed by the results of the Wechsler Intelligence Scale for Children which gave these results:

Verbal IQ	134
Performance IQ	108
Full-scale IQ	124

Day-by-day observation confirmed the test estimates of his mental ability. The teacher noted that John has an excellent listening and speaking vocabulary. He demonstrates ability to think and to solve verbal problems. He is alert and shows a wide range of interests, which embrace chess and space travel. These are not the traits or interests of a dull child. His low reading performance is not due to lack of mental ability.

To ascertain more precisely the nature of John's reading difficulty, a minute analysis of his reading was made by means of a series of diagnostic tests and inventories:

Word recognition test

The informal reading inventory (see Chapter 10)

Visual discrimination tests, visual memory, and speed of perception

Auditory discrimination tests

The Dolch Basic Sight Word Test

The Cooper Diagnostic Word Analysis Tests—a systematic series of tests of phonic and structural analysis

On the word recognition test John began to encounter difficulty on the first-grade level. When asked how he attacked a new word, he said he tried to "spell it out" or sound it out letter by letter. He could make sound-letter associations for initial consonants but was not sure of blends, especially when they came at the end of a word.

On the informal reading inventory he maintained 95 per cent comprehension but made an increasing number of word perception errors through the fourth grade. On the fifth-grade level his reading became so labored that he was not asked to go on after the first two sentences. In twenty-five running words he had two repetitions, two hesitations, and four word perception errors. The following reading levels were indicated by the informal reading inventory:

Basal: First grade

Independent level: Second grade

Instructional level: Third grade

Frustration level: Beginning at fourth grade and definitely at the fifth

When selections on the fifth-, sixth-, seventh-, and eighth-grade levels were read to him, John showed excellent comprehension and eighth-grade capacity level, which confirmed the impression gained from the Durrell-Sullivan Reading Capacity Test and the Wechsler Intelligence Scale for Children.

It now appears still more clear that John is a bright youngster with a high reading capacity. He has difficulty in associating sounds with symbols and has no system of figuring out strange words except to go by initial consonants and context clues.

An informal visual discrimination test revealed no difficulty in identifying printed symbols, in discriminating differences and similarities in letter and word forms, or in remembering a letter or word that he had just identified. He was also good on speed of perception.

The test of auditory discrimination did not confirm the results of the readiness test given in the second half of the kindergarten year. On an informal test of ability to associate a sound with its corresponding letter, John's performance was excellent on initial consonants, initial blends and digraphs, and on final consonants and blends. He was quite good at identifying the two words that rhymed in a group of three and excellent on auditory fusion and in hearing sounds at the beginning, end, or middle of words. In general, his auditory discrimination was surprisingly good.

Of the 335 words in the preprimer, primer, and first reader vocabularies, John recognized on the tachistoscope all but 11. His difficulty in pronouncing these seemed to be that he did not know the vowel principle involved in such words as *Jane, pets, hope, party,* and *tall.* Of the Dolch list, John missed 9 of the 220 words. Here again his difficulty seemed to be with the short vowel sounds.

The Cooper Diagnostic Word Analysis Test of word attack skills gave more detail about some of the strengths and weaknesses revealed on the diagnostic tests and inventories previously given. The need for specific instruction and practice was indicated with such blends and digraphs as *str, br, thr, tw, shr,* and *sw* and with final endings like *ck* and *nk.* The vowels gave him the most trouble; short *e, o,* and *u* and the long vowels *e* and *o;* he found it hard to differentiate between the long and short vowel and vowel digraphs and diphthongs. He was quite unable to apply phonetic principles, although he knew several rules of syllabication.

To summarize: John has superior intelligence, good visual and auditory acuity, and no speech defect that might hinder his reading growth. Yet, at twelve years of age, he is reading on the third-grade level and his oral reading on material that is at all difficult is characterized by many repetitions. These may represent the corrections he makes as he gets meaning from context clues, which is his best method of word attack. He also makes good use of initial consonants but encounters difficulty with certain blends and digraphs and with vowel sounds.

John's failure in reading seems to be the result of a combination of factors: a general immaturity, initially poor visual and auditory discrimination, prolonged absence from school during his first two years, which caused him to miss a great deal of beginning reading instruction, and insufficient help as he progressed through the grades.

If the diagnosis of emotional and social factors had been as thorough as the diagnosis of visual and auditory discrimination, vocabulary, and word attack skills, specific emotional difficulties might also have been uncovered. It is not unrealistic to assume that seven years of failure in reading must have had some effect on John's attitude toward himself and his ability to read. However, he now seems to have a strong desire to read.

In working with John, it should not be difficult to give him practice in the specific letter-sound associations which, according to the diagnosis, are causing him difficulty. For example, the "Phono-Word Wheels" published by the Steck Company, Austin, Texas, are a useful device; and similar devices may be constructed by teachers and students to give specific practice in such consonant blends and digraphs as *str, br, thr, tw, shr, sk, sw, er, ser, wr, fr, shr, fl,* and *bl.* Other word games and practice exercises can be used in teaching the vowel sounds, vowel digraphs such as *ai, ow, ea, ai,* and *oa* and the vowel diphthongs *oo, au, oi, ou,* and *ow.* John should be given this practice in connection with words in which these sounds appear. He may join a small group of other students, who are having similar difficulty, for practice in these skills using games and exercises. The teacher may ask a good reader to serve as assistant instructor of this small group. When John meets unfamiliar words in his reading, he should be expected to apply his phonetic skills as needed to get their meaning.

It would be well to have John do a certain amount of oral reading and dramatized reading, which would help to develop thoughtful phrasing. It would also detect difficulties he may be having in silent reading.

John may also be given opportunity to discover and apply the principles of pronunciation and syllabication that govern a large proportion of words. For example, he is familiar with words such as *am, ham, sat, at, cat, mat.* He can note that each word has only one vowel at the beginning or in the middle and that in all these words the vowel has the short sound. He can then state the principle himself: When a word has only one vowel at the beginning or in the middle, the vowel is usually short. Experiences of this kind help a student to find underlying principles or patterns in related experiences and show him that it is possible to organize a world of separate things.

On a higher level, the same values are attained by practice in outlining, summarizing, making inferences, anticipating meaning, and applying the knowledge gained in reading to present problems. In teaching these skills it is essential to make the students aware of the methods by which they are learning, to help them understand the strategy behind the campaign, so to speak.

Much silent reading of easy, interesting material will help John to develop smoothness, rapidity, and fluency; will decrease obvious vocalization; will reinforce the mastery of words and parts of words already learned; and will give him an opportunity to recognize new words.

While working with John, the reading teacher, without prying or probing, may get glimpses of emotional difficulty to which he will respond, not as a clinical psychologist, but as an understanding human being. For example, if John expresses anxiety about his mother's illness, the teacher may encourage him to talk about ways he can help at home. One of the best ways to relieve anxiety is to do something constructive about the anxiety-arousing situation.

By using methods and techniques such as these, the reading teacher should be able to help John attain his very considerable reading potentialities.

SEQUENTIAL DIAGNOSTIC PROCEDURE

A more technical purpose of these specific appraisal and diagnostic procedures is to ascertain the individual's pattern or profile of sequential strengths that can be reinforced and deficiencies that can be corrected by appropriate instruction. For example, the following list represents such a functional sequence in the phonetic word recognition skills:

DIAGNOSIS OF PHONETIC WORD RECOGNITION SKILLS

The printed word presented.
See it clearly.
Identify sounds in the words.
Distinguish different sounds in words.
Know letter names.
Associate sounds with letters.
Pronounce the word.
Associate spoken word with previously acquired meanings.
Attach these meanings to the printed word.
Check correctness of meaning by context.
Make verbal or motor response to the word that shows comprehension of its meaning.

The diagnosis of a student's word recognition skills should obtain evidence on each of these steps. Visual acuity is tested as a routine matter. Informal tests of visual and auditory discriminations of sound-symbol associations, ability to pronounce the word, understanding of spoken words, and ability to associate the meaning with the printed word can be given to a child having difficulty in word recognition.

Similar diagnostic sequences could be made for other aspects of reading development, such as getting the literal meaning of a selection:

DIAGNOSIS OF COMPREHENSION OF A SELECTION

The printed selection
Recognizing own purpose
Recognizing author's purpose
Recognizing key words
Recognizing and giving proper weight to key words
Grouping words into thought units (phrasing)
Recognizing sentence structure
Recognizing paragraph structure
Seeing relations—main ideas and supporting details, contrasting points
Reading aloud with good phrasing, accent, etc.
Making outline, making summary, answering thought-provoking questions

With such sequential diagnostic information it would be possible to identify any factor in the sequence that was blocking the individual's total reading achievement. Ideally, prevention and correction would be based on such diagnosis of many factors in a functional sequence. To neglect any important factor in this sequence would make remedial work ineffectual; to expend effort on factors in which the individual is already proficient would be a waste of time.

READING RECORDS

Records of Student Progress

The techniques of reporting students' progress in reading parallel the two general procedures described in Chapter 1. If the reading teacher has obtained information about the student's reading achievement before beginning to work with him, the usual method of appraising his progress is to administer a comparable form of the tests initially given and report the gains he has made. When appraisal is interwoven with instruction, the teacher may note progress by keeping a continuous record and chart. This might include a day-by-day graph of scores on comparable exercises, a growing list of words recognized at sight, reports of books read, and dated tape recordings of early and later readings of similar material. These and other kinds of continuous records that show the ups and downs of progress are enlightening to the student, the teacher, and the parent.

Perhaps the least helpful forms for reporting students' progress are the checklist of general items such as comprehension, pronunciation, expression, etc., and speed-of-reading charts. Unless adequate comprehension can be assumed, a record of speed alone has little significance. More useful is the record that shows rate of comprehension for materials of varying difficulty and different types—study-type and free or recreational reading.

Records of Instructional Needs

Various forms of checklists have been used to summarize the student's reading level and instructional needs. Most of these checklists emphasize certain observable and somewhat mechanical reading errors rather than comprehension and appreciation.

A useful, compact four-page Remedial Reading Record was developed by the Philadelphia reading staff.[1] Pages 1 and 2, reproduced here, give specific information about reading levels and test scores and analysis of difficulties in oral and silent reading,

[1] Reproduced with permission of Rosemary G. Wilson, Assistant Director of Curriculum, the Board of Public Education, School District of Philadelphia.

	DATE OF BIRTH			ROOM OR GROUP NO.				
	MO.	DA.	YR.					

LAST NAME		FIRST NAME				
SCHOOL	DIST.	SCHOOL	DIST.	ADM. TO REM.	DIS. FROM REM.	

READING ANALYSIS

	INFORMAL READING INVENTORY						ADDITIONAL FORMAL READING TESTS			
LEVELS	DATE						DATE	NAME OF TEST		SCORE
	IND.									
	INS.									
	FRUS.									
	CAP.									

	CHECK LIST	DATE						CHECK LIST	DATE				
ORAL	POINTING							METHOD OF ATTACK					
	POOR PHRASING							FAILS TO USE:					
	POOR COMPREHENSION							CONFIGURATION CLUES					
	IGNORES PUNCTUATION							PICTURE CLUES					
								CONTEXT CLUES					
SILENT	POINTING						**WORD RECOGNITION**	PHONETIC ANALYSIS					
	VOCALIZATION							STRUCTURAL ANALYSIS					
	POOR COMPREHENSION							GLOSSARY & DICT. SKILLS					
	RATE TOO SLOW							USES SPELLING ATTACK					
	LACKS ABILITY TO:							NO METHOD					
	LOCATE INFORMATION							SUBSTITUTES					
STUDY SKILLS	EVALUATE & INTERPRET							REVERSES					
	ORGANIZE							REPEATS					
	REMEMBER & USE MATERIAL							OMITS OR INSERTS					

SIGNIFICANT MEDICAL AND PHYSICAL FACTS

FORM HV 68—REMEDIAL READING RECORD—SCHOOL DISTRICT OF PHILADELPHIA   (MAY 1954)

CUMULATIVE RECORD—GRADES 1 TO 6

TERM ENDING	19		19		19		19		19		19		19	
	JAN.	JUNE	JAN.	JUNE	JAN.	JUNE	JAN.	JUNE	JAN.	JUNE	JAN.	JUNE	JAN.	JUNE
GRADE-SECTION														

RECORD EACH TEST SCORE BY ENTERING CODE LETTER, E.G., R, OPPOSITE ATTAINED STD. SCORE

	VERBAL ABILITY V	OTHER TESTS	13+		13+		13+		13+		13+	
READ. COMP. R			12		12		12		12		12	
LOCATING INFOR. L			11		11		11		11		11	
SPELLING S												
ARITH. PROB. P	10		10		10		10		10		10	
ARITH. FUND. A												
MAPS & GRAPHS M	9		9		9		9		9		9	
HANDWRITING H												

GRADE EQUIVALENTS / STANDARD SCORES

(4A) — 8
(3B) — 7
(3A) — 6
(2B) — 5
(2A) — 4
(1B) — 3
(1A) — 2 / 1 / 0

RECORD AGE ONCE A YEAR IN TERM BIRTHDAY OCCURS (COUNT JULY OR AUGUST AS JANUARY TERM). ENTER AGE, E.G., 6, OPPOSITE APPROPRIATE STANDARD SCORE (6 YR. AT 2, 7 AT 4, 8 AT 6, 9 AT 8, ETC.)

| I.Q. | | | | | | | | | | | | | | |

TEST SCORES—GRADES 7 TO 12*

TERM ENDING	19		19		19		19		19		19		19		
	JAN.	JUNE	JAN.	JUNE	JAN.	JUNE	JAN.	JUNE	JAN.	JUNE	JAN.	JUNE	JAN.	JUNE	
6+															6+
5—															5—
4+															4+
4—															4—
3+															3+
3—															3—
2+															2+
2—															2—
1															1

* INDICATE SUBJECTS BY INITIAL LETTER. USE CODE OF GRADES 1 TO 6 WHERE IT APPLIES.

MARKS—GRADES 7 TO 12

TERM ENDING	19		19		19		19		19		19		19	
	JAN.	JUNE	JAN.	JUNE	JAN.	JUNE	JAN.	JUNE	JAN.	JUNE	JAN.	JUNE	JAN.	JUNE
GRADE														
ENGLISH														
MATHEMATICS														
SOCIAL STUDIES														
SCIENCE														
CO-OPERATION														

A somewhat similar form is used in the elementary school.

word recognition, and study skills. There is space at the bottom of page 1 for significant medical and physical facts. Page 2 provides space for test results from grades 1 through 12 and for marks from grades 7 through 12. The last two pages are left blank for dated comments made by different persons who have had contact with the student.

The Reading Diagnostic Record (Strang and others, 1952) was designed to encourage high school and college students to study and appraise their reading and to plan for its improvement.

Records of Special Diagnostic Study

In school systems that employ reading teachers with a Master's degree in reading or its equivalent, a system-wide diagnostic clinic is sometimes set up. To this clinic are referred all reading cases that require expert, specialized diagnosis. After the diagnosis is completed, a report is sent to the reading teacher in the school where the referral originated. The following is an outline for the report following a reading analysis (form developed by Dr. Helen Carey and Dr. Dorothy Withrow in the Reading Clinic serving the Philadelphia schools):

I. Identifying data
II. Scores of tests administered
III. Interview with parent and with subject
    A. Time of arrival, general attitude, speech pattern, other evidence of socioeconomic background
    B. Reading problem as seen by parent
    C. Health and developmental history
    D. Relationships with other children
    E. Reading problem as seen by subject
    F. School
        1. Best liked subject or activity
        2. Least liked subject or activity
        3. Spelling
        4. Arithmetic
    G. Educational and vocational goals
    H. Interests and activities outside of school
    I. Subject's appearance, his interview and test behavior
IV. Significance of test results
    A. Skills
        1. Oral reading
        2. Silent reading

       3. Phonic skills

       4. Number skills

  B. Capacity

       1. Auditory comprehension

       2. Vocabulary

       3. Verbal intelligence

       4. Nonverbal intelligence

       5. Evidence of projective tests

       6. Lateral dominance

V. Prognosis

  A. Positive factors

  B. Negative factors

  C. Summary

VI. Recommendations

  A. To the principal

       1. Placement

       2. Retention in grade

       3. Further referral

       4. Candidacy for clinical instruction

  B. To the remedial teacher

       1. Methods

       2. Materials

       3. Professional reading

       4. Interests, skills, and abilities of subject which may serve to suggest method of instruction

  C. To classroom teacher

       1. Methods

       2. Materials

  D. To counselor

       1. Direction that guidance should take

       2. Participation in remedial instruction

       3. Educational and vocational guidance

       4. Further exploration of environmental factors

       5. Further referral

       6. Development of referral readiness in parent and subject

  E. To parent

       1. Discussion of test results

       2. Help parent may give

  F. To pupil

       1. Discussion of test results

       2. Positive factors which may be emphasized

Using this outline, the following prognosis and recommendations were made for Tony, aged nine years seven months, in grade 4:

Prognosis for Tony. The prognosis for eventual good achievement in reading and writing is, in Tony's case, excellent. The positive factors far outweigh the negative factors. On the credit side are (1) the high level of auditory comprehension, vocabulary development, and verbal intelligence in general; (2) the relatively high level in every area of mental functioning, verbal and otherwise; (3) the interest and cooperation of the home; (4) Tony's own excellent motivation; (5) the well-developed number skills; (6) the chronological age, which makes it possible to plan a long-range program of remedial instruction before the disability becomes too firmly established and before its adverse effect on scholastic achievement "snowballs."

Negative factors are (1) Tony's tension and anxiety in relation to learning activities, (2) pressure which is possibly too great from the home (the parents' tensions and anxieties will aggravate the child's; their unskilled teaching methods and inappropriate choice of materials may hinder rather than help learning), (3) the possibility of slight brain damage, which will necessitate highly specialized methods and materials.

Recommendations. The program recommended for Tony is as follows:

1. Retention in the school's adjustment class—Tony may need individual instruction to supplement group instruction.

2. Consideration for membership in the Summer Workshop Reading Clinic—Tony is apparently offering the school an opportunity to salvage a really good mind for eventual school achievement. He should not be denied any appropriate special service which the schools have at their disposal. His retardation is not so severe as that of some clinic cases, but it should be measured against his vocabulary level and not against his grade placement and his chronological age. Also, if the disability is not corrected, the discrepancy between achievement and capacity may become much greater than it is now.

3. Training in auditory perception and in auditory discrimination—rhyming games and other phonic games might be used. There are many excellent ones on the market.

4. Phonic instruction in general, beginning on the reading-readiness level—Tony needs help with everything phonic, beyond initial consonants.

5. A great deal of practice in silent reading to supplement

and reinforce the oral work in phonics and phonic analysis; an attempt should be made to provide plenty of high interest level-low readability level material, preferably books, for Tony to select from. There are many books with factual content for young readers which should appeal to a boy who thinks he might like to become a "science man." The use of the SRA Elementary School Reading Laboratory is also suggested, although it is not in book form. The reading selections have high interest value, and they make it possible to progress from one level of difficulty to the next as rapidly as competence is developed.

6. Experimental use of V-A-K-T techniques (a modification of the Fernald method); they should prove particularly helpful in improving spelling.

7. Practice in spelling on the second-grade instructional level—words should not be assigned for study beyond this level until Tony is *independent* with second-grade words. On the other hand, he should not be forbidden the opportunity of adding a relatively long and difficult word to his spelling vocabulary, if he finds a word which interests him and he voluntarily decides to learn to spell. It is good V-A-K-T practice to begin with words which the subject wishes to learn.

8. Help for the mother in bringing less pressure to bear on Tony. He is sturdy enough to take some pressure, but there may be too much.

9. Help for the mother in selecting and securing books and other reading materials for Tony to use at home; the mother presents a real need in this area and a real willingness to use help. Perhaps the young uncle, who is also Tony's godfather, can be persuaded to buy him some books, but the uncle probably will have to have a list from which to select.

10. Reassurance for the mother that Tony is not a mentally retarded child; her fears may be, and almost certainly are, communicating themselves to Tony and interfering with learning.

11. Help for Tony in overcoming his tensions, anxieties, and tendency to nervous excitement; this calls for counseling service or for a guidance approach to remedial instruction.

When possible, the diagnostician who reports the reading analysis discusses the case with the person assigned to work with it, usually the reading teacher in the school but sometimes the counselor or psychologist. Such an interview enables the diagnostician to give additional information, clarify details, and see whether his recommendations are feasible in the school situation.

Even more valuable is a case conference that includes not only the reading teacher but also the student's regular teachers, the principal, the school nurse, and others who may be helpful. A case conference is a learning experience for all the participants. The specialists learn what the teachers can and cannot do. The teachers gain understanding from the specialists' interpretations and recommendations. The case conference is also a valuable form of in-service education.

USES OF DIAGNOSTIC SUMMARIES

The diagnostic formulation made at any stage of working with the student is useful in many ways:

1. Knowledge about the individual's potential reading ability gives the teacher a sense of direction in working with him. The teacher's self-assurance, in turn, gives assurance that improvement is possible; this is an important factor in the successful treatment of a case.

2. An understanding of the reading difficulty and the conditions that seem to have given rise to it helps all those involved in the case to do something about the underlying factors, rather than merely treating surface symptoms. The diagnostic information may eliminate certain possible factors by establishing, as in John's case, that the subject has adequate mental ability, good oral comprehension, no evident auditory or visual difficulties.

3. Definite information about the student's actual reading level enables the teacher to begin instruction with reading material that is a little below the student's present level.

4. An analysis of the student's reading skills enables the teacher to give him practice and instruction that are truly functional and will be applied in his daily reading.

LIMITATIONS OF DIAGNOSTIC SUMMARIES

We must recognize that the diagnostic summary has certain limitations. It is never complete. As we have noted, while diagnostic tests may definitely point to difficulties in vocabulary, word recognition skills, or comprehension, they do not identify the emotional factors that cause an individual to resist or to be unable to profit from instruction and practice that might remedy these deficiencies. The usual diagnostic procedure may also fail to describe attitudes, values, and motivations that are basic to improvement in the individual's reading.

Remedial procedures cannot be determined once and for all. Any diagnostic summary should be constantly revised as new information is obtained. Much of this information is gained through continuous sensitivity to the individual's response to various techniques and materials.

Most diagnostic formulations involve some degree of inference. For any given effect, several causes are possible. As a guide to his treatment of the case, the reading teacher selects the most plausible explanation or hypothesis and tries it out.

Many diagnoses contain discrepancies that must be ironed out. For example, what parents say about their relations with their children may not agree with what the children say. The way in which children perceive their parents' attitudes and behavior is important, however inaccurate this may be, for children respond to the home situation *as they perceive it*.

CONCLUDING STATEMENT

Interpretation and syntheses of data are the most difficult steps in the diagnostic process. They involve an understanding of the possible significance of each item and ability to keep in mind related items and to organize them into clusters or patterns. From these patterns, one derives hypotheses from which the treatment of the case tentatively stems. These hypotheses are modified as new information and insights are gained in working with the case. Each reading case offers a unique creative experience to the teacher or clinician.

While not abandoning the established clinical procedure of analyzing the reading process, uncovering possible causes, then trying to synthesize the information collected and formulate hypotheses from this compilation of facts, might we not experiment with a more dynamic clinical method of studying students' reading? A proposed method would recognize the continuing development of the client's reading, his inner urge to improve, the environmental conditions that are inhibiting or facilitating improvement, and his interaction with the clinician and with other people in school and at home. The clinician would begin working with the reading problem as the client sees it and assist him through tests and interviews in clarifying it. He would teach the client methods of learning which he can apply to himself and try to change conditions that are inhibiting his progress.

Suggested Problems
Practice and Demonstration

1. Demonstrate a comprehensive diagnostic procedure with two children of different ages and reading problems, going through the process of interpretation and synthesis of the information obtained.

2. Report a number of different kinds of current cases, first giving the diagnostic information available, then letting the class formulate their hypotheses and recommendations for treatment, and finally reporting the case as it was actually carried out.

3. Demonstrate or play a recording of a case conference on a reading problem, showing the exchange of information and ideas among the various participants.

4. Study the cumulative reading record illustrated in this chapter and adopt, adapt, or create one that you can use in your school or clinic situation.

5. Read some of the case studies reported in the additional references at the end of this chapter. Extract from them ideas concerning the significance and use of various kinds of diagnostic information.

6. Read Kirk's chapter in the report of the Annual Reading Conference (The University of Chicago Press, Chicago, 1962) for more detailed understanding of the idea of sequential diagnosis.

7. Summarize the values and the limitations of diagnostic summaries.

8. What applications of this chapter can a teacher make to his work with reading problems within a class group?

References

Dressel, Paul L.: "Counseling Caprices," *Personnel and Guidance Journal,* 33:4–7, September, 1954.

Koester, G. A.: "A Study of the Diagnostic Process," *Educational and Psychological Measurement,* 14:473–486, Autumn, 1951.

Ledley, Robert S., and Lee B. Lusted: "Reasoning Foundations of Medical Diagnosis," *Science,* 130:9–21, July 3, 1959.

Strang, Ruth, and others: *Reading Diagnostic Record for High School and College Students,* Bureau of Publications, Teachers College, Columbia University, New York, 1952.

Tanyzer, Harold J.: Case presented by Mr. Tanyzer in an advanced case study course at Teachers College, Columbia University, New York, 1956.

Suggested Readings

Fry, E.: "Reading Clinic Reports: Its Results and Methods," *Journal of Educational Research,* 52:311–313, April, 1959.

Jansky, Jeannette: "A Case of Severe Dyslexia with Aphasic-like Symptoms," *The Reading Teacher,* 15:110–113, November, 1961.

Kress, Roy: "Case Study of Reading Retardation: The Diagnosis and Correction," *Conference on Reading,* University of Pittsburgh Press, Pittsburgh, 1960, pp. 75–91.

Mayhew, Lewis B.: "Critical Incidence Technique in Educational Evaluation," *Journal of Educational Research,* 49:491–598, April, 1956.

Newman, Ruth, and others: *Technical Assistance in a Public School System,* School Research Program, P.H.S. Project OM-525, Washington School of Psychiatry, Washington, D.C., 1962.

Robbins, M. H.: "Case Study of a Retarded Child," *Education,* 82: 230–231, December, 1961.

Rogers, Carl R.: *On Becoming a Person,* Houghton Mifflin Company, Boston, 1961.

Roth, Robert M.: "The Role of Self-concept in Achievement," *Journal of Experimental Education,* 27:265–281, June, 1959.

Shedd, Charles L.: "The Diagnosis and Treatment of Symbolic Confusion," *Changing Concepts of Reading Instruction,* International Reading Association Conference Proceedings, vol. 6, Scholastic Magazines, Inc., New York, 1961, pp. 97–102.

Spache, George D.: "Diagnosis of Reading Problems in the Classroom," *Education Digest,* 26:47–49, November, 1960.

"Symposium: Contributions to the Diagnosis and Remedial Treatment of Reading Difficulties," *British Journal of Educational Psychology,* 30:146–179, June, 1960; 31:79–105, February, 1961.

Sequential Tests of Educational Progress, Educational Testing Service, Princeton, New Jersey. A new series of achievement tests, STEP measures the ability of students to *use* what they have learned in the classroom. There are four levels with two forms each ranging from grade 4 through the sophomore year of college. Each test is 70 minutes in length (divided into two 35-minute units), so that individual students are measured reliably on the depth and power of their skill. The four levels are: level 4—grades 4 to 6; level 3—grades 7 to 9; level 2—grades 10 to 12; level 1—freshman and sophomore years of college.

The STEP Reading Tests were chosen for these reasons:

1. They measure critical skills in *application* of learning.
2. Their purpose is to evaluate student ability to read new materials with comprehension, insight, and critical understanding.
3. They measure important aspects of reading ability:
   a. Ability to understand direct statements made by the author
   b. Ability to interpret and summarize the passage
   c. Ability to see the motives of the author
   d. Ability to observe the organizational characteristics of the passage
   e. Ability to criticize the passage with respect to ideas, purposes, or presentation
4. The material on which the tests are based contains these important features:
   a. High interest value
   b. Similar to that which pupils encounter in their classrooms
   c. Representative of a variety of types of reading
   d. Of a length to insure unity in content and opportunity to employ the skills being measured
5. Instructional value of test: It is possible for the teacher to analyze the weaknesses and strengths in reading for the entire class, since items for each passage are constructed to identify a particular skill.
6. Percentile bands are used as a safeguard against interpreting a score as more precise than it really is.
7. The design of the test and the test questions themselves were formulated by teachers who have had first-hand experience in coping with students' learning problems.

[1] Prepared by Dr. Amelia Melnik, University of Arizona. Similar analyses may be made from the test manual, Buros's latest *Mental Measurements Yearbook,* and other sources.

8. They have been built as power tests rather than speed measures.

VALIDITY: General validity for STEP rests entirely upon content validity based upon the combined judgments of the educators who designed and built the tests. They listed the kinds of learning that were central and continuous in the field and then devised test situations that would call forth these kinds of learning. If the goals of instruction in a class or school are similar to those included in the test, then the test would have specific content validity for that class or school. It is expected that additional evidence pertaining to several kinds of validity will be reported as it accumulates.

RELIABILITY: Reliabilities reported are results of internal analyses. Correlation between scores on alternate forms or test-retest scores have not been obtained. Reliabilities were estimated for four samples tested in the norms program. Analyses were done separately for grades 5, 8, 11, 13 only on Form A. Kuder-Richardson Formula 20 was used to estimate all the reliabilities and standard errors of measurement.

Test, reading	Grade	Number of items	N	Total group		100-case sample mean	Relia-bility	SE meas.
				Mean	S.D.			
Formula 1A	13	70	106	46.45	11.54	46.25	.91	3.42
Formula 2A	11	70	488	43.58	11.82	41.10	.92	3.39
Formula 3A	8	70	480	35.60	11.23	37.30	.90	3.62
Formula 4A	5	70	277	40.92	14.84	40.25	.95	3.45

In computing the reliability estimates, the raw-score statistics were obtained for all students in the norms group for the grade. The item statistics were based on 100-case samples drawn at random from the total norms group for the grade. The minor differences between the two groups are not sufficient to affect the reliability estimated.

Additional data are not presently available. However, the manual points out that the test contains many questions and samples the student's achievement many times and in many ways to provide a reliable estimate of the student's achievement. Furthermore, the manual points out that a score earned by a student is not interpreted as a single point on the score scale but as a band interval. Thus a band of scores takes into account the reliability characteristics of the test and in this way avoids overinterpretation of small score differences.

With the exception of one article, there is no literature available pertaining to STEP in published sources, according to *Psych. Abstracts* and *Educational Index*. In a descriptive article, "New Tests of Scholastic Aptitude and Achievement" (*Journal of the National Association of Women Deans and Counselors,* vol. 22, October, 1958, pp. 2–7), John Dobbin cites three central characteristics of STEP:

1. Comparability: tests are comparable at all levels because the standardization was done at all levels at the same time with the same students.

2. Centrality: the tasks elicit the kind of behavior that is at the center of the educational process and that challenges the student to demonstrate how well he can apply his knowledge to new situations.

3. Continuity: tests are constructed so there is a continuity in content, testing, and interpretation at all grade levels. "Standardization insures the continuity of interpretation by affording a single continuous score scale to which all levels and forms in each field are equated."

GENERAL COMMENT: The following features of STEP are of particular significance from a reading teacher's point of view:

1. *Purpose:* ETS emphasizes, and rightly so, the instruction value of STEP which is in line with the recent recognition of the need for developing techniques which can be used for the improvement of classroom instruction as well as for evaluative purposes.[2] As suggested in their manual, the very taking of STEP may increase the student's awareness of what is involved in the reading process. Furthermore, an analysis of the questions can provide clues as to the nature of the skill involved. The material is varied; the questions are appropriate and present problems in a clear way and at a vocabulary level appropriate to the student. The discussion of these questions can serve as an excellent springboard for further instruction.

2. *Content:* Traxler points out that standardized tests represent a misleading oversimplification of the reading process. STEP is moving in the right direction by focusing on growth in the higher levels of abilities expected in the upper grades—abilities to comprehend relationships—in passages long enough to call for sustained attention to organize content, to draw inferences, and, too often neglected, to apply what is read.

3. *Use:* STEP is making a pioneering attempt toward realistic interpretation of test scores by reporting ranges of percentile ranks instead of grade level standings, which give the erroneous impression to those who know little about testing that a student's test score is a completely accurate and stable measure of his reading ability. The use of the percentile band is one way of preventing misconceptions of meaning of a score.

OTHER TESTS: Some additional standardized tests are as follows:

[2] Paul Dressel, "Problems of Evaluation," in *Proceedings of 1951 Invitational Conference on Testing Problems,* Educational Testing Service, Princeton, N.J., 1952.

Kelley-Greene Reading Comprehension Test for senior high schools and college freshmen. Three forms: AM, BM, CM. Victor H. Kelley and Harry A. Green, Harcourt, Brace & World, Inc., New York, 1953.

This test is designed "to provide an over-all measure of reading comprehension for high school students and college freshmen."

Time on test samples varies from 3 to 20 minutes, suitable for high school students (grades 10, 11, and 12) and college freshmen.

Machine scored or hand scored, separate answer sheet.

Materials interestingly written, but are limited and weighted heavily in science reading. No diagnostic value beyond paragraph comprehension, directed reading, and memory. No direction given for using it for diagnostic purposes.

Reliability was fairly consistent, .91–.95 when used on six different small groups of students in three different states.

Claims to give accurate measure in various areas that are comparable.

Norms are set up for grades 9, 10, 11, and 12 and raw scores for tests 1, 2, and 3, and for the total raw score. The norms on tests 1 and 3 are given for the spring of the year, while test 2 and the total scores are given for twice a year, November and April.

The pupil reads passages and then answers questions about the passages.

Exercises were selected from materials used in three experimental tests used as a pretest.

Directions are clear. Norms are furnished. Use of test is claimed but no directions are given for diagnostic use.

Print too small. Not listed in Buros' *Mental Measurements Yearbook*.

Stanford Achievement Tests, intermediate and advanced, in forms J, K, L, M, and N. Truman L. Kelley, Richard Madden, Eric F. Gardner, Lewis M. Terman, Giles M. Ruch, Harcourt, Brace & World, Inc., New York, 1953.

Designed to measure "the important knowledges, skills, and understandings commonly accepted as desirable outcomes of the major branches of the elementary curriculum."

There are two tests for measuring reading achievement: comprehension, and vocabulary and word meaning.

This test was validated upon the per cent of correct response made in groups high and low in reading comprehension. This specific procedure is recognized as one that selects questions which differentiate the good readers from the poor readers.

A study based on the Spearmon Brown formula for grade X

showed a reliability test rate close to .90. This is higher than the reliability of most reading tests. These tests are better for judging the difficulties of a group than of an individual and better as a general test of knowledge than as a reading test.

The two sets of norms are:

1. Modal-age grade norms, recommended for interpretation of individual scores.

2. Total-group grade norms, recommended for interpretation of group averages.

The questions on both tests are multiple choice. The pupil answers directly on the question booklet, filling in the spaces between lines under the number corresponding to the correct solution.

The test items were selected from an analysis of the most widely used textbooks in various subjects and through research of the literature on child development. Specialists on each particular subject judged the actual questions. The tests were given in connection with intelligence tests to check the ability equivalence of various groups.

There is a manual in the form of a booklet with directions for administering the battery. This booklet contains the norms and scoring directions as well. The directions are clear, concise, and very complete with respect to administration, scoring, and interpretation of the norms.

The legibility and understandability of the tests are good.

Diagnostic Reading Tests, published by the Committee on Diagnostic Reading, Mountain Home, N.C., 1947.

A. Grade 7 through college freshman, 8 forms
B. Attempts to measure:
   1. Reading rate
   2. Vocabulary—multiple choice
   3. Comprehension—study-type reading skills
   4. Word attack
   5. Reading of social sciences
C. Validity:
   1. Rate—material one type only and not long enough to evaluate rate in relation to purpose
   2. Comprehension—asks for details only
   3. Vocabulary—fair selection
D. Reliability: .91 overall (8 forms aid in this)
E. Diagnostic value: not too good for use with individual student; has value as a screening test for class
F. Norms: none available in the general bulletin
G. General information:
   1. Time, 50 minutes.

2. Mechanically, test is good with excellent instructions.
3. Publisher has added additional costs by putting pertinent information in a number of separate bulletins.

Iowa Tests of Educational Development, E. F. Lindquist (ed.), published by Science Research Associates, Chicago (1942–1959).
A. Grades 9 through 12, 2 forms
B. Purposes:
   1. Measurement of individual
   2. Study of curriculum
   3. Identification of gifted students
   4. Prediction of college success
C. Attempts to measure:
   1. Understanding of social concepts
   2. Knowledge of natural sciences
   3. Power of expression
   4. Quantitative thinking
   5. Vocabulary
   6. Use of sources of information
   7. Reading of social studies
   8. Reading of natural sciences
   9. Reading of literary material
D. Validity (7.5): not high enough for predicting individual success
E. Diagnostic value: not too good for use with individual student, thought to be an excellent battery for general school use
F. Norms: based on 50,000 pupils; also compared favorably with Iowa group in tests given to 30,000 entrants into the Army
G. General information:
   1. Time: long form, 9 hours; short form, about 50 minutes
   2. Three manuals, most complete
   3. Good directions, but tests vary as to legibility, ease of use of answer sheet, etc.

Traxler Silent Reading Test, published by Public School Publishing Company, Bloomington, Illinois, 1942 and 1943.
A. Grades 7 through 10, 4 forms
B. Attempts to measure:
   1. Reading rate
   2. Story comprehension—high level of interest material
   3. Word meaning—use of sentences
   4. Paragraph meaning
   5. Total comprehension
C. General critical thought states that the manual is poor with insufficient data on validity, reliability, and equivalence of forms.
D. Norms based on 25,000 pupils who are not classified as to grade, etc.

E. The test is thought to be useful for surveys, not for individual diagnosis.
F. General information:
1. See note C on manual
2. Time, 55 minutes

Traxler High School Reading Test, published by Public School Publishing Company, Bloomington, Illinois, 1938 and 1942.
A. Grades 10 through 12, 2 forms
B. Attempts to measure:
1. Rate of reading
2. Comprehension of individual units—words, phrases
3. Comprehension of main idea—considered good
4. Vocabulary
C. Validity: fair
D. Reliability:
1. .90 rate
2. 172 main idea comprehension
3. .80 other comprehension
E. Some diagnostic value for individual use
F. General information:
1. Time, 50 minutes
2. Excellent manual with descriptive information on validity, reliability, and percentile norms for each score, each grade level, plus suggestions for interpretation of test results

APPENDIX B *Checklist of Instructional Needs*[1]

Nonreader or Preprimer Level

Needs help in:

1. Listening comprehension and speech
   _____ Understanding of material heard
   _____ Speech and spoken vocabulary
2. Visual perception of word elements
   _____ Visual memory of words
   _____ Giving names of letters
   _____ Identifying letters named
   _____ Matching letters
   _____ Copying letters
3. Auditory perception of word elements
   _____ Initial or final blends
   _____ Initial or final single sounds
   _____ Learning sounds taught
4. Phonic abilities
   _____ Solving words
   _____ Sounding words
   _____ Sounds of blends—phonograms
   _____ Sounds of individual letters
5. Learning rate
   _____ Remembering words taught
   _____ Use of context clues
6. Reading interest and effort
   _____ Attention and persistence
   _____ Self-directed work
7. Other

_____ _____
_____ _____
_____ _____
_____ _____
_____ _____

[1] Donald D. Durrell, *Durrell Analysis of Reading Difficulty*, new ed., Individual Record Booklet, Harcourt, Brace & World, Inc., New York, 1955, p. 2.

Primary-grade Reading Level

Needs help in:

1. Listening comprehension and speech
   - ———— Understanding of material heard
   - ———— Speech and spoken vocabulary
2. Word analysis abilities
   - ———— Visual memory of words
   - ———— Auditory analysis of words
   - ———— Solving words by sounding
   - ———— Sounds of blends, phonograms
   - ———— Use of context clues
   - ———— Remembering new words taught
3. Oral reading abilities
   - ———— Oral reading practice
   - ———— Comprehension in oral reading
   - ———— Phrasing (eye-voice span)
   - ———— Errors on easy words
   - ———— Addition or omission of words
   - ———— Repetition of words or phrases
   - ———— Ignoring punctuation
   - ———— Ignoring word errors
   - ———— Attack on unfamiliar words
   - ———— Expression in reading
   - ———— Speech, voice, enunciation
   - ———— Security in oral reading
   - ———— ——————————————————
   - ———— ——————————————————
   - ———— ——————————————————
4. Silent reading and recall
   - ———— Level of silent reading
   - ———— Comprehension in silent reading
   - ———— Attention and persistence
   - ———— Unaided oral recall
   - ———— Recall on questions
   - ———— Speed of silent reading
   - ———— Phrasing (eye movements)
   - ———— Lip movements and whispering
   - ———— Head movements, frowning
   - ———— Imagery in silent reading
   - ———— Position of book, posture
   - ———— ——————————————————
   - ———— ——————————————————
   - ———— ——————————————————

5. Reading interest and effort
    _____ Attention and persistence
    _____ Voluntary reading
    _____ Self-directed work, workbooks

Intermediate Grade Reading Level

Needs help in:

1. Listening comprehension and speech
    _____ Understanding of material heard
    _____ Speech and oral expression
2. Word analysis abilities and spelling
    _____ Visual analysis of words
    _____ Auditory analysis of words
    _____ Solving words by sounding syllables
    _____ Sounding syllables, word parts
    _____ Meaning from context
    _____ Attack on unfamiliar words
    _____ Spelling ability
    _____ Accuracy of copy, speed of writing
    _____ Dictionary skills: location, pronunciation, meaning
    _____ _____
    _____ _____

3. Oral reading abilities
    _____ Oral reading practice
    _____ Comprehension in oral reading
    _____ Phrasing (eye-voice span)
    _____ Expression in reading, speech skills
    _____ Speed of oral reading
    _____ Security in oral reading
    _____ Word and phrase meaning
    _____ _____
    _____ _____

4. Silent reading and recall
    _____ Level of silent reading
    _____ Comprehension in silent reading
    _____ Unaided oral recall
    _____ Unaided written recall
    _____ Recall on questions
    _____ Attention and persistence
    _____ Word and phrase meaning difficulties
    _____ Sentence complexity difficulties
    _____ Imagery in silent reading
    _____ _____

5. Speeded reading abilities
   —— Speed of reading (eye movements)
   —— Speed of work in content subjects
   —— Skimming and locating information
6. Study abilities
   —— Reading details, directions, arithmetic
   —— Organization and subordination of ideas
   —— Elaborative thinking in reading
   —— Critical reading
   —— Use of table of contents, references
7. Reading interest and effort
   —— Voluntary reading
   —— Variety of reading
   —— Self-directed work

APPENDIX C

Date of Application_____

Boy_____
Name of Applicant_____ Girl_____ Age_____

Address of Applicant_____

Telephone_____Place of Birth_____

Birthday_____ Age of entrance to kindergarten_____first grade____

Father's Name_____Place of Birth_____

Father's Occupation_____Education_____

Mother's Name_____Place of Birth_____

Mother's Occupation_____Education_____

Marital Status of Parents_____

Health of Applicant_____

Other Children (List in order)

Name	Birth Date	Sex	Health	Highest Grade Reached
_____	_____	_____	_____	_____
_____	_____	_____	_____	_____
_____	_____	_____	_____	_____
_____	_____	_____	_____	_____

Language Spoken in the Home_____

Do any of the other children have a reading problem?_____

Referred to Reading Center by_____Address_____

Education (Name and address of the school you have attended last or are attending now.)

_____

Have you received special help in reading before this time? When and by whom?

Source of Help   Person in Charge   Date   Length of Time

_____

_____

_____

(OVER)

Marks in Each Subject in Last Grade Attended_____

_____

_____

Kindergarten-Nursery School Attended_____

Elementary School_____

High School_____

Future Educational Plans_____

Future Vocational Plans_____

History of your reading interests - from the time you first began to read, how much
and what kinds of reading have you done through the grades up to the present?

_____

_____

_____

_____

Your present interests - how you spend your free time

_____

_____

_____

What are your dissatisfactions with your present reading and study methods?

_____

_____

_____

_____

_____

Just what do you want to accomplish at the Reading Center - what are your specific
goals? Please state them simply and definitely.

_____

_____

_____

Filled out by_____

Relationship to Applicant_____

Address_____

Reproduced with permission of Max G. Rubinstein, Assistant
Superintendent in charge of the New York City Junior High School
Division.

NAME INDEX

Abet, L. E., 263
Abrams, Elias N., 222, 227
Alexander, Theron, 263
Alpert, Harvey, 146
Ammons, Robert Bruce, 212
Anderson, Harold H., 48, 58
Anderson, Irving, 38
Artley, A. Sterl, 38
Austin, Mary C., 24, 208

Barbe, Walter B., 38
Baron, D., 148
Beck, Harry S., 180, 183
Bellak, L., 255, 262–263
Bellak, Sonya S., 255, 262
Bender, Lauretta, 179, 184
Bernard, H. W., 148
Bernstein, Margery R., 101, 113
Betts, Emmett Albert, 25, 197, 208
Bianchi, Martha Dickinson, 23
Bing, Lois B., 185–186
Blair, Glenn M., 25
Bloomer, R. H., 38
Bond, Guy L., 25, 131, 134, 146, 185, 205, 208
Bonsall, Marcella R., 96
Botel, Morton, 205
Bracken, Dorothy, 39
Brooks, Harold F., 218, 227
Brooks, Nelson H., 72
Bruce, Paul, 218, 227
Brueckner, Leo J., 25, 208
Bullock, Harrison, 96, 244, 246, 250
Buros, Oscar K., 132, 148, 208
Burt, Cyril, 228

Burton, William H., 38
Buswell, Guy, 185

Carey, Helen, 280
Carrigan, Patricia M., 162
Carter, Homer, 38
Cason, Eloise B., 208
Cassel, Russell N., 226–227
Cleland, Donald L., 225, 228
Clymer, Theodore A., 148, 205, 228
Coleman, James H., 15, 24, 106, 113
Collier, Mary Jeffrey, 105, 113
Conant, James Bryant, 24
Conant, Margaret M., 148
Crane, Marian M., 168, 184
Crombach, Lee, 58
Cruickshank, William, 161

Dallman, Martha, 38
Davidson, Helen H., 89, 96
Dawson, Mildred A., 72
Dearborn, Walter, 38
DeBoer, John J., 38
Dechant, E. V., 209
Deighton, Lee C., 38
Delacato, Carl H., 162, 180, 194
Della-Piana, Gabriel, 73
Denny, E. C., 96
Dewey, John, 99, 113
Diederich, Paul B., 25
Dolch, Edward W., 10, 24, 64, 72
Dreikurs, Rudolf, 159, 161
Dressel, Paul L., 266, 286
Driscoll, Gertrude P., 58
Durkin, Dolores, 58, 229

303

Durrell, Donald D., 24, 170, 182, 184, 190, 205, 208, 215–216, 228

Eagan, Paul J., 90, 96
Eames, Thomas H., 165, 168, 184, 186
Early, Margaret J., 37, 141, 147
Ebel, R. L., 148
Eiserer, Paul E., 263
Ephron, Beulah K., 162, 247, 250
Estes, Eleanor, 49
Ewalt, H. Ward, 186

Fernald, Grace M., 162, 208
Figurel, J. Allen, 6, 24, 114, 166, 184
Flanders, Ned A., 48, 59
Frank, George H., 250
Fry, E., 287
Furst, E. J., 148

Gaier, Eugene L., 105, 113
Galisdorfer, Lorraine, 184
Gates, Arthur I., 190, 205, 208
Gilmore, John U., 205
Goins, Jean Turner, 170, 184, 229
Graham, Ellis E., 219, 228
Graham, Grace, 148
Gray, William S., 25, 38, 62, 72, 73, 204
Guilford, J. P., 215, 228

Haddox, Genevieve, 227
Hagen, Elizabeth, 59
Hammil, Carrie E., 259
Harris, Albert J., 25, 162, 180, 184, 209
Havumaki, Sulo, 59
Henry, Florence, 106, 113
Herrick, Virgil, 73
Hildreth, Gertrude, 25, 209
Hill, E., 73
Hinds, L. R., 59
Holmes, Jack A., 12, 24
Howe, Edmond S., 250
Hoyt, C. J., 132, 134, 146, 205
Hunt, Jacob T., 133, 147

Ingram, Winifred, 186
Inhelder, Barbel, 96

Jacobs, Leland, 73
Jansky, Jeannette, 287
Jastak, Joseph, 189, 208
Johnson, Eleanor, 190, 208
Jungblut, Ann, 106, 113

Karp, Etta E., 64, 72
Kelley, Charles R., 165, 184
Kephart, Newell C., 186
Kirk, Samuel A., 64–65, 208, 228, 286
Knox, G. E., 186
Koester, G. A., 266, 286
Kottmeyer, William, 38
Kress, Roy, 287

Lang, Gerhard, 89, 96
Larrick, Nancy, 114
Larson, Lola, 184
Leavell, Ullin W., 179–180, 184, 205
Ledley, Robert S., 267, 286
Lee, L. G., 148
Leestma, Robert C., 184, 186, 190
Letton, Mildred Celia, 96
Lindquist, Donald, 39
Lowrance, Robert Bruce, 250
Lusted, Lee B., 286
Luttell, Barbara J., 262
Lytton, H., 27, 37

McCarthy, James J., 64, 208
McConville, Carolyn B., 180, 184
McCord, H., 186
McCullough, Constance M., 25, 39, 72, 148
McGuinnes, Dorothy, 38
Machover, Karen, 260, 262
McKim, Margaret G., 38
Mackintosh, Helen K., 114
Mary Josephine, Sister, 25
Matson, Charlotte, 184
Mayer, Robert W., 141, 147
Mayhew, Lewis B., 287
Mearns, Hugh, 38
Meckel, Henry C., 25

Melnik, Amelia, 131, 147, 289
Mills, Robert E., 134. 147
Monroe, Marian, 209
Moore, Mary R., 250
Moustakas, Clark E., 48, 59, 263
Murray, H. A., 255, 262

Natchez, Gladys, 63, 72
Nelson, M. J., 96
Neville, Donald, 218, 228
Newman, Ruth, 287
Newton, John R., 38
Nichols, Ralph, 148
Norvell, George W., 114

Odell, C. W., 148
Ogden, Charles Kay, 96
Olson, Willard C., 25

Park, G. E., 182, 184
Parsley, K. M., Jr., 140, 147
Pascal, Gerald R., 262
Patterson, Donald G., 186
Perry, William G., Jr., 186
Peterson, Eleanor M., 101, 113
Piaget, Jean, 96, 226, 228
Piekarz, Josephine A., 96
Pope, Benjamin, 250
Popham, W. James, 250
Porterfield, O. V., 15, 24
Powell, Marvin, 140, 147
Pronovost, Wilbert L., 73

Quast, Wentworth, 251

Rabinovitch, Ralph D., 179, 185
Rappaport, David, 218, 228
Renshaw, Samuel, 170, 185
Richards, I. A., 96
Robbins, M. H., 287
Roberts, Paul, 73
Robinson, H. Alan, 65
Robinson, Helen M., 25, 38, 73, 114,
    161–162, 165, 185–186
Roby, D. L., 251
Rogers, Bernice, 38
Rogers, Carl R., 287
Rorschach, H., 255, 262

Roth, Robert M., 287
Ruesch, Jurgen, 73
Russell, David H., 25, 38, 63–64, 72,
    96, 148

Sargent, Helen, 254–255, 262
Saunders, David R., 228
Schlichting, H. F., 15, 24
Schneidman, E. S., 255, 262
Schonell, F. J., 209
Scott, William R., 159, 161
Shaffer, Laurance F., 254, 262
Shedd, Charles L., 287
Sheldon, William D., 24
Shepherd, David L., 111, 113, 121,
    131, 147
Shoben, Edward J., 254, 262
Simpson, Glenn O., 24
Smith, Donald E. P., 162
Smith, Henry P., 209
Spache, George D., 9, 24, 38, 72,
    186, 287
Spitz, René, 156
Staiger, Ralph C., 26, 182, 185
Stevens, Leonard, 148
Strauss, Alfred H., 186
Studholme, Janice, 159, 161
Sullivan, Harry Stack, 157, 161
Sullivan, Helen Blair, 24, 170, 182,
    184
Sweeting, Orville J., 168, 185
Sweetland, Anders, 250
Swenson, Esther J., 148
Symonds, P. M., 255, 263

Tanyzer, Harold J., 270, 287
Taylor, Edith, 186
Thompson, Alfred Leete, 23
Thorndike, Robert, 59, 106, 114
Thurstone, Thelma Gwinn, 229
Tillman, Chester E., 186
Tinker, Miles A., 39, 148, 175–177,
    185–186, 208
Toussaint, Isabella H., 228
Traxler, Arthur E., 140, 147, 162
Triggs, Frances O., 148
Tyler, Fred, 39

Vernon, M. D., 26, 161, 180, 185
Vernon, Philip E., 142, 147–148, 218, 228–229
Vorhaus, Pauline G., 161

Walters, Richard H., 14, 24
Wechsler, David, 218, 228
Weiss, Jerry M., 39
Westover, Frederick L., 148
Wharton, William P., 101, 114
Whitlock, Charles P., 186
Wilson, Rosemary G., 277

Withall, John, 48, 59
Withrow, Dorothy, 280
Witty, Paul, 39, 105, 107, 114
Wolfe, Don M., 39
Wollner, Mary Hayden Bowen, 115
Wood, Dorothy Adkins, 148
Woolf, Jeanne A., 162
Woolf, Maurice D., 162
Wright, E. Muriel J., 59
Wrightstone, J. W., 26

Zollinger, Marion, 72

SUBJECT INDEX

Activities for retarded readers, 30, 32
Affective motivations, relation of, to
   achievement and intelligence,
   226–227
American Foundation for the Blind,
   169
American Optometric Association,
   166
American School Arithmetic Test,
   225
Analysis of reading tests, 135–137,
   289–295
Aniseikonia, 167
Application forms, 238, 301–302
Appraisal of student's progress, 56
Approaches to diagnosis, 7–9
Attitudes, 14, 203
   of parents toward children, 241
   toward reading, 67
Auditory efficiency, 181
   improvement of, 182
   tests of, 181
Auditory-perception technique, 190
Auditory and speech difficulties, 181–
   182
   importance of, 181
   tests of, 181–182

Bender Visual Motor Gestalt Test,
   179, 261, 269
Bilingual background, 13
Bilingual children, 182
Binocular coordination, 165, 167,
   169
Broad view of reading related to di-
   agnosis, 6
Brown-Carlsen Listening Compre-
   hension Test, 224

Buros Mental Measurements Yearbook, 207
California Mental Maturity Tests,
   140, 212
Case conference, 284
Case data, diagnostic summary of,
   270–275
   interpretation of, 265–286
   kind of, 267–270
   synthesis of, 265–286
Cases, particularly baffling, 157–158
Causes of difficulties (see Reading
   difficulties)
Cautions in use of diagnostic information, 36
Checklist, directions for using, 51
   of instructional needs, 297–299
   of oral and silent reading performance, 198–199
   record of observations, 52–55
Chicago Community Child Guidance
   Centers, 159
Chicago Non-verbal Examination,
   213
Child guidance clinic, referral to, 204
Children's drawings and paintings,
   259–262
Class discussion, of reading interests,
   112
   of test results, 120
Classroom situations as source of information, 43–50
Classroom teacher, information obtained by, 11–12
   role of, in diagnosis, 27–28
   (See also Teacher)
Clinical diagnostic study, 280–284

Clinician, role of, in diagnosis, 154, 159
Coefficients of correlation between group intelligence and reading tests, 140–141
Committee on Diagnostic Reading Tests, 134
Complexity of diagnosis, 22
Comprehension, abilities in, 12
factors in, 7, 12–15
Comprehension skills, sequence of, 276
Concept formation, 217
Controlled Reader, 173–174
Cooper Diagnostic Word Analysis Test, 272–273
Coordination, eye-hand, 179
tests of, 179
Counseling procedures, 266
Counselor, referral to, 204
Creative response question, 67, 120
rating of responses on, 69–70
Criticism, response to, 5–6

Daily schedule, 92–94, 247
Daily schedule clinic, 94–95
Davis-Eells games, 212
Developmental picture of reading progress, 83–84
Diagnosing, over-, 20
Diagnosis, complexity of, 22
dynamics of, 5, 7
medical, 267
related to remediation, 9–10
Diagnostic information, obtained, in group instruction and discussion, 47
in interaction between student and teacher, 48
by listening to story, 45
by oral reading, 45–46
in oral reports, 44, 48
by silent reading, 45–46, 49–50
by talking with teacher, 50
about the reader, 4
sources of, 36

Diagnostic information, from standardized reading tests, 136–140
use of, 207
cautions on, 36
immediate, 29–30
Diagnostic interviews, 247
Diagnostic procedures, individual, 16–17
Diagnostic reading tests, 134
Section II, Comprehension: Silent and Auditory, 224
Diagnostic self-appraisal teaching procedure, 131
Diagnostic summaries, limitations of, 284–285
uses of, 284
Differential diagnosis, 64
Dolch Basic Sight Word Test, 16, 63–64, 272
Doren Diagnostic Reading Test, 134
Drawings, children's, 259–262
Durrell Analysis of Reading Difficulty Test, 190, 198
Durrell-Sullivan Reading Capacity and Achievement Tests, 13
Durrell-Sullivan Reading Capacity Test, 225, 271–272
Dynamic view, 154

Educational deprivation in reading difficulty, 155
Educational Development Laboratories, 171–172
Effort and interest, 190
Emotional difficulties, 14, 274–275
in relation to reading difficulty, 155–156
Emotionally disturbed children, 98
interviews with, 237
Emotions, 203
Employed mothers, influence of, 268
Errors, in judgment, 143
of measurement, in testing, 143
Eye-hand coordination, 179
tests of, 179
Eye movements, conclusions from study of, 175
nature of, 174

Eye movements, observation of, 176–177
  photographs of, 175–176
  training of, 177–178
  (*See also under* Visual)
Eye span, 167

Failure, effect of, 4–5
Family, facts about, 268
Far-sight (hyperopia), 165
Favorite stories, 105, 109–110
Fears, 14
Finger painting, 256
Flexible use of standardized tests, 142
Free response question (*see* Creative response question)

Garrard Press, The, Champaign, Illinois, 30
Gates Oral Vocabulary Test, 189
Gates Reading Diagnostic Tests, 190
Gates Reading Survey, 225
Gilmore Oral Reading Test, 205
Gray Oral Reading Paragraphs, 271
Gray Oral Reading Tests, 204
Gray Standardized Oral Reading Check Test, 168
Group diagnostic procedures, 16
Group reading inventory, 120–131
  for English, 121–125
  for science, 127–129
  for social studies, 125–127

Harvard Reading Films, 172
Hearing (*see under* Auditory)
Home conditions, 15, 155
Homeroom teacher, information obtained by, 10
Hyperopia, 165

Illinois Test of Psycholinguistic Abilities, 64, 205
Importance of reading in getting a job, 98
Improvement in reading, reasons for, 248–249
Inability to read, multiple cause of, 3–4

Inability to read, relation to other problems, 3
Incomplete lateralization (*see* Mixed dominance)
Incomplete sentence, 256–258
Individual diagnostic procedures, 16–17
Individual differences in response to praise and critism, 5–6
Individual intelligence tests, 212–214, 218–221
  (*See also* Intelligence tests)
Individual methods, advantages of, 160
  levels of complexity of, 153–154
Individual reading inventory, 187–207
  criteria for judging, 191
  example of, 191–196
  instructions for administering, 200
  interpretations of, 201–203
  main features of, 188–199
  recommendations based on, 203–204
  understanding gained in, 188
  values of, 200–201
Individualization of instruction, 22–23, 33
Individualized reading, 63
Information, needed, 10–15
  skills, location of, 12
  sources of, 15–17
  synthesis and interpretation of, 17–20
  uses of, 20–22
Instruction, following diagnosis, 63
  indications of, that can be observed, 217–218
  individualized, 22–23, 33
  relation between reading and, 215–217, 219
Intelligence quotient (IQ), interpretation of, 213–214, 217, 269
Intelligence test scores, effect of environment on, 214
  fluctuation in, 213
  interpretation of, 216–217
    to parents and students, 224

Intelligence test scores, practice effect on, 214
  relation of, to IQ level, 215
    to reading level, 215–216, 219
  significance of, 268–269
  unreliability of, 213
  validity of, 213
Intelligence tests, caution in use of, 212–214
  diagnostic value of, 218–221
  effect of reading skills on, 141
  effect on self-esteem, possible, 218
  requiring little or no reading, 212–213
  uses of, 222–224
    clinical, 218
    in determining need for reading instruction, 141
  vocabulary section of, 219
Interest, and comprehension, 101–102
  cultivation of, 102
  as dynamic force, 98–99
  and effort, 99–100
  and memory, 101–102
  and personality development, 100
  and readiness, 100
  and reading ability, 102–103
  sex differences in, 106
  relation of, to intelligence, 106
  using information about, 110–112
  ways of ascertaining, 103–110
  and wide reading, 100–101
Interest inventories, 107
Interest questionnaires, 107–110
Interest rating, of fictitious titles, 106
  of real books, 106
Interests, 13–14, 203–204
Interpretation, test of, 119
Interviews, 17
  diagnostic, 247
  evaluation of, 248
  examples of, 239–240, 244–246
  exploratory, 243–246
  initial, 238
  with parents, 232–233, 236–242
  personal, 158–159
  purposes of, 232–233

Interviews, quotations from, 240–242
  taking notes during, 235
  techniques of, 231–235
  therapeutic, 247–248
  voluntary, 238–239
Introspection based on test responses, 137
Iowa Reading Films, 172
Iowa Silent Reading Tests, 134, 140, 248, 271

Keystone View Company, 172
Keystone Visual Screening Test, 270
Keystone Visual Survey Telebinocular, 168

Language experience approach, as source of diagnostic information, 30–31
Learning capacity, 13
Learning Methods Test, 134–135
Learning rate, 13
Leavell Analytical Oral Reading Test, 205
Leavell Hand-Eye Dominance Test, 179
Lee-Clark Reading Readiness Test, 140
Levels of reading ability, 197
  (See also Reading levels)
Linguistic abilities, 13, 155
Listening comprehension, 13, 269
  relation of, to reading, 198
    to reading comprehension, 225
  section of the STEP tests, 224
  test of, 36, 198, 224–225
Location of information skills, 12
Lorge Readability Index, 101, 107

McCullough Word Analysis Test, 20, 64, 207
Machover Draw-A-Figure Test, 260
Main idea, test of selecting, 118–119
Massachusetts Vision Test, 168
Mature readers, characteristics of, 175
Medical diagnosis, 267

Medical treatment of reading problems, 182–183
Mental ability, 12–13
  clues of, 202–203
  in relation to reading difficulty, 155
Mental hygiene clinic, referral to, 204
Mental potential, 141
Mentally retarded children, 98
Methods of work with individuals, effect of, 158
Metropolitan Life Insurance Company, School Health Service, 166
Metropolitan Reading Test, 135
Michigan Speed of Reading Test, 134
Miles A-B-C Vision Test of Ocular Dominance, 180
Mirror reading (see Mixed dominance)
Mixed dominance, 179–181
  corrective exercises for, 180–181
  tests of, 180
Monroe Reading Aptitude Test, 270
Motivations for reading, 88
Myopia, 164–165

National Society for the Prevention of Blindness, 169
Neurological factors, 15
  and reading difficulty, 155, 179–181

Observation, advantages of, 42
  checklist of, 51–56
  in classroom, 41–58
  global approach to, 56, 58
  during individual reading inventory, 188
  interpretation of, 57
  during interview, 249–250
  limitations of, 42–43
  method of, 56
  recording of, 50–51, 56
  of students' reading interests, 103
Oral reading paragraphs, 190–197

Oral reading as technique, 10, 11–12, 34, 61–71
  in elementary school, 62–65
  in high school and college, 65–71
  uses of, 61–62
Orthoptic training, 169
Over-diagnosing, 20

Paintings, children's, 256, 259–262
Paragraph analysis, 69–71
Paragraph comprehension, kinds of errors, 68–69
Parent-child relations, 240–241, 258
Parents, cooperation with, 204
  discussions with, 159–160
Perception, influence on behavior, 89–90
Personal development through reading, 7
Personal interview, 158–159
  (See also Interviews)
Personality tests, 226
  and social insight test, 226
Philadelphia Reading Record, 277–279
Philadelphia Self-appraisal Program of Guidance, 266
Phono-Word Wheels, 274
Physical conditions reported in interviews, 240, 258
Physical factors, 14–15
  in diagnosis of reading, 163–186
  in reading difficulty, 154–155
Positive approach, 10
Praise, response to, 5–6
Preliminary conversation, 189
Pressure methods and machines, 178–179
Primary Mental Abilities Test, 225
Probable error of a difference, 213–214
Procedures for working with cases, 20–23
Projective methods, 16–17, 253–262
  administration of, 255–256, 260
  informal, 255–261
  interpretation of, 255, 261
  levels of, 254–255

Projective methods, nature of, 254
    purpose of, 254–255, 261
Projective picture stories, 258–259
Psychotherapy, 266
Purposes in reading, 14

Reader's Digest Skill Builder, 31
Reading, attitudes toward, 67
    importance of, in getting job, 98
    improvement in, reasons for, 248–
        249
    individualized, 63
    motivations for, 88
    oral, 45–46
    purposes in, 14
    as related to diagnosis, broad view
        of, 6
    relation, between instruction and,
        215–217, 219
        between thinking and, 7
    silent, 45–46, 49–50
    as visual task, 164–165
        psychological factors in, 165
Reading aloud to children, 90
Reading Analysis Tests, 205–206
Reading autobiography, 76–84
    diagnostic information from, 83–
        84
    examples of, 80–85
    questions answered in, 76–79
    student reaction to, 76
    unstructured type of, 79–84
    values of, 76, 84, 90
Reading case, prognosis, 282
    recommendations, 20, 282–284
Reading Clinic serving Philadelphia
    schools, 280
Reading Diagnostic Record, 280
    for high school and college stu-
        dents, 65
Reading difficulties, causes of, 3–4,
    9–10, 237–238
    conditions that lead to, 154–156
    detected by tests, 137–139
Reading expectancy, 216–217
Reading interests, patterns of, 99,
    112
    study of, 98–99

Reading inventory, group, 120–131
    individual, 187–207
Reading lesson as source of diagnos-
    tic information, 28–30
Reading levels, 197, 200–201, 206
Reading materials, easy, interesting,
    275
    for persons of limited vision, 169–
        170
    for poor readers, 30
    suited to individual, 204
Reading performance, oral and silent,
    checklist, 198–199
Reading potential, 12–13, 211–227
    measures of, 198
Reading process, 6
    complexity of, 154
    difficulty in diagnosing, 132
    introspective study of, 86–87
    retrospective study of, 85–86
    students' analysis of, 85–86
    visual factors in, 163
Reading Profile, 142, 144, 145
Reading status, 11–12
Reading teacher, information ob-
    tained by, 11
Reading test scores, interpretation of,
    269–270
Reading tests, analysis of, 135–137,
    289–295
    choice of, 135
    coefficients of correlation between
        group intelligence and, 140–
        141
    Committee or Diagnostic, 134
    purposes of, 118–119
    standardized, 132–143, 204–206
    teacher-made, 36, 118–120
        advantages of, 119
        in each subject, 119–120
Recommendations for reading cases,
    20, 282–284
Records, checklist form, 277–279
    of student progress, 277
Referral, to child guidance clinic,
    204
    to counselor, 204

Referral, counselor's responsibility for, 242
to mental hygiene clinic, 204
Relationship with pupil (*see* Teacher)
Reports of students' reading, 103–104
Respect for pupil (*see* Teacher)
Retarded readers, individual cases, 33–35, 49–50
Revised Beta Examination, Psychological Corporation, 212
Role of teacher (*see* Teacher)
Rorschach test, 255
indications of intelligence from, 222
Roswell-Chall Diagnostic Test of Word Analysis Skills, 134

SCAT, 141
Schedule, daily, 92–95, 247
School conditions, 15
School marks, 268
School relations, 241–242
School Vision Tester, 168
adapted to school use by Bausch and Lomb, 168
Science Research Reading Laboratories, 248
Self-appraisal, 75–76, 112, 119, 121, 131, 142–143, 266
information obtained from, 15–16
responsibility for, 9
Self-concept, 89–90
Self-evaluation questions, 87–88
Sequential development of reading skills, 28
Sequential diagnostic procedure, 275–277
Short-answer questions, 120
Silent reading, 12
paragraphs, uses of, 197, 206
tests of, 118
Simpson, My Reading Design, 20
Skimming, test of, 118
Slow learners, 269
self-evaluation of, 88–89
Snellen Chart, 36

Spache Binocular Reading Test, 168–169
Spache Diagnostic Reading Scales, 134
Special reading class as source of diagnostic information, 31–33
Speech, reading and, 182
relation to personal adjustment, 182
Speech difficulties, 181–182
Speed of Reading Tests, 134
SRA Primary Mental Abilities Test, 213
SRA Reading Laboratory, 31
Standardized reading tests, abilities measured by, 132–134
abilities not measured by, 132
compared with informal procedures, 206
diagnostic information from, 136–139
kinds of tests available, 132–135
oral, 204, 205
use and misuse of, 140–143
Stanford-Binet, 216, 225, 269
Stanford-Binet Intelligence Test, 34, 140
STEP (Sequential Test of Educational Progress), 141, 225
Manual for Interpreting Reading Scores of, 136, 141
Stories, favorite, 105, 109–110
Student-centered approach, 21
Student's background, information about, 36
Student's reaction to reading autobiography, 76
Student's evaluation of reading instruction, 91
Student's use of time, 94
Subjective essays, 89–91
Success, effect of, 4–5
experience of, 204

Tachistoscopic training, 170–174
effectiveness of, 174
instruments for use in, 171–172

Tape recordings, uses of, 266–267
Teacher, information obtained by, 11–12, 50
  and pupil, relationship with, 5
  respect for, 4–5
  role of, in diagnosis, 27–28, 37, 91, 143, 197–200
  in parent interviews, 238–240
Teacher diagnosis, values of, 35
Teacher-made tests, 36, 118–120
Technical diagnosis, 35
Test, of ability to pronounce printed words, 189–190
  of basic sight vocabulary, 63–65
  of knowledge of spoken words, 189
  (*See also* Intelligence tests; Reading tests; names of tests)
Thematic Apperception Test, 255
Therapeutic effect, 9
Thinking and reading, 7
Thorndike-McCall Reading Test, 140
Three-wishes techniques, 260, 262
Thurstone's Primary Mental Abilities Test, 12
Traxler Silent Reading Test, 134

Unfavorable home and neighborhood conditions, 155
University of Chicago Clinic, 165

Values, 14
Visual defects, frequency, 165
  kinds of, 165
  study of, 165, 176
  teacher's observation to detect, 166
Visual factors, 164–170
  instruments and methods used in studying, 163, 166–167
  in reading difficulty, 165–166
  relation of, to reading, 165–166
Visual screening tests, 36, 157–159
  criteria for judging, 169
  study of, 168–169
Vocalization, 201–202

Wechsler Intelligence Scale for Children, 33, 202, 216, 218–221, 227, 271–272
Wepman Auditory Discrimination Test, 182
Western Electric Company's Model 4 C Audiometer, 181
Wide Range Achievement Test, 189–190
Wirt Stereo Test, 168
Word attack skills, 64
Word calling, 201–202
Word meaning, 202
Word recognition skills, 202
  sequence of, 276